A Cloud of Other Poets

Robert Frost and The Romantics

Mario L. D'Avanzo

UNIVERSITY
PRESS OF
AMERICA

Lanham • New York • London

Copyright © 1991 by
University Press of America®, Inc.
4720 Boston Way
Lanham, Maryland 20706

3 Henrietta Street
London WC2E 8LU England

Acknowledgement is due to Henry Holt and Company for
permitting me to quote from the following under their control:

From *The Poetry of Robert Frost* edited by Edward Connery Lathem.
Copyright 1916, 1928, 1930, 1934, 1939, 1947,
© 1969 by Holt, Rinehart and Winston.
Copyright © 1964, 1967, 1970, 1975 by Lesley Frost Ballantine.
Copyright 1936, 1942, 1944, © 1956, 1958, 1962 by Robert Frost.
Reprinted by permission of Henry Holt and Company, Inc.

And to Jonathan Cape Limited, for British Commonwealth permission.

Library of Congress Cataloging-in-Publication Data

D'Avanzo, Mario L., 1931-
A cloud of other poets : Robert Frost and the Romantics /
Mario L. D'Avanzo.
p.   cm.
Includes bibliographical references and index.
1. Frost, Robert, 1874-1963—Criticism and interpretation.
2. Frost, Robert, 1874-1963—Knowledge—Literature.
3. English poetry—Appreciation—United States.
4. American poetry—English influences.
5. Romanticism—United States.
6. Romanticism—Great Britain.
I. Title.
PS3511.R94Z614   1990   811'.52—dc20   90–45737 CIP

ISBN 0–8191–7997–3 (alk. paper)
ISBN 0–8191–7998–1 (pbk. : alk. paper)

 ™ The paper used in this publication meets the minimum requirements of
American National Standard for Information Sciences—Permanence
of Paper for Printed Library Materials, ANSI Z39.48–1984.

For Sylvia and Michael D'Avanzo

ACKNOWLEDGEMENTS

I am grateful to the late Professor George Frost of Dartmouth College; he was the first to introduce me to poems of Robert Frost (no relation)-- in the very place that the poet lived when an undergraduate and in the very year that Robert Frost published his complete poems. The poems have stuck like burrs over the years. During that time I have contemplated the "glory" of the poetry.

I acknowledge with pleasure the advice and encouragement of Professors Rene Fortin and Rodney Delasanta of Providence College. Their reading of the text was helpful and insightful. My thanks also goes to Professor Barbara Horn of Nassau Community College for improving and proofing the manuscript.

I wish to acknowledge the encouragement of the late Hyatt H. Waggoner, whose professionalism in all things scholarly and academic showed the way. I would also like to thank Richard Furman for being letter-perfect in preparing these pages.

Table of Contents

CHAPTER I
INTRODUCTION

At the 1955 Dartmouth College commencement, I heard Robert Frost admit to deliberate literary adaptations as the basis of his poetry-making:

> I'm going to tell you that every single one of my poems is probably one of these adaptations that I've made. I've taken whatever you give me and make it what I want it to be. That's what every one of the poems is.[1]

Frost was to repeat his indebtedness to literary tradition again and again, not simply to aver his place in literary history, but to assert a principle of aesthetics: His poems are to be read and appreciated in relation to the poetry of the past. This literature he describes as "a cloud of other poets," a cloud of minute particles of poetic water gathering force and power for the creative moment.

> The manner of a poet's germination is . . . like . . . that of a . . . waterspout at sea. . . . He has to begin as a cloud of all the other poets he ever read. That can't be helped. And first the cloud reaches down toward the water from above and then the water reaches up toward the cloud from below and finally cloud and water join together to roll as one pillar between heaven and earth. The base of water he picks up from below is of course all the life he ever lived outside of books.[2]

This important passage acknowledges the creation of his poetry as an energetic joining of the life in books and the world of reality.

Frost's admission, then, serves as the title and subject of my book. First, it introduces one of my central ideas--that Frost's involvement with the "cloud" of American and British Romantic writers is at the center of his major poetic achievements. My purpose is to read many of the poems through the focus of Frost's Romantic predecessors --Thoreau, Emerson, Wordsworth, Coleridge, Shelley, and Keats. Seen in relation to their Romantic origins, many of Frost's poems--both those widely known and many less familiar, unfold to richer meanings.

But the passage speaks of more than Frost's dependence on books for his poetry-making. For the cloud metaphor reveals Frost's Romantic attitude toward the role of the poet and the imagination. The passage describes the poet in the act of creation as a *pillar* of cloud and water joining heaven and earth, spirit and matter. The pillar of cloud alludes to the almighty creator Yahweh, the miracle-maker of Exodus and, as well, the Primary imagination of Coleridge: "I AM." The cloud metaphor thus brings me to my second basic idea in this study: that many of Frost's poems show a profound awareness of Romantic assumptions concerning the poet, the imagination, the relations between mind and nature, visionary questing and insight, and the supernal power of mind to create value and form--the form of poetry.[3]

My intention is to examine the variety of responses that Frost's poems make towards these Romantic themes of the poet, mind and nature, spiritual value, and form-making. Many of Frost's poems show both kinship and differences with Emerson, Thoreau, Wordsworth, Shelley, Coleridge, and Keats. I distinguish between Romantic and "anti-Romantic" poems, showing that not only do individual poems proceed by dialectic but that a good deal of Frost's poetry, seen as a larger whole, also proceeds dialectically. As a result, I am able to organize my discussion around clusters of poems, related in outlook, theme, and controlling symbol. For example, Frost's flower poems reflect a rich, positive Romantic heritage. However, for every flower poem attending some tentative visionary insight there stands a poem of darker mood, such as the profoundly moving and significant "Leaves Compared to Flowers," and other poems of diminishment, annihilation, and negativism. Likewise, in a later chapter (VI) "The

Visionary Quest," I follow a course moving from those poems of tentative affirmation to those of increasing negation. What emerges is a poetic voice of great range in its uncertainty, ambiguity, and powerful irony. In grouping the poems around a common theme or controlling symbol (such as birds and birdsong), my key notion is that a typical Frost poem plays against one or more Romantic predecessor poems. Knowing those Romantic poems enables the reader to discover the shape and lines of Frost's dialectic with his poetic heritage.

The Romantics helped shape the psyche of Frost, and it is important to know in what ways his poems show differences and affinities with these poets. The typical structure of a Frost poems I have described as dialectical, in that he uses the very language and figures of his source. Frost means it when he confesses to taking "whatever you give me" and making "it what I want it to be." The organic relation between Frost's poems and the older literature they ride is singularly illuminating. Seen in relation to their sources, many poems extend their meaning a range further than has yet been noticed, often revealing a dimension of deliberate, studied irony that is vitally tied to the language and ideas of the Romantic that Frost is debating or resisting. These sources, therefore, are referents on which the verbal form and direction of his argument depend. Often his poems use the language and symbolism of Romanticism while denying or reconceiving its doctrines.

An example of Frost's use of sources will further explain my method of discussing the poems. One of Frost's well known poems, "Dust of Snow," appropriately illustrates the further range of meaning a source often reveals. Taken by itself, the poem simply expresses a sense of delight in an experience in nature.

> The way a crow
> Shook down on me
> The dust of snow
> From a hemlock tree
>
> Has given my heart
> A change of mood

> And saved some part
> Of a day I had rued.

Seen against a parallel scene from Thoreau's Journal, the poem shows the transcendental overtone of the poet's joy:

> As I stand by the hemlocks, I am greeted by the lively and unusually prolonged *tche-de-de-de-de-de* of a little flock of chicadees. The snow has ceased falling, the sun comes out, and it is warm and still, and this flock of chicadees . . . feeling the influence of this genial season, have begun to flit amid the snow covered fans of the hemlocks, jarring down the snow. . . . Nature is moderate and loves degrees. Winter is not all white and sere. Some trees are evergreen to cheer us. . . . Some evergreen shrubs are placed there to relieve the eye . . . [and] keep the semblance of summer still.[4]

In "Dust of Snow" nature likewise restores Frost's spirit, not through the ear, as birds often do, but through the eye. Frost modifies and diverges from the tone of his forebear. The recasting of bird and color is suggestive; seemingly, the details of nature serve to break the frozen wintry scene, thus saving some part of the day. The parallel in Thoreau indicates how Frost departs from transcendental experience; but his hemlock tree also has the primary effect of cheering and elevating by revealing the eternal green underneath. And it is an esthetic response in the colors that Frost emphasizes, bringing some joy to a day he has rued. The poem plays against the prose passage and illustrates the ways of the poet's imagination. ("Turn it your way," Frost advised.)[5] It also characterizes his modest transcendental epiphany, or grace, gotten from nature, and his allegiance to a Romantic tradition of discovering spiritual experience in the cooperation of nature and man.

It is important to remember that *both* Romantic and anti-Romantic elements are *always* present in the body of Frost's poetry, and he holds both in suspension throughout his career. In each of Frost's volumes we find contrasting poems, one of affirmative vision answering one of dark skepticism, one positive about nature countering a negative point of view. *A Witness Tree* , for example, contains the visionary "The Quest of the Purple Fringed" and its opposite "Come In." Since Frost admitted that "anything I ever thought I still think . . . . I don't even grow,"[6] there can be very little argument for a development in the poetry, as, say, the poems of Eliot show an evolution. It seems apparent that his ideas and attitudes, for the most part, were formed before *A Boy's Will*, and subsequent volumes deepen his responses to certain Romantic beliefs. Yet Frost's poems are no doubt visitations of the hour, occasioned by a mood. We need to remind ourselves that poets are often philosophers but do not write as philosophers, with a coherent world view or larger plan in mind throughout the body of their work. Frost made it clear that he was not a philosopher but a philosophic poet. He is impelled by various feelings--"a lump in the throat"--as Frost would say--which become clarified in "momentary stay[s] against confusion."[7] The different volumes of Frost's poems reflect oppositions in mood, tension, arguments with himself, and a variety of perspectives. My method of grouping the poems in a spectrum from his positive Romanticism to uncertainty and tentativeness of vision to those poems of darkness and despair will best show Frost's dialectic with himself over a poetic career.

My method of proceeding in this study is, first, to establish the Romantic leanings of Frost. Chapter II discusses the poet's relation to the Romantic writers, using his letters and essays as references. Chapters III and IV discuss a number of poems that establish Frost's positive Romantic character. Poems of Shelleyan and Emersonian visionary experience, intuition and the poetic imagination, and the mind's relation to nature all bespeak a Romantic heritage. Beginning with Chapter V, I examine Frost questioning his Romantic beliefs, or, more precisely, those of his forebears. He asks, in effect, if such notions are delusions. In Chapters V, VI and VII, I show those poems, both early and late, that indicate an anti-Romantic, skeptical, or nihilistic mood. Throughout these poems of limited insight, uncertainty, tentativeness and negation, Frost presents tough, sometimes despairing arguments about Romanticism, in which a spiritless interior mirrors the void "out there."

Implicitly he asks: What does a man do without revelation, his Wordsworth, Emerson, and Shelley having failed him? He tries to frame a spiritual and creative life around discordant revelations. They are discordant partly because of the ruin or blank in his own eye looking on nature. The mind that is not whole cannot see the world whole. In this group of poems, transparency, or vision--usually through nature--ends in surmise or incompleteness. Yet there is always the impression that he yearns for a deeper vision or wisdom and that he is attuned by nature to a Romantic credo that he intentionally masks. My impression is that Frost admired the Romantics in the same way and for the same reasons that Matthew Arnold did: they united the naturalistic and the moral worlds in their poetry. However, both poets found themselves too far removed in time and condition from such heroic vision. Whatever the outcome of Frost's quest for transcendency, the experience is all-important. But if his visionary power failed him, his Thoreau did not.

From Thoreau he learned that "a true account of the actual is the rarest poetry." A "fact" could be "mean" or "sublime"; the important thing is that we work on it with our intellect and feelings, and also our hands and senses in order to know it by experience and be able to give a true account of it. The hoped-for unity that Frost can expect is ultimately a poem, out of which the fact and the experience of the fact emerges. From Thoreau Frost found not only a work ethic but a work esthetic. Out of farm labor, vigorously recommended by Thoreau for all writers, would come Frost's basic metaphors for the imaginative process and poetry-making. A writer must labor vigorously in the field, according to Thoreau:

> Learn to split wood. . . . Every stroke will be husbanded, and ring soberly through the wood; and so will the strokes of that scholar's pen, which at evening record the story of the day, ring soberly, yet cheerily, on the ear of the reader, long after the echoes of his axe have died away. The scholar may be sure that he writes the tougher truth for the calluses on his palms. They give firmness to the

> sentence. Indeed, the mind never makes a great and
> successful effort, without a corresponding energy of
> the body. . . . Plainness and vigor and sincerity, the
> ornaments of style, were better learned on the farm
> and in the workshop than in the schools.[8]

No wonder Frost values so highly the vigorous labor of wood-chopping in "Two Tramps in Mud Time." Physical labor initiates the unification and perfection of the soul.

Chapter VIII is pivotal to an understanding of Frost's poetry; it discusses the interrelation of labor, art, and imagination in key poems and the importance of Thoreau to that interrelationship. In Thoreau, Frost finds his mentor and fashions a spiritual and physical life based on Thoreau's concept of self-culture. More than any other writer, Thorea taught Frost how to bring his whole soul into activity for creative purpose. Knowing and sensing reality is not only an emotional and intellectual interreaction with fact but also a physical working on it. Experiencing fact in labor will have its reward: apples and the dream of apples. This is how a fact will one day flower into a spiritual truth for Frost. This concept of creative effort radically departs from Coleridge, Wordsworth, or Emerson by calling for an intensification of sense experience. For Frost, a high spiritual and creative life begins in and grows out of labor--farm work--that is, the close interaction with the real and mundane. The moment of unity lies in effort, "the essay of love"; in the chaos of the world that he sees continually around him he knows there is still the possibility of artistic and self-perfection. It is clear that Thoreau was a passion for Frost. John Aldridge correctly identifies Thoreau as Frost's courage maker during severe depression and *Walden* as the "justification for becoming the kind of poet he wished to be."[9]

Adding to the discussion of Thoreau's importance in the poetry, Chapter IX discusses four visionary poems that best summarize Frost's Romantic heritage and constitute his most positive Romantic statements. Each in its own way is concerned with Frost's belief in the oneness of God, self, and art. "Directive" effectively summarizes Frost's Romanticism in advocating the esthetic wholeness that is integral to spiritual unity.

Though it is not my intention to discuss Frost as a modern poet, but, rather, how his poems relate to a past literary tradition, it seems necessary to note that only recently have we come to appreciate the extent of modern poetry's debt to Romanticism. Jay Parini is the most recent to assert that modern poetry has strong ties to a romantic tradition:

> Modernism was not a reversal of romanticism; it was an extension of it, a modification. . . . Granted Frost's rugged singularity, remains true that his most fundamental notions about poetry, its nature and function, comes from the romantic mainstream. He is especially an American romantic.[10]

In short, like the Romantic, Frost, in attempting to reintegrate fact and value, makes explorations into the universe; any moments of insight are taken as temporary and tentative and limited. The poet holds the meaning of his experience in suspension, subjecting his insight to constant revision, modification, and testing. He is an explorer of the enigma he senses within and without. Frost's poems measure the different degrees of receptivity and resistance to a possible "something" in nature, always retaining its mystery while accepting and relishing its physical reality.

In addition to Parini and Charles Carmichael, David Perkins, *A History of Modern Poetry*, and Richard Foster, *The New Romantics,* Morse Peckham, *The Triumph of Romanticism*, and others indicate the common ground and continuity between the Romantics and many major writers of the nineteenth and twentieth centuries, who have the same situation of confronting a valueless world and, out of their doubt and skepticism, finding it necessary to look at reality and impose some tentative value on it through imagination. This interrelation between mind and world, which is a central concern of the literature of the past two centuries, continues the explorations into meaning and value initiated by the Romantics. The imagination in perception and creativity fuses the idea to reality, creating a temporary order. This creative act is healing, unifying, and salvific. Frost's definition of poetry as a "momentary stay against confusion" reasserts what Arnold said in "The Study of Poetry" (1880) about the function of poetry in man's spiritual life: It provides a "stay" against confusion. Arnold wrote:

> The future of poetry is immense because in poetry, where it is worthy of its high destinies, our race, as time goes on, will find an even surer and surer stay. There is not a creed which is not shaken, not a received tradition which does not threaten to dissolve.[11]

In the face of spiritual chaos we have poetry to rely on as value maker. Out of this treasured cloud of other poets (which is also the poet's experience), poetry making provides a "stay" to Frost's sometimes shaky spirit, first, in that as an ordering, it overcomes the sense of chaos within the self and, secondly, it imposes meaning and value on the chaos without, for the moment, that we may also be enlightened. Valuing the rawness he has to draw on, the pertinacious poet says:

> Let chaos storm!
> Let cloud shapes swarm!
> I wait for form.

Here again are the clouds of other poets and poems in the midst of the poetic process. They mix with the chaos of earth in form making. This quest for form is of inestimable importance, for it delivers the poet from the larger excruciations of formlessness within and the void without.

CHAPTER II
EMERSON, THOREAU, AND THE ENGLISH ROMANTICS: FROST'S PROSE

Robert Frost lived twenty-six years in the nineteenth century, when the cloud of Emerson, Thoreau and English Romantic poetry were ascendant in popularity and prestige, many poems having already been established as classics in the language. Frost's essays, letters, and talks indicate his relation to his forebears. They are detailed and informative, and provide a first step in 1) explaining the reasons for his life-long interest in the previous literature, and in 2) examining the themes and artistic achievement of his own poems.

1. THE AMERICAN ROMANTICS

EMERSON

Emerson's presence in Frost's thought is so solidly established that there is no need to review the points of contact. Frost's essay on Emerson is the clearest statement of the influence; the Harvard seminar he taught on Emerson is academic evidence of a lifelong interest. Frost read in Emerson that the mind, because God-reliant, is the origin and reference for all knowledge, thought, and speculation. From the fundamental Romantic assumption that the self is the source and basis of value and order flows Frost's Emersonian Romanticism and an ordering principle of his poetry.[1] But a basic tension often shows in the poems. He does not always believe that once the communion between man and God has been established, it is invariably there for the mind to draw on in the form of revelation or inspiration. For Frost, insight, creativity--in fact his spiritual life itself--involves a constant striving to reattain that communication. Because "God-belief" wavers, so do all the other beliefs. The poems repeatedly measure the shifting gradients of the self's potentiality to know and believe, ranging from momentary insight to doubt and skepticism.

In stating that "in the beginning was the word," Frost identifies language with spirit in a highly Emersonian way.[2]   The mind's centrality to all creation makes it the divine Logos expressing itself through the form of words, *i.e.*, the mediant logos of metaphor. "The Constant Symbol" voices this divine function of imagination, stating, "the bard has said in effect, 'Unto these forms did I commend the spirit.'"[3] Similarly the frontispiece to *In the Clearing* defines poetry as like "God's own descent/ Into flesh," the subtantiation of spirit that forever renews the world by repeated rebirths of poetry. Clearly, the incarnation of spirit (or idea) into metaphor expresses a concept of poetry echoing Shelley and Emerson. Emerson states, "There seems to be a necessity in spirit to manifest itself in material forms."[4] (Shelley also specifically defines poetry as an "incarnation of the spirit."[5])

It is perhaps Emerson most of all who impressed upon Frost that a poem is a constant symbol and microcosm of the world and an embodiment of spirit. The soul is self-reliant because creative; for Emerson it is a type of the "One Mind," ordering what it discovers in the self and projecting it into form. That form is "a nature passed through the alembic of man,"[6] a nature ordered as it is filtered through the mind and will to produce a little cosmos of organic form. A poem is therefore an "abstract or epitome of the world. It is the result or expression of nature, in miniature."   Emerson further states that "every spirit builds itself a house . . . a world . . . a heaven" by altering, moulding, and remaking. Through us is nature perfected. The poem therefore becomes the Emersonian emblem of spirit, or a constant symbol of perfected nature.   Frost aptly expresses this Emersonian principle: "In us nature reaches its height of form and through us exceeds itself. When in doubt there is always form for us to go on with."[8] Creating forms is salutary in that it spares man from the "larger excruciations." This claim about the supportive force of forms engendered by the spirit is also Emersonian. "The Over-Soul" asserts that "the least activity of the intellectual powers redeems us in a degree from the conditions of time."[9]   This is precisely Frost's claim. In the form of a poem lies a constant symbol of all that is creative and heroic about humanity in its repeated confrontations with the facts of experience. The poem is a "heterocosm," a little self-contained world like God's own creation, in which the creator expresses and conceals himself.[10] Frost's "Revelation" is just such an expression of the "play" and anguish of "hide-and seek."

Of "self-belief" Frost says: "A young man knows more about himself than he is able to prove to anyone. He has no knowledge that anybody else will accept as knowledge. In his foreknowledge he has something that is going to believe itself into fulfillment, into acceptance." Similarly, "literary" or "art-belief" begins in "something more felt than known." These intuitions, known but not articulated, are modes of the divine teaching, a spiritual power that is akin to the visitations of the Over-Soul. Emerson has so described the self: "One mode of the divine teaching is the incarnation of the spirit in a form,--in forms, like my own."[11] The self intuitively understands its common nature with other souls and the common bond of love that unites them. In being drawn to other souls (Frost's equivalent to "love-belief") the soul apprehends a third party, God, arching over humanity. Man's widsom lies in this spiritual knowledge; the self is shaped and fulfilled by it even though the intuitions and feelings of self-belief remain inarticulated. The self's intuitive knowledge is a potentiality that will be believed into being. Frost's notion of "self-belief "is derived from Emerson, who states:

> The action of the soul is oftener in that which is felt
> and left unsaid than in that which is said in any
> conversation. . . . We know better than we do. We
> do not yet possess ourselves, and we know at the
> same time that we are much more.[12]

The knowledge of "self-belief" is a divine gift flowing into the soul through the mysterious channels of feeling. It will be believed into fulfillment and acceptance. Likewise, "art-belief" is the formalizing of the gift of inspiration, allowing the poet to say more than he thought possible. This is a peculiarly Emersonian notion: "For the soul's communication of truth is the highest event in nature, since it then does not give somewhat from itself, but it gives itself, or passes into and becomes that man whom it enlightens; or, in proportion to that truth he received, it takes him to itself."[13']

Frost often speaks of this divine correspondence of souls. When he talks of the poem (or "real art") as being written by belief instead of "cunning" or "craft," he refers to the idea put forth in "The Over-Soul" that "Omniscience" and the grace of inspiration are required for great art. Genius is inspired. Emerson states:

> Among the multitude of scholars and authors we feel
> no hallowing presence; we are sensible of a knack
> and skill rather than of inspiration. . . . Their talent is
> some exaggerated faculty . . .so that their strength is
> a disease. . . . But genius is religious . . . . There is
> in all great poets a wisdom of humanity which is
> superior to any talents they exercise. . . . The soul is
> superior to its knowledge; wiser than any of its
> works.[14]

These are precisely Frost's borrowed ideas on "art-belief" in "Education by Poetry."

He suggests that "self-belief," "love-belief," and "art-belief" are closely related to "God-belief," "that the belief in God is a relationship you enter into with Him to bring about the future," and the hereafter.[15] Frost's confidence in the realization of one's beliefs is rooted in Emerson's ideas on the concomitance of belief and action in God's revelation to man. To both writers, the mind is both receiver and projector, believing and fulfilling at once. For believing is not merely preliminary to, but coincident with Emersonian fulfillment:

> We distinguish the announcements of the soul . . . by
> the term *Revelation*. . . . This communication is an
> influx of the Divine mind into our mind. . . . In these
> communications the power to see is not separated
> from the will to do, but the insight proceeds from
> obedience, and the obedience preceeds from a
> joyful perception. . . . Revelation is the disclosure of
> the soul. . . . They are solutions of the soul's own
> questionings.[16]

The influx of spirit, or inspiration, into man's soul is both perceived and felt, and answers the questions which the understanding asks, according to Emerson. Frost, following Emerson, brings about the future by assenting to work, process, and creativity, and by concerning himself with "truth, justice, love, which are the attributes of the soul." These are man's truly relevant moral concerns. We "believe the future in" by addressing ourselves to these subjects, expressing them artistically, and practicing them. They are God; they are the hereafter. Frost's future and hereafter are solidly based on "The Over-Soul." He distills its difficult idealism into a concept of belief, relating it to art, life, love, and God; his poetry pursues and tests these Emersonian ideals by which he finds his home with God.

If "art-belief" is closely linked to "God-belief", what evidence in Emerson does Frost have to justify that claim of the momentary spiritual wholeness that poetry gives the soul? Art, love, and self are the divinity that shapes our ends. In this Emersonian idealism Frost finds his spiritual origins and belief. One final task remains: how to know whether "art-belief" and "self-belief" finally give evidence of Frost's assertion that the poet sheds light on his fellows. He bases this claim on Emerson, who states of the poet,

> If he have not found his home in god, his manners, his forms of speech, the turn of his sentences, the build, shall I say, of all his opinions will involuntarily confess it, let him brave it out how he will. If he have found his centre, the Deity will shine through him, through all the disguises of ignorance, of ungenial temperament, of unfavorable circumstance. The tone of seeking is one, and the tone of having is another.[17]

Expression and art are related to "God-belief." If Frost believed this statement--and I am convinced that he did, if I read "Education by Poetry" correctly--one understands how poetry can be considered his test, the evidence of his grace, and the testament of his fidelity to the truth that his imagination conceives. Poetry is altogether a serious matter of "God-belief," as we shall see in discussing "Two Tramps in Mud Time." There is evident here, too, a tinge of Puritan determinism as to who the elect are, but it appears to be based as much on the evidence of the creative soul doing good works of art as on the man of faith alone.

"Education by Poetry" is essentially transcendental in thought, for therein Frost argues that intuition, inspiration, and spirit are the sources of art and imagination. And the root impulse of the four beliefs (self, love, art, God) is emotion. These beliefs are creative, leading to related kinds of fulfillment; in Romantic theory all are aspects of imagination.

We have not fully accounted for emotion itself in Frost's canon of beliefs. Emerson speaks of visitations of fervor, enthusiasm, and joy that come with divine apprehension. It is the emotion of love that believes itself into fulfillment, or, to put Frost's and Emerson's notions into an English Romantic equivalent, the imagination is unique in its prefigurative power: it can adumbrate a reality or truth to come, until, as Shelley says, it creates the thing it contemplates. Frost is perhaps thinking of Keats's celebrated description of the prefigurative mind, creative in the extreme, because impelled by love, the generative power of the universe.[18] (It is noteworthy that Keats is the only poet mentioned in "Education by Poetry.") Keats talks about surprise as a part of the creative experience, as do Frost and Emerson, but common to all three poets is the Romantic idea that the mind foreknows, foreshadows, and brings into being through belief and desire. Love in its sublime form is creative of aesthetic, philosophical, and eschatological verities--beauty and truth in Keatsian terms. Frost is on occasion concerned with these Romantic ends, finding love his agent or means. Love is the source of his visionary questing, as in "Two Look at Two." It is the uniting power of all form, as in "The Silken Tent," and the source of creative power in mind and universe, as in "Prayer in Spring" and "Mowing."

THOREAU

If Emerson left an intellectual heritage, Thoreau left all that too, and an exemplary life. Frost's kinship with Thoreau is so strong that I believe he attempted to model his life, thought, and art after Thoreau's example, and, moreover, that much of his poetry derives from the record of that life. Late in life Frost remarked in confidence: "You know, I have come to think he was a greater one than Emerson, after all."[19]

Thoreau represents the integrated man, a philosopher, naturalist, poet, and sage, and an artist in prose who is a fountain for Frost's imagination. Both were Latinists, teachers, lecturers, botanizers, farmers, and laborers. Harvard and the Concord and Merrimack Rivers nourished them. Frost looked upstream (in time) to Concord for an example of freedom and the "one man revolution" which Thoreau carried on. If Frost's poetic strategy was "to return to the wilderness of abandoned experience,"[20] it was perhaps Thoreau's example of the uses of the past that turned Frost's head backward so often. *A Week on the Concord and Merrimack Rivers* begins and proceeds in an aura of other poets, observing that a good author will "consult . . . with those who have gone before."[21]

More than any other work *Walden* -- "that great, great book, that sacred book"--awakes Frost's repeated admiration throughout his career": It "surpasses everything we have in America"; its prose is "unversified poetry.[22] Not only is its subject matter of intrinsic excellence but its narrative form is "always near the height of poetry."[23] As with every work which he found useful for his own art, he assigned *Walden* to his students, reading it aloud in class.[24] It is a curious fact that as Frost lived in the pages of *Walden* and the Journals and intensified his admiration for the man and his work, above all others, his life took on the characteristics of his mentor, especially in his later days of creative thought. Then, Frost withdrew into his one-room Ripton cabin to write and think in days of wifeless solitude, relishing, perhaps, the consolations of that solitude outlined in Chapter 5 of *Walden.*

The Journal record of Thoreau's daily experiences commanded Frost's attention;[25] he regarded the entries as uncut gems. Lawrance Thompson's biography identifies Thoreau as the single writer most helpful to the poet's understanding of his craft. He learned immensely from Thoreau's radically inventive metaphors in *Walden* and the Journals. It is stunning to observe how Frost takes the Journals' raw naturalistic facts and works them up into form--resulting in poems such as "the Oven Bird," "Build Soil" and "An Encounter." Entries gave the poet model accounts of the process of contemplating facts to understand their shifting overtones. Thoreau taught Frost how to live and observe as a natural philosopher, exploring the meanness or sublimity of facts and how to give a true account of them through experience. As a poet this deliberation is what Thoreau lived for, as did Frost. He also learned from Thoreau his symbolic manner of writing, by which he might keep the over-curious from the privacy of his soul. Thoreau, as Emerson observed, "piqued the curiosity to know more deeply the secrets of his mind. He had many reserves, an unwillingness to exhibit to profane eyes what was still sacred in his own, and knew well how to throw a poetic veil over his experience."[26] In sum, Thoreau exemplified the high poet and defined his true task.

A poem is the constant symbol of the mind playing freely and taking risks in attempting to achieve form. The ordering process is a reconciling labor, and the core of the form created is metaphor, which unites spirit and matter, as Frost indicated many times. The character of his figurative language describing this process, which is my concern in Chapter VIII, is Romantic, but of a distinctly American brand, deriving from the metaphors and images of Thoreau. Thoreau especially saw the poet as earth-bound, firmly rooted in a farmer's and naturalist's angle of vision, and tasked to make his thought and art out of his experience with the soil and farm. It was not romantic soaring that he taught Frost, but digging. Unlike the English Romantics, who often contemplated nature in wise passiveness, or abandoned it for apocalyptical apprehension, Frost, guided by Thoreau, found the ordering process and insight to be tied to, and dependent on, arduous labor and cultivation of the soil. This is Frost's idea of the Romantic notion of interchange or "correspondence" with nature, though several poems play around the idea of a possible deeper interchange with the "spirit" of Nature. He learned that physical involvement begins the cooperative process of self and nature, leading to the unity of soul that he sought, and the creative potentiality which is its reward. He therefore wanted the immediate experience--bodily and psychic--with the physical world, out of which he hoped to achieve order, spiritual value, and imaginative insight--in short, poetry. *Mens sana in corpore sano* summarizes Frost's golden rule in the pursuit of self-perfection. The experiences and processes leading to this goal of unity are of practical importance to the poet, as Thoreau well knew in remarking: "Some must work in fields if only for the sake of tropes and expression, to serve a parable-maker one day."[27] I believe Frost took up farming to be a writer, following the recommendation of Thoreau. The labor poems discussed in Chapter VIII are pervaded by the cloud of Thoreau, particularly the Thoreau of the Journals.

I can find no more provocative journal entry by Thoreau than the following parabolic advice to the writer to build up the fertile soil within him, that his "harvest" of poems may be full, rich, and accomplished.

> It is a great art in the writer to improve from day to day just that soil and fertility which he has, to harvest that crop which his life yields, whatever it may be. . . . He should be digging, not soaring. Just as earnest as your life is, so deep is your soil. If strong and deep, you will sow wheat and raise bread of life in it.[28]

This passage transmutes into the imaginative richness and depth of "Build Soil," a poem that itself shows a pervasive fertility of mind within the poet.

In some of his best poems Frost is to be seen in the tradition of the earth-anchored Transcendentalism of Thoreau, a tough-minded rather than passive, grace-expectant later Romantic. He is the model of the practical poet who does not separate action and experience from speculation. After Thoreau's example Frost learned how to assay the limits and powers of the mind to know, order, and envision. Often the tone of inquiry is playful or guarded or serious or ambiguously argumentative or contradictory, indicating the variety of ways by which Frost delights in the brilliant play of ideas. He is a Romantic scion, drawing from the vitality of the past, and repeatedly finding in it ways to be new.[29]

2. THE ENGLISH ROMANTICS

In his revealing talk, "A Tribute to Wordsworth," Frost's repeated references to Wordsworth's contemplation of "glory" accentuates the importance of the spiritual basis of great poetry and renown. He says:

> Contemplate glory till it burns your eyes out. . . . The one human thing that won't prove to be vanity: glory. . . . It's the great religious word. The glory of God is all the God there is. The word glory is what fills Him with meaning.[30]

Frost goes on to say where he acquires this highest voice of expression and insight, which is the source of his own verse. It is in the poetry of the past, including the nimbus of Wordsworth. "You give yourself years of poetry to realize what glory is. Years of poetry! . . . you read poem A the better to read poem B. You read B the better to read C. C the better to read D. D the better to read A."[31] The word "glory" alludes not to the spiritual quality of those poems celebrating the beauteous forms of nature, as we might expect, but to the splendor of the spiritual intimations of the child in nature. Glory calls up the splendor of childhood and the visionary gleam in Wordsworth's great ode, "Intimations of Immortality."

Frost finds in Wordsworth's poems celebrating man's redemptive memory of the glory and unity of being of childhood a model for his own poetry. It is the visionary gleam and joy of the child that gives the adult, alien from his God, comfort:

> Those first affections
> Those shadowy recollections, . . .
> Are yet the fountain light of all our day,
> Are yet a master light of all our seeing.

"The Master Speed," as shall be seen, is just this "master light," whose "speed" celebrates the mind's power to swiftly perceive the source of all things. Likewise, "In a Vale" locates the Wordsworthian place of origin of virtue, truth, and poetry. Again, the romantic vision of "The Trial by Existence" presents Wordsworth's notion of the loss of Eden as "a sleep and a forgetting." In this same poem we note the influence of Shelley in the description of the heavenly realm.

In "Birches" we fine a subtle Wordsworthian dimension to the speaker's "dream" of going back to be a youthful birch-swinger, whose glad animal movements tend *toward* heaven. Frost treats the desire to go back as a spiritual intimation of the lost glory; at the same time he treats the climb up the tree as a Shelleyan gesture toward the empyrean, as we shall see in discussing the Romanticism of "Birches" in Chapter V.

In *The Excursion* and "Michael" Wordsworth provided Frost with the pastoral source to his moral imagination. It is so profound a debt that Frost in his great poem "Directive" would acknowledge Wordsworth's role as a guide to the sources of poetry and as redeemer of ruin and the past.

Shelley's and Keats's poems of Romantic abandonment to a richer world of harmony and ease were dangerously attractive to Frost. Keats's nightingale and Shelley's west wind and empyrean realm of "Adonais" beckon to migration, escape, and suicide; it is to this dimension of abandon in their poems that Frost is drawn in a dialectic yet must resist as illusory. Frost's poetic responses are powerful.

Frost's last volume *In the Clearing* adapts the themes and meter of Shelley's "The Skylark," subtitling "Kitty Hawk" "A Skylark . . . in Three-Beat Phrases." Frost's question on Shelley's animism, "How about as a Shelleyan principle of spirit coeternal with the rock part of creation, I ask,"[32] also underlies the enigma of nature in a number of Frost's poems.

Equally problematical is Coleridge's great moral imperative of charity and brotherhood in "The Rime of the Ancient Mariner." Frost carries on the drama of the ballad by asking the question of the limits of charitable responsibility in "Love and a Question."

Frost, like Coleridge, is concerned everywhere with opposites in his works and life. The poet's sense of order lies in the act of imaginative reconciliation. Opposites must be fused in one orientation. He writes in a notebook in England:

> I can hold in unity the ultimate irreconcileable spirit
> and matter, good and evil, monism (cohesion) and
> dualism reaction), peace and strife. It o'er rules the

> harsh divorce that part things natural and divine. Life
> is something that rides steadily on something also
> that passes away. . . . All a man's art is a bursting
> unity of opposites.[33]

This little *biographia poetica* is pure Coleridge, following his idea of
the synthetic power of imagination, which "reveals itself in the balance
or reconciliation of opposite or discordant qualities: of sameness, with
difference; of the general, with the concrete; the idea, with the image;
the individual with the representative."[34] These reconciliations are
always on the point of "bursting" but for the record of them in a poem.
No wonder a poem is the ultimate achievement for Frost, and as such
it explains why he writes poems about poetry and imagination, such
as "The Silken Tent." "Greatest of all attempts to say one thing in
terms of another is the philosophic attempt to say matter in terms of
spirit, or spirit in terms of matter, to make the final unity. . . ." It is the
height of poetry . . . the height of all poetic thinking."[35] The agent
bridging these opposites and reaching that height is the imagination.
    One need only read Frost's essay "A Romantic Chasm" to discern
a Coleridgean concern for opposites and the metaphoric vitality of
poetry. The chasm derives of course from "Kubla Khan," the foremost
poem on the Romantic idea of imagination. The pleasure dome is an
artifice in which all opposites are reconciled, while the source and
center of all life in imagination's domain is the "romantic chasm" which
forces a mighty fountain. This chasm is analogous to the creative
mist of Genesis, and thus the origin of all things. Frost significantly
refers to the ultimate beginning as "the word." In a letter, he again
refers to the site of creation and reconciliation as a savage place like
Coleridge's chasm: "Life sways perilously at the confluence of
opposing forces. Poetry in general plays perilously in the same wild
place."[36] That wildness and vigor reiterate the cloud metaphor out of
which poetry is born.
    Frost's accounts of creative experience repeatedly show a
familiarity with the Romantics' moments of inspiration. He remarks
that "Shelley writes of 'spirit of delight--rarely comest thou.'" He
describes these Shelleyan visitations as "delight," "ecstasy,"
"wildness," "wonder," "unexpected supply," and ""a revelation" in "The

Figure a Poem Makes," a remarkable essay on Romantic attitudes about imagination, spontaneity, feeling, surprise, and poetry-making.

Shelley analogizes poetry as a microcosm and an ordering out of chaos: "It makes us the inhabitants of a world to which the familiar world is a chaos. . . . It creates anew the universe, after it has been annihilated in our minds by the recurrence of impressions blunted by reiteration."[37] The poet orders out of chaos. A poem is a check against it, creating anew the unverse, as Shelley asserts in "A Defense of Poetry." Frost too made many defenses.

On his ideas of form-making Frost seems instructed by Keats. Frost read Keats's *Hyperion* as a poem about the process of achieving form, stating, "Keats . . . set out to show you the great revolution of form getting the better of power."[38] In the same letter he states, "Every day and every new poem of a poet is a revolution of the spirit." Frost means, among other things, turning spirit into form. He needs only "freedom" of imagination "to summons aptly from the vast chaos of all [he] has lived through." This statement is all the political theory Frost needs. Freedom to create will prove to be an esthetic declaration of independence in "Build Soil," which is a poem about poetry-making and metaphor building.

Frost's seminal essay, "Letter to *The Amherst Student"* serves as a fitting summary to the discussion of form-making and poetry in this chapter. The letter celebrates the creative act as the projection of mind on chaos. The "form" achieved is "everything" to Frost, the symbol of all that is heroic and original in our spirit:

> The background in hugeness and confusion shading away from where we stand into black and utter chaos; and against the background any small man-made figure of order and concentration. What pleasanter than that this should be so? . . . We don't worry about this confusion; we look out on [it] with an instrument or tackle it to reduce it. It is partly because we are afraid it might prove too much
> for us. . . . But it is more because we like it, we were born to it, born to use it and have practical reason for wanting it there. To me any little form I assert upon

> it is velvet, as the saying is, and to be considered for
> how much more it is than nothing.[39]

Of all "man-made figures," a poem is the height of form and thought, a constant symbol for all that a person can imagine, seek, and achieve. It is a pure assertion of form, a projection of identity through imagination. The poet is the source of value, whose artifice rescues one from the surrounding illimitable blackness.

Like the cloud of other poets, which give impetus and direction to Frost's poetry, the clouds of nature are given shape by our own imagination. When Frost asserts that we all have this ability to find "suggestions of form in the rolling clouds of nature," he is attributing the most noble and spiritual faculty within us all; for "in us nature reaches its height in form."[40] The following chapters amplify on Frost's quest for form.

CHAPTER III
THE VISIONARY MIND; THE FIGURE OF THE POET; THE POETIC IMAGINATION

And for a moment all was plain
That men have thought about in vain.

Our concern here is to establish the Romantic heritage of Frost's poetry by investigating those poems concerned with the mind's visionary power, the nature of its revelations in confronting and interpreting nature, poetic inspiration, self-reliance, originality, and the creative imagination. Noting Frost's Romantic sources illuminates the character of his ideas and language. To define and dramatize his concept of the mind and imagination, and his delineation of the poet by various metaphors and myths, he draws predominantly from the language of Emerson and Thoreau.

We have noted how some of Frost's poems speak in the tone of Wordsworth in his great Ode. They imply "there was a time" of earlier flight and insight before the visionary gleam darkened and earth enveloped the man. Frost once believed that "Thought has a pair of dauntless wings" taking him past the sun to "Sirius' disc." "Bond and Free" sets up the recurrent antinomies of heavenly "Thought" and earthly "Love." In "The Bear" Platonism is the "one extreme" that attracted him in his subjective youth. In "To Earthward" he recalls the ecstasy of youth when "I lived on air." "Canis Major" humorously celebrates a night of cosmic unity with the brightest star in the heavens. These poems intimate Frost's Emersonian and Shelleyan visionary phase that other poems rejected or diminished or found compelling enough to take up and test with great subtlety. Such a poem as "Unharvested" would continue to "live on air" more obliquely than "To Earthward" but is like it in its attempt to sense some deeper significance in nature's scents. Essence, as we shall see, is often a Frostian preoccupation.

Frost's first volume of poems should remind us that a boy's will is not quite the same as a man's will, and in their difference lies a lesson. A boy is inclined to hold Romantic ideals before his maturity and experience tell him differently. Several of the poems in *A Boy's Will* are Romantic in their subjectivity and themes, and quite maskless. Flower poems, "Into My Own," "In a Vale," "My Butterfly," and "The Trial By Existence," recount youth's will to believe in an idealism rooted in the Transcendental - Romantic tradition. Later volumes are skeptical of this tradition in which Frost grew up, but there is evidence that he never abandoned his Romantic sympathies, or, indeed his doubts, which also appear in his first volume. As the poet said about his beliefs, "I take nothing back." One of his enduring tents is an Emersonian concept of mind.

1. THE VISIONARY MIND

"All Revelation"
A head thrusts in as for a view,
But where it is it thrusts in from
Or what it is it thrusts into
By that Cyb'laean avenue,
And what can of its coming come,

And whither it will be withdrawn,
And what take hence or leave behind,
These things the mind has pondered on
A moment and still asking gone.
Strange apparition of the mind!

But the impervious geode
Was entered, and its inner crust
Of crystals with a ray cathode
At every point and facet glowed
In answer to the mental thrust.

Bring out the stars, bring out the flowers,
Thus concentrating earth and skies
So none need be afraid of size.
All revelation has been ours.

"All Revelation" is an affirmative poem in the sense that in revealing the relationship between mind and matter, it asserts that the mind's quest for meaning in nature is our highest pursuit. Meaning depends on the "mental thrust." It is Frost's most Emersonian poem; it tests the idealism found in *Nature* and "The Over-Soul," using Emerson's very language in answering his claims. These essays regard the mind as the locus of all things, the maker of value and form. Through the Understanding and the Reason (Emerson's two modes of knowing derived from Coleridge'), the mind reduces nature to unity. "Revelation is the disclosure of the soul," and nature serves as the "apocalypse of the mind."[1] "All Revelation" regards the mind, aided by the discipline of science, as the agent and power which perceives a correspondence between man and nature and, indeed, can "concentrate," reconcile, or see relationship in all things and trumpet its findings in the language of art. In Emerson's words, "nothing but is beautiful in the whole. A single object is only so far beautiful as it suggests this universal grace. The poet, the painter, the sculptor, the musician, the architect, seem each to *concentrate* this radiance of the world in one point."[2] Man's mind is, then, an "alembic, distilling or concentrating" into form "earth and skies." Frost probes Emerson's claim that "One after another [man's] victorious thought comes up with and reduces all things, until the world becomes at last only a realized will."[3] On one level of meaning, then, the poem celebrates the creative mind of the artist, the one whose insight takes on form. On another level, the geode is simply a complex grain of sand; but the point of the poem is to play with the Romantic idea: "To see the world in a grain of sand."

The triumph of the modern mind lies in the discipline of science, whose findings may help man apprehend reality, if not a teleology. Frost and Emerson agree that "All science has one aim, namely, to find a theory of nature," by which man may "enjoy an original relation to the universe."[4] In this way science offers a means of revelation, for it fuses knowledge, reason, and intuition in an act of mind, of poetry, that Frost, expanding Emerson's epistemological notions, considers fully imaginative.

The first two stanzas are concerned with mental thrust into material reality, via the "Cyb'laean avenue" of earth, in the mind's quest for insight into ultimate mystery: the meaning, purpose, origins, and ends of nature. Ever conscious of the enigma of its being, the mind has nowhere to probe but the element in which it is immersed. Our questing and questioning spirit considers the "where," "what," and "whither" of things. This is the dramatic inquiry of philosophical idealism anticipated by Emerson in *Nature* :

> Three problems are put by nature to the mind: What is matter? Whence is it and Whereto? . . . Idealism saith: matter is a phenonenon, not a substance. Idealism acquaints us with the total disparity between the evidence of our own being and the evidence of the world's being. The one is perfect; the other, incapable of any assurance.[5]

He goes on to say that nature is a creation of the mind, which is a part of the universal mind. All things exist for each spirit and the "all in each." If "behind nature, throughout nature, spirit is present," then, "the Supreme Being does not build up nature around us, but puts it forth through us." Since matter is spirit, it then follows that "the noblest ministry of nature is to stand as the apparition of God."[6]

Frost's sturdy reliance on the individual, interpretive, creative mind is not relativistic here, for he implicitly subscribes to Emerson's basic idea that self-reliance is God-reliance.

Thus, Emerson's epistemology is the subject and reference to "All Revelation"; the mind's relation to the "Cyb'laean avenue" prompts the profoundest questionings in Frost and is the abiding "strange apparition of the mind." For both writers, nature perceived and weighed by the mind is an "apparition"--an appearance ghosting of God for Emerson, and a phenomenon of spirit for Frost. Equally relevant, too, is the mind's awareness of itself and its powers of perception and understanding; its own advent and being is a "strange apparition."

The key third stanza symbolically probes the dynamic relationship between mind and matter. It refers to more than a "television tube," or epistemology and sexuality, or an unaccountable scientific experiment.[7] The poem is indebted to Emerson's descriptions of the qualities of mind and matter found in *Nature*. The "ray cathode" irradiating the "impervious geode" symbolizes the projecting mind illuminating the world, here represented as a dark, crystalline cavity. As a cathode ray projects a stream of electrons so as to ascertain the highly organized matter and form of the microcosmic geode, so the mind illuminates the macrocosmic world. Frost's geode is the equivalent to Emerson's crystal, which, as the "marrow" of nature reveals, when rightly perceived, the moral and spiritual world:

> Every chemical change from the rudest crystal up to the laws of life . . . shall hint or thunder to man the laws of right and wrong. . . . A leaf, a drop, a crystal . . . is related to the whole, and partakes of the perfection of the whole.[8]

The marrow of Frost's geode objectifies Emerson's "center of nature" wherein lies the moral law, which is

> the pith and marrow of every substance, every relation, and every process. All things with which we deal, preach to us. . . . Each particle is a microcosm, and faithfully renders the likeness of the world.[9]

If "every property of matter--in its solidity or resistance [analogized in the ray's penetration of the geode]--is a school for the understanding," the cathode ray[10] itself is Frost's equivalent to the Emersonian mind in its relation to nature. Emerson states: "Man its an analogist, and studies relations in all objects. He is placed in the centre of beings, and a ray of relation passes from every other being to him."[11]

The interchange between mind and matter is symbolized by the glow of the geode's inner crust, acted upon by the "ray cathode." The crystals "At every point and facet glowed/ In answer to the mental thrust." The lines dramatize Emerson's remark that there exists a "radical correspondence between visible things and human thoughts."[12] Truth, or knowledge, clearly lies in the mind's exercise on matter. The third stanza objectifies the working of the mind, to state in symbolic form Emerson's statement that "all spiritual facts are represented by natural symbols."

The role of the poet as both discoverer of correspondence and communicator of his discovered truths is the theme of the last stanza.

His eyes seek rays of relation everywhere; as Emerson further remarks: "A man's power to connect his thought with its proper symbol, and so to utter it, depends on . . . his love of truth and his desire to communicate it without loss."[13]   The eye, Emerson's analogue for the creative mind, is the agent of such correspondence-making, performing its god-like role of integrating all reality into a verbal whole. Near and far, center and circumference, large and small, earth and sky come under the suzerainty of the creative eye. The relationship between it and the natural universe--*i.e.,* between the ray cathode and the geode--now becomes clearer, and is spelled out in Sherman Paul's discussion of Emerson's epistemology:

> When one tries to diffuse the focus of the eye, and thereby 'to embrace the whole field' objects lose their solid-convexity and the whole field becomes concave: the horizon literally becomes circular, as Emerson felt when he viewed 'the bending horizon.' The 'limit,' Ortega says, 'is a surface that tends to take the form of a hemisphere viewed from within.' And this concavity begins, as Emerson also noted, at the eye. The result was the exhilaration of feeling one's centrality and penetration of space, and Emerson felt this in viewing the landscape and the heavens. He noted Aristotle's notion of space as a container and pictured the world as 'a hollow temple,' the beauty and symmetry of which depended on the eye.[14]

The eye, always positioned at the center of material reality--the hollow sanctum of the geode in "All Revelation"--brings everything to it, seeks to impose form and relation on what it sees, as the will forever seeks to exert a response from the mind's eye. In sum, the mind is a lens converging and concentrating matter into form.[15] Since the mind has this magical power, "none need be afraid of size/ All Revelation has been ours." But is revelation ours presently? The use of the perfect tense in the last line indicates that the apocalypse of the mind has always been and still is ours but that perhaps man, dominated by mechanistic, philosophical systems rather than Romantic idealism, has not always assented to the doctrine of the unity of mind and nature. But science, being a construct of the mind, can serve idealism. Frost is intent on assuring us that Emerson is highly relevant to our day, for he regards *Nature* as an appropriate manifesto for science and modern epistemology. The essay asserts: "Every property of matter is a school for the understanding,--its solidity or resistance. . . . Reason transfers all these lessons into its own world of thought, by perceiving the analogy that marries Matter and Mind. Nature is a discipline of the understanding in intellectual truths."[16] Whitehead and Einstein would surely agree with this statement, for all scientific investigation ultimately leads man to a revelation of the unity that underlies the universe. Heriocally and intrepidly the mind thrusts itself into material reality in a most Emersonian confrontation. That confrontation is the source and substance of "All Revelation," and others of Frost's quest poems.

"AN UNSTAMPED LETTER IN OUR RURAL LETTER BOX"

Call it revelation or intuition, Frost often expresses his belief in the visionary moment, but nowhere so affirmatively as in the voice of the philosopher-poet of "An Unstamped Letter in Our Rural Letter Box." He tells of his moment of transcendental vision in which the external world coalesces with the life of the mind, or soul. The fusion of two stars in a brilliant flash analogizes two memories coming together in an intense inner clarification. The experience also refers to a poet's creative moment, the flash marking the rare occasion of inspiration, so described in "How Hard it is to Keep from Being King . . ."

> This perfect moment of unbafflement ,
> . . . . .
> [A] summons out of nowhere like a jinni.
> We know not what we owe this moment to,
> It may be wine, but much more likely love--
> . . . . .
> It's what my father must mean by departure,
> Freedom to flash off into wild connections.
> Once you have known it nothing else will do.
> Our days all pass awaiting its return.

The "wild connections" of poetic metaphor are likewise described in "An Unstamped Letter":

> Inside the brain
> Two memories that long had lain,
> Now quivered toward each other, lipped
> Together, and together slipped.

The experience is at once visionary and creative; the letter is a report to the semi-Philistine farmer, who is like the tramp-visionary poet in that he too has had similar, but lesser, ordering experiences in daily farm tasks:

> Things must have happened to you, yet,
> And have occurred to you no doubt,
> If not indeed from sleeping out,
> Then from the work you went about
> In farming well--or pretty well.

The labors of farming, as we shall see, are analogous to the poet's ordering.

In "An Unstamped Letter" the poet stands a constant, attentive watch on the thoughts that flash and fuse within his mind. The central occupation of his life is to record these stellar illuminations as they come. Like Keats's watcher of planetary skies, he regards poetic thought as heaven-sent rather than reflections of sublunary, conventional modes of thinking. Thoreau has so described the poet as an astronomer of the mind, whose occupation is to chart carefully the stars of thought flashing in him:

> The poet must be continually watching the moods of
> his mind, as the astronomer watches the aspects of
> the heavens. . . . The humblest observer would see
> some stars shoot. . . . Catalogue stars, those
> thoughts whose orbits are as rarely calculated as
> comets. It matters not whether they visit my mind or
> yours,--whether the meteor falls in my field or in
> yours,--only that it come from heaven.[17]

Different in tone from Thoreau's straightforward self-assuredness, the poem can be read as Frost's transcendental self addressing a verse message to his more proprietary, conventional alter-ego. If the tone is playful, even pixieish, it is because the man of letters cannot comfortably proclaim or "boast" *ex cathedra* as visionary the apocalypse in his mind and its correspondence in nature. His letter, like his office, has no official stamp or imprimatur to it. A man of "letters," he must speak as a "tramp astrologer," *sotto voce* :

> Please, my involuntary host,
> Forgive me if I seem to boast.
> 'Tis possible you may have seen,
> Albeit through a rusty screen,
> The same sign Heaven showed your guest.

In this guise of a pauper, like Shakespeare's motley fools, Frost speaks of the highest truth and has fun in the process of dealing with this traditionally serious poetic theme.

"UNHARVESTED"

> A scent of ripeness from over a wall.
> And come to leave the routine road
> And look for what had made me stall,
> There sure enough was an apple tree
> That had eased itself of its summer load,
> And of all but its trivial foliage free,
> Now breathed as light as a lady's fan.
> For there there had been an apple fall
> As complete as the apple had given man.
> The ground was one circle of solid red.
>
> May something go always unharvested!
> May much stay out of our stated plan,
> Apples or something forgotten and left,
> So smelling their sweetness would be no theft.

I have already said that Frost's Romanticism has as its object the apprehension of an essential truth. In "Unharvested" he talks about essences, the real and yet ideal knowledge that the tree yields to the sensitive, transcendentally attuned mind. Despite its title, this sonnet records a rich poetic harvest of meaning abstracted from the apple fall, "as complete as the apple had given man." The line "May something go always unharvested" rejects mere commodity as the only gift of nature. The "something" in the "scent" and "smell" perceived from a distance, or over the wall, bespeaks an essence--both literally and metaphysically--divined by the poet, who reacts affirmatively to what he senses. The poet alone plucks such knowledge of ultimates from the real.

Thoreau's Journal spells out the transcendental meaning attached to the effluence of apples and helps illuminate the poem:

> The mystery of the life of plants is kindred with that of our own lives. . . . The ultimate expression or fruit of any created thing is a fine effluence which only the most ingenious worshipper perceives at a reverent distance. . . . Only that intellect makes any progress toward conceiving of the essence which at the same time perceives the effluence. . . .
>
> There is no ripeness which is not, so to speak, something ultimate in itself, and not merely a perfected means to a higher end. In order to be ripe it must serve a transcendent use. The ripeness of a leaf, being perfected, leaves the tree at that point and never returns to it. It has nothing to do with any other fruit which the tree may bear, and only the genius of the poet can pluck it.
>
> The fruit of the tree is neither in the seed nor the timber,--the full grown tree,--but it is simply the highest use to which it can be put.[18]

Frost, as "ingenious worshipper," finds an effluence and "transcendent use" of his Thoreauvian apples; his intellect conceives of an "essence" and "higher end" in so outwardly simple a scene. The poem is typical of an indirection in talking about ultimates and the import of natural fact (wherein olfactory essence yields Platonic essence). The poem speaks of ultimates guardedly; fragrant, extravagant nature bespeaks a transcendental, but deftly disguised belief.

2. THE FIGURE OF THE POET

Frost's figures of the poet enact the virtues of self-reliance, instinctual wildness, integrity, and daring. These are often inspired by an Emersonian conception of the poet, whose calling is filled with difficulty, struggle, and isolation; the poems remain positive in their Emersonian regard for the poet's role as guide and hero.

"RIDERS"

The surest thing there is is we are riders,
And though none too successful at it, guiders,
Through everything presented, land and tide
And now the very air, of what we ride.

What is this talked-of mystery of birth
But being mounted bareback on the earth?
We can just see the infant up astride,
His small fist buried in the bushy hide.

There is our wildest mount--a headless horse.
But though it runs unbridled off its course,
And all our blandishments would seem defied,
We have ideas yet that we haven't tried.

The metaphor of riding in "Riders" refers not only to man's inventiveness in utilizing nature (an inventiveness guided by the *idea* of science) but also to the philosopher-poet's being borne away by instinct, inspiration, and poetic feeling and not always knowing where he is going but relishing the Pegasian flight wherever it may take him. The metaphor appears in several of Emerson's essays. In "Montaigne," Plotinus, Fenelon, Pindar, and Byron are philosophers who get astride an idea, but "each of these riders drives too fast,"[19] whereas Frost maintains that "We have ideas that we haven't tried" to ride, and that cavalier testing is the essence of sport and adventure.

In his essay "Inspiration," Emerson prefers abandonment to control, which is precisely the "wild" "free" quality that Frost wants as a poet.[20] Emerson's poet employs as signs the facts of all branches of knowledge,"for in every word he speaks he rides on them as the horses of thought."[21] From Emerson Frost learned to disdain tameness and to trust instinct and intuition in riding a poetic thought. The last stanza of "Riders" renders the idea in "The Poet" that we trust not the Understanding (the head) but the Reason, Emerson's term for instinct and creative intuition, symbolized in horse sense:

> As the traveller who has lost his way throws the reins
> on his horse's neck and trusts to the instinct of the
> animal to find his road, so must we do with the divine
> animal who carries us through this world.[22]

The divine animal is, of course, "instinct" and inspiraton, manifestations of the One Mind and Nature, of which man's mind is a part. "The Poet" notes that "Plato calls the world an animal;"[23] it is to be mastered by thought and language. Frost's headless horse to which reins cannot be attached further intensifies the virtues of wildness and unpredictability.[24] It also represents an unbridled idea and the free language to express that idea, for as Emerson remarks in "The Poet," "all language is vehicular and transitive, and is good, as ferries and horses are, for conveyance."[25]

In riding nature, which is also a vehicle of thought for Emerson, Frost's poet is a "guider," often "none too successful at it." Emerson assigns the poet the function of guide--"yield[ing] us a new thought" and "unlock[ing] our chains and admit[ting] us to a new scene."[26] Frost's misgivings about the poet's ability as "guide" are Emerson's. Emerson states: "the winged poet can carry man to heaven but does not always have the ability or know the way; and as a consequence I tumble down again into my old nooks . . . and have lost my faith in the possibility of any guide who can lead me thither where I would be."[27] Guiding man through land, tide, and air, Frost's creative man assumes, once again, the Emersonian task of the poet who is addressed as "thou true land-lord! sea-lord! air-lord!"[28]

Continuing Emerson's analogue of the poet, the second stanza of

"Riders" pictures an infant astride the horse, clutching its sides. The infant is Emerson's "wildly wise" child[29] of unified, innocent mind, passing through the world, "pursu[ing] the game" in adventurous flight, illuminating the darkness with his eyes, and giving musical order to all things. The talked-of mystery of birth is merely "being mounted bareback on the earth" whereby the individual soul controls nature and in turn is shaped by it. Whether referring to the birth of a baby or a poem, the soul has only nature to ride.

In "The Poet" Emerson expounds on the mystery of birth and the interaction of soul and nature, stating, "all facts of the animal economy, sex, nutriment, gestation, birth, growth, are symbols of the passage of the world into the soul of man, to suffer there a change and reappear a new and higher fact."[30] The perfected soul and the shaped poem are the issue of this "passage." To the degree that the poet rides nature instinctively, the form of his ideas will be correspondingly excellent. Frost is saying we have ideas that we haven't tested yet because we have not realized the potentiality of the soul's intuitions. "The Poet" asserts that the true poet "speaks somewhat wildly," a point which clarifies Frost's stress on departure and wildness in poetry; poets sponsor untried thought, which is "the intellect released," taking "its direction from its celestial life."[31] Frost would be like Emily Dickinson, "inebriate of air," carried to realms of inspired poetic thought and utterance. Such unpredictable creative riding (or writing) is the figure the imagination and a poem make.

"A LONE STRIKER"

Self-reliance and commitment to the vocation of poet are the subjects of "A Lone Striker." The speaker not only goes on strike against an "institution" but also strikes out on his own, making a new beginning in his resolve to think and "re-renew a love"--*i.e.,* the getting back to his dearest concerns. His formative decision takes place on a cliff[32] "among the tops of trees," where nature serves as the stage for the speaker's resolve to transcend his former life. The lines describing the trees and this elevated rebel--"their upper branches round him wreathing,/ Their breathing mingled with his breathing"--suggest his identification with nature. As in "Directive" the poet seeks the pastoral source of intellectual vitality; the upward path, the spring, and the hoped-for renewal of love prepare the poet for later creative action. The Lone Striker's "path" and "spring that wanted drinking" lead to an inspirational, meditative resurgence. His resolution is not just talk: "With him it boded action, deed." The speaker is mindful, perhaps, of Emerson's admonition, "'good thoughts are no better than good dreams, unless they be executed!'"[33] The confluence of thought and action is poetry, the final integration of all things related to the self. As in "Two Tramps in Mud Time" (which will be discussed in a later chapter), thought and action, love and need, vocation and avocation, must finally unite to occasion the highest creativity.[34]

The speaker would live in this higher sphere. The factory is not "divine"; but the renewal of love and thought in the woods is. Frost does not demean the task of wool spinning ("man's ingenuity was good"); it simple does not release his potentiality.

The Lone Striker is a self-reliant soul. He must be a striker if he is to grow. On the formation of great men Emerson remarks that the stronger are "reactive and "inhabit a higher sphere of thought. . . . The true artist has the planet for his pedestal."[35] We find this strength and purposefulness in the Striker's firm withdrawal from the "institutions" of machines[36] to a higher sphere in which the tree cliffs become his pedestal. In sum, he is a Romantic who transcends the values of his society and validates his role as poet.

"PAUL'S WIFE"

The figure of the poet in this higher sphere of beauty and love is more fancifully delineated in "Paul's Wife," a fairy tale about a mythic craftsman's marriage to the principle of beauty. Paul is a hero and an artist with an ax--a poet, that is, who not only releases the spirit of beauty--a naiad--but also becomes her possessor. In adapting an American tall tale about Paul Bunyan, Frost illustrates his own ideas about the character of the true backwoods hero. Paul exists alternately in the loggers' world and in an ideal realm of beauty, symbolized in his marriage. Like the poet in "Two Tramps in Mud Time," he has integrated his inner and outer, public and private, vocational and avocational lives (and loves). He can do "wonders," such as "slip[ping]/ The bark of a whole tamarack off whole" with his

37

ax, master nature, and even defy physical laws, according to the tall tales about him. He is both folk hero and an artist shaping nature to his purpose.

Paul, his wife, and their courtship are departures from the American legend. There is something mythical about her role as naiad and Paul's deed of sawing a hollow pine log, extracting a "pith" or "skin a snake had cast," and delicately metamorphosing it into a girl. We are reminded of Prospero's magical power over nature in *The Tempest*.[37] He too releases the "imprisoned" spirit of fancy, Ariel, from a "rift" in a "cloven pine." "It was mine art/ When I arrived and heard thee, that made gape/ The pine and let thee out" (I. ii, 291-93). The hollow pine imprisoning Paul's wife, similarly, has "no entrance"; her metamorphosis and emergence as a water nymph from a sheath of pith identifies her with Ariel, who is first instructed by Prospero to "go make thyself like a nymph o' the sea" (I,ii,301). The pith or snakeskin is the mysterious essence on which Paul works his magic, bringing forth his spirit of beauty. This detail reinforces our understanding of the girl's fairy nature; for fairies traditionally live in snakeskins, as Shakespeare indicates in *A Midsummer Night's Dream*: "And there the snake throws her enamell'd skin,/ Weed wide enough to wrap a fairy in" (II,i, 255-56).

Paul's romantic role now changes from creator to lover. Whatever his wife is--muse, inspirer, idealized beauty, or imagination--she ascends with Paul "half-way up a cliff," radiant like a star. Perhaps Frost wants to dramatize the correspondences Emerson makes between the love for a woman and the love of beauty. The essay "Love" identifies a woman's beauty with ideal beauty, or divinity, to which poets would wed themselves and "find the highest joy."[38] This conception of love and beauty explains the secrecy and sanctity of Paul's marriage. His "business" is with beauty, a private affair in which only he, in creative acts, can "praise her" and "name her." Paul is a "terrible possessor" who "wouldn't be spoken to about a wife/ In any way the world knew how to speak." This passion for privacy reflects the poet's secrecy in his personal life and in his verses, the most famous statement of which is his remark to Sidney Cox: "I have written to keep the over curious out of the secret places of my mind both in my verse and in my letters to such as you.[39]

3. THE POET AND IMAGINATION

Frost's Romantic heritage also accounts for the figures taken from nature, by which he expresses his concept of imagination. Again, Thoreau is his exemplar, one who describes inner states of mind through natural phenomena. From the evidence of Frost's borrowings, he carries on this tradition of using Romantic metaphors to describe creative power. Wind, thaw, flow, and moon mirror mind and spirit in generative motion; the seasonal shift from frost to mud time has its internal analogue in the creative moment. Frost also treats Transcendental ideas about time and space and the imagination's power to reconcile opposites. He writes celebratory poems about how poetry itself has the magical power to give to the spirit unity and form, an artifice like a silken tent bound by ties of love and thought to everything on earth.

"A HILLSIDE THAW"

"A Hillside Thaw" celebrates the power of the creative spirit to sculpt nature. The moon, a stock Romantic symbol for the imagination, casts its magical "spell" to achieve a momentary stay, much like the frozen pastoral beauty of a Grecian Urn. (The moon is a "witch" whose "gentle cast," like that of Shelley's Witch of Atlas, represents the power of imagination.) Frost, the moon's magical "chill effect," fixes the lizards. Nature outdoes the poet's imagination ("The thought of my attempting such a stay!"), yet the poem itself makes a similar momentary stay.

Frost's poem derives from the hillside thaw described in the chapter "Spring" in *Walden*. Nature's artistry is a sign of the creative spirit abroad and within us. Frost's thronging silver lizards are forms cognate to the organic designs of the thaw in *Walden* . That these "innumerable little streams overlap and interlace one with another," like friezework of Grecian art,[40] prompts Thoreau to feel that he stands "in the laboratory of the Artist who made the world and me . . . where he was still at work, sporting on this bank and with excess of energy strewing his fresh designs about."[41] Each "meandering channel" making up a "little silvery stream glancing like lightning"[42] metamorphoses into Frost's glittering, wriggling lizards. They are

39

analogous to "the frost [that] comes out of the ground like a dormant quadruped from its burrow, and seeks the sea with music."[43]

The ingenious designs flowing from the thawing frost was a fact (which Thoreau emphasizes) of special relevance to Frost. For the mysterious force creating beauty is the poet's namesake, *frost.* [44] This punning further suggests that outer nature is the mirror of an inner creative spirit. The idea that frost corresponds to the poetic imagination stems from Thoreau's observation that

> Nature . . . is mother of humanity. This is the frost
> coming out of the ground; this is Spring. . . . These
> foleaceous heaps lie along the bank like the slag of
> a furnace, showing that Nature is "in full blast" within.
> The earth is . . . living poetry.[45]

"A Hillside Thaw" presents nature as a symbol of mind; thaw analogizes imaginative vitality. Thoreau summarizes: "Thus it seemed that this one hillside illustrated the principle of all the operations of Nature. . . . What Champolion will decipher this hieroglyphic for us?[46] Frost not only deciphers but also transforms it into poetry in a celebration of the self--*himself*, if one accepts the punning on his name. The study of nature yields self-knowledge and provides the poet his figures.

"TO THE THAWING WIND"

This poem uses the same metaphor of melting to suggest the poet's inner transformation. His thoughts would thaw as does nature, whose outer weather "bring[s] the singer," "gives[s] the buried flower a dream," and makes his window "flow." This change from ice to thaw mirrors an inner weather of creative change. Thoreau also asserts that

> We too have our thaws. They come in our January
> moods, when our ice cracks, and our sluices break
> loose. Thought that was frozen up under stern
> experience gushes forth in feeling and expression. . .
> Our thoughts hide unexpressed, like the birds under

their downy or resinous scales. . . . My winter
thoughts are like . . . blossom buds which . . . will
not expand into leaves and flowers until summer
comes.[47]

Frost's invitation to the wind--

> Burst into my narrow stall;
> . . . . .
> Run the rattling pages o'er;
> Scatter poems on the floor;
> Turn the poet out of door--

carries Thoreau's figurative meaning. New thoughts and feelings
invoke new poetry. Driving the poet from his hermitic "stall," the wind
scatters the old leaves of verse. Severely restricted by his winter life,
the poet must be "turn[ed] . . . out doors," a phrase Thoreau uses in
advising that we rid ourselves of stultifying winter "conscience," which
"is instinct bred in the house" and which makes thought and feeling
"an unnatural breeding in and in." "I say, turn it [conscience] out of
doors."[48] There is renewal in the creative thaw that comes naturally:
"Would you know your own moods, be weather-wise. . . . Let all things
give way to the impulse of expression. It is the but unfolding, the
perennial spring. As well stay the spring. Who shall resist the thaw.[49]

"THE FREEDOM OF THE MOON"

> I've tried the new moon tilted in the air
> Above a hazy tree-and-farmhouse cluster
> As you might try a jewel in your hair.
> I've tried it fine with little breadth of luster,
> Alone, or in one ornament combining
> With one first-water star almost as shining.
>
> I put it shining anywhere I please.
> By walking slowly on some evening later,
> I've pulled it from a crate of crooked trees
> And brought it over glosssy water, greater,

> And dropped it in, and seen the image wallow,
> The color run, all sort of wonder follow.

This is also a poem on imagination, but it stands in exact contrast to "A Hillside Thaw" in that the new moon (a mere crescent of light) has no symbolic value. It shines but does not magically fix. It is simply an object of nature, material which the poet freely arranges and orders. This outdoor fooling with the moon is "play," an imaginative game.

Frost's role here fits Emerson's poet, who "conforms things to his thoughts . . . esteem[ing] nature . . . as fluid, and impresses his being thereon."[50] The poem also suggests the poet's Orphic role which Frost in a letter describes as controlling nature "by the power of music like Amphion or Orpheus. It is an old occupation with me. The trees have learned that they have to come where I play them to. I enjoy the power I find I have over them . . . the trees dancing obedience to the poet.[51] "The Freedom of the Moon" dramatizes this free, experimenting and arranging of visiual effects, suggesting in the action of "I've tried," I put," "I've pulled," "brought," and "dropped." The central eye is Frost's subject here and parallels Wordsworth's identification of imagination as "creation in the eye" and "powers . . . that colour, model and combine/ The things perceived with . . . an absolute/ Essential energy."[52] This energy is what "The Freedom of the Moon" is about. The poet's activity, a passion for finding relationships, raises him above the astronomer's cold, passive observation of the factual heaven.

The poet's last and most satisfying act is to drop his moon in water and observe the colorful "wonder" that follows. Thoreau also describes the visual wonders attending

> the reflections of the moon sliding down the watery
> concave . . . [,] myriad little mirrors reflecting the disk
> of the moon with equal   brightness to an eye rightly
> placed. The pyramid . . . of light . . . is the outline of
> that portion of the shimmering surface which an eye
> takes in.[53]

Seen in relation to this source, the poem suggests that wonder lies in the eye's proper positioning, a dictum at the heart of Thoreau's exact observation of Walden Pond.

"CARPE DIEM"

"The Freedom of the Moon" concerns the spatial imagination; "Carpe Diem" may be considered a companion poem in its concern for the temporal imagination. More than a critique of hedonism, or any way of life that adheres to sense and the present, it is about the imagination's perspective on past, present, and future. The poem refers to the long-imposed theme of gathering rosebuds ""while ye may," advice given from the point of view of "Age." Thus Herrick's "Gather-roses burden" is an admonition that youth be made intellectually aware of the love and happiness they presently have:

> 'Twas Age imposed on poems
> Their gather-roses burden
> To warn against the danger
> That overtaken lovers
> From being overflooded
> With happiness should have it.
> And yet not know they have it.

Thus, to "seize" the present is to take advantage of life, not only physically but also intellectually. This, youth cannot do, for the mind requires time to attach meaning to experience. The imagination lives more in the future and most in the past, which it interprets and shapes; for

> the present
> Is too much for the senses,
> Too crowding, too confusing--
> Too present to imagine.

"Carpe Diem" gives minimal importance to Herrick's rosebud hedonism. Like "Build Soil" it calls for a poetry of reflection, delay, and perspective. As the chaotic present becomes the past, the imagination is able to order and interpret it. The very last word of the poem, "imagine," suggests its real concern: the imagination as value maker. Frost perhaps borrowed this view from Thoreau, who distinguished between the understanding's bald perception of "what is actually present and transpiring" and the imagination's power to idealize an event or fact:

> It is not simply the understanding now, but the imagination that takes cognizance of it. The imagination requires a long range. It is the faculty of the poet to see present things as if, in this sense, also past and future, as if distant or universally significant.[54]

"Carpe Diem" dramatizes this distinction between common sense and imagination.

"THE SILKEN TENT"

This is, foremost, a love poem in traditional Shakespearean rhyme, with one extended simile comparing the woman to the delicate structure of a tent. The focus of the poem is the tent's form and beauty which suggest the human attributes of thought and love. But "she" refers to more than a woman since there is considerable reference to aesthetic structure, balances, and order--in short, to Frost's first love, poetry itself. The silken tent is thus the artifact of the imagination: a poem. Frost has elsewhere used feminine gender to describe an abstraction. In "Birches," for example, truth breaks in "with all her matter-of-fact." The silken tent can be regarded as a symbol for a poem, defined by Frost as "the preservation of the spirit in the material."[55] The tent embodies many of the poet's essential ideas on poetry as artifice. For example, the reconciling power of the imagination, which "Carpe Diem" asserts, reveals itself in the order and balance of a poem.

A poem, like a tent, is "a bursting unity of opposites," a formal reconciliation of spirit and matter, desire and reason; it "sways perilously at the confluence of opposing forces."[56] The silken tent symbolizes a temporary "stay," containing under its light "sway" "everything on earth the compass round." One is reminded of Kubla

Khan's pleasure dome, "a miracle of rare device," reconciling diverse elements as it arches over the fertile landscape of the imagination. Built by thought and music, it too must exist momentarily, like Frost's tent of silk, suggestive of poetry's fine and lustrous texture.

Frost's structure is less "Romantic" than Kubla's dream-born dome, having as its main support a "central cedar pole" thrusting "heavenward," signifying "the sureness of the soul." Like the soul, this pole is really an axis, and made of the most durable of woods to suggest permanence. Everything depends on it for support, and, conversely, the spirit, like the pole, cannot exist without the forces set by its members to which it stands related. The tent is a dynamic, interacting totality. Like the form and spirit of a poem, the pole

> Seems to owe naught to any single cord,
> But strictly held by none, is loosely bound
> By countless silken ties of love and thought
> To everything on earth . . . .

These ties root the tent in earth, exerting a downward tug in opposition to the pole's "heavenward" thrust. Symbolically, the meaning and form of a poem are not dependent on one part, nor is its music reducible to one chord (another signification of "cord"); rather, the whole is greater than the sum of its parts.

"Ties of love and thought" are the language of poetry--the words that make concrete the felt thoughts of the poet. Frost says of poetry that "theme alone can steady us down," and that it is "wildness" or "enthusiasm tamed to metaphor." With its ties giving constancy and order, strength and stability, the poem arrests emotion temporarily, as a tent achieves a transitory stay in a tension of opposites. Emerson makes a similar comparison in the essay "Love," stating, "Our affections are but tents of a night."[57] Frost has repeatedly remarked that love is the root of poetry and that a poem begins as a compelling emotion akin to love-sickness;[58] emotion becomes tamed by metaphor.

The figure a poem makes depends on its sureness of meter, sound, and metaphor; they steady feeling and thought, just as the center pole and ties stabilize a tent. The analogy indicates that a poem is the sum of its interacting verbal and musical patterns. The words of a poem attach themselves to earth "the compass round," tying feeling and thought to concrete images. Poetry, in fine, is an arching unified tent. Earth is truly the poem's and the imagination's center and circumference, and the right place for love. In Coleridgean fashion, Frost likens the mind's reconciling, spanning power to a "strut"; the figure is akin to the silken tent's center pole and ties:

> The philosopher values himself on the inconsistencies
> he can contain by main force. They are two ends of
> a strut that keeps his mind from collapsing. He may
> take too much satisfaction in having once remarked
> the two-endedness of things.[59]

Freedom-within-bondage, which describes the outward appearance of the silken tent, is yet another way poetry reconciles. The tent's "ropes relent," allowing it to "gently sway." It is "loosely bound," but in the summer air goes "slightly taut," manifesting "the slightest bondage." These references to restiction and freedom point to the poem's own sonnet form which, although limited, allows some freedom of arrangement. Note that the poem is one long sentence, the syntax being an example, therefore, of restriction and freedom, subjects that the Romantics often wrote *about* in sonnets. For instance, Wordsworth, whose criticism Frost studied, wrote that "poetry is, like love, a passion" and a "pleasing bondage,"[60] suggesting that pleasure arises from the strict containment of emotion in formal patterns.

"The Silken Tent," then, is in the tradition of sonnets about sonnets, such as Wordsworth's "Nuns Fret Not At Their Convent's Narrow Room," which uses the cloister cell as a symbol of the restrictive Petrarchan form. Almost a Shakespearean sonnet, "The Silken Tent" offers more freedom of rhyme and demarcation than Wordsworth's. In this way it parallels Keats's "On the Sonnet"; the "fetter'd" form, the chaining of English rhymes, and the "constrain'd" poet recall the bondage of the silken tent. Frost concludes that the sonnet's ties produce the "slightest bondage"; Keats has the similar conclusion that "if we may not let the Muse be free/ She will be bound with garlands of her own."

CHAPTER IV
WILD FLOWERS--THE FLOWERING MOMENT

The butterfly and I had lit upon,
Nevertheless, a message from the dawn.

The last chapter examined poems dealing with the mind's relation to nature and with the possibility of "all revelation" in confronting phenomena. Our purpose here is to note an array of flower poems which further establishes Frost's Romantic regard for nature. These lyrics provide clear evidence that the poet operates in a Transcendental tradition which envisions flowers as the magical evidence of timeless beauty. In their flowering moments, they spiritualize the observing poet.

Wild flowers recurrently attend visionary insight or stand as mysterious harbingers of spirit. They may strike the poet with wonder, occasioning in him a correspondent flowering of thought. Just as a flower represents the fullness of a divine moment, the mind may blossom forth with a thought. Intuition or wisdom may derive from wild flowers, which seem objects of worship in "Rose Pogonias" and "A Prayer is Spring." A qualified message of unity radiates from a tuft of flowers. Frost's symbolic blossoms compare to Wordsworth's daisy, which has a "function apostolic . . . administering both to moral and spiritual purposes."[1]

Wild flowers, like St. Matthew's lilies of the field, hint at glories beyond Solomon, not the least of which for Frost is the concord these flowers allow between man and man, and man and God. One of Frost's early, unpublished poems claims that forest flowers inspire humility, brotherhood, and communion.[2] Men are therefore "flower-guided"[3] to deepest thoughts. Flowers feed the spirit. "In a Vale" indicates that wild flowers bring to man "things of moment," such as news of "Where the bird was before it flew/ Where the flower was before it grew," perhaps pointing back to the Elysian "Wide fields of asphodel fore'er" of "The Trial by Existence." Though "Nothing gold

47

can stay" in Frost's mutable world, the flower in bloom is the momentary, vestigial evidence of Paradise.[4] However, "A Boundless Moment" quickly resists any wishful thinking based on false evidence; the Paradise-in-bloom, we are assured, does conform to the schedule of nature and necessity. Some poems contain muted thoughts of Paradise, for which the soul yearns. Nature sometimes serves as a provisional second Paradise to satisfy this desire, and thus consoles us, providing flowers as earth's equivalent to that state of beauty and unity before the fall. "The Flower Boat's" "Elysian freight" wittily intimates that former perfection, as does Emerson's *Nature* , which notes that "the flowers . . . reflected the wisdom of [man's] best hour as much as they had delighted the simplicity of his childhood."[5]

Thoreau more precisely spells out the flower's role as the visible correspondent to man's thoughts, making an important transcendental assumption that illuminates the meaning of several of Frost's flower poems: "Every new flower that opens, no doubt, expresses a new mood of the human mind. Have I any dark or ripe orange-yellow thoughts to correspond? The *flavor* of my thoughts begins to correspond."[6] Some of Frost's poems entertain the possibility of these correspondences. Rose pogonias either correspond to, educe, or occasion a radiant, worshipful mood in the beholder. The steeple bush, or hardhack (Thoreau's "homely, but dear plant"),[7] and the meadow sweet ("an agreeable, unpretending flower")[8] analogize Frost's sere and yellow mood--the sense of an autumnal, diminished nature. He loves these flowers not only for what they are but also for what thoughts and attitudes they represent.

Correspondence is only achieved in a mood of generosity, especially in the early flower poems, where Frost, in an often guarded, allusive manner, is inclined to regard every bloom as the reflected image of a thought. Thoreau noted that men pursue every actual flower, but asked, "Have they with proportionate thoroughness plucked every flower of thought which it is possible for men to entertain?"[9] The finest flower of thought is poetry; Romantic poetry identifies "poesy" and "posy" as the same.[10] Thought, inspiration, and poetry-making are not only associated with but also induced by flower-questing. Wordsworth's three poems to the daisy, for example, dramatize its power to stimulate the poetic imagination to "play" to refine the spirit.[11]

1. FLOWER-GATHERING AND FLOWER-GUIDANCE

"FLOWER-GATHERING"

    This poem concerns the gathering of thoughts or poetry; it is a harvest requiring isolation. The speaker leaves his beloved in the morning, saddened by her reluctance to separate. Gaunt and grey with roaming, he returns, questioning her silence. The poem is an apology and an offering of the "flowers" he has gathered.

> They are yours, and be the measure
> Of their worth for you to treasure,
> The measure of the little while
> That I've been long away.

One meaning of his flower-gathering sharpens in the light of Emerson's "The Apology," a poem about the gathering of thought-flowers in isolation:

> Every aster in my hand
>   Goes home loaded with a thought.
> There was never mystery
>   But 't is figured in the flowers;
>   . . . . .
> A second crop thine acres yield
>   Which I gather in a song.

That second crop of thought and song is like Frost's gift in "Flower-Gathering." His flowers are the "measure," connoting, in part, the musical essence of poetry. The gift is offered as a gesture of love. In sharing his thought with his beloved, the poet doubles the correspondence of the day, and this is Frost's significant difference from the Romantics' tendency to be bachelors of nature.

"THE TELEPHONE"

IV - Wild Flowers; Flower Gathering

Floral correspondence between man and wife is also the subject of "The Telephone." The poem humorously plays on the threadbare Romantic tradition of regarding a flower as God's herald. Yet the poem allows a mysterious, though purely human, communion to be achieved through the flower, much as the telegraph pole in "An Encounter" connects person to person, not to a sublime Presence. Love does indeed communicate--a wife calls her husband home through the medium of a trumpet flower (perhaps a daffodil, which resembles the speaker unit of early telephones). If a divine correspondence between man and nature is doubtful, at least Frost acknowledges a mysterious, flower-transmitted, unvoiced message between wife and husband at "an hour all still."

In many of Frost's flower poems a time of stillness occasions instruction of deeper insight. "The Quest of the Purple-Fringed," "Rose Pogonias" and "A Prayer in Spring" all reveal a floral moment of arrest that attends worship, communion, a revelation, or an insight into nature. Counter-love comes not in a great wave sweeping over nature or man and woman, as in "Two Look at Two," but as a silent, cerebral correspondence in which a mysterious "*Someone* said 'Come.'" For Frost, ESP through flowers may be as inscrutable and interestng as any Romantic perception of larger, hoped-for correspondence.

"IN A VALE"

However fugitive are the adult's intimations of immortality and however diminished is the celestial gleam, the poet may still feel confident of being flower-guided to deepest thoughts. As Wordsworth admitted, "To me the meanest flower that blows can give/ Thoughts that do often lie too deep for tears."[12] These flower-inspired thoughts stem from the primal time of childhood where the glory, the vision, and the dream exist whole in the imagination and remain the "master light" of all our future days, however obscured by age and time. Wordsworth says this time of unity and joy comes on "a sweet May-morning" when "children are culling/ On every side/ In a thousand valleys far and wide/ Fresh flowers; while the sun shines warm."

"In a Vale" is Frost's "Intimations" poem of childhood unity and visonary joy that are flower-guided and flower-taught. The vale corresponds not only to Wordsworth's "fields of sleep" and flowered "valleys far and wide," but also to Thoreau's fen and mist, the holy ground and natal place of unity and love," as this passage from "Walking" indicates: "Live free, child of the mist,--and with respect to knowledge we ar all children of the mist. . . . The highest that we can attain to is not Knowledge, but Sympathy with Intellegence."[13] Frost's vale, ringing all night, is a Paradise where the soul is instructed in ultimate matters ("things of moment") by maidens in long garments, who come every night to the child's window. These maidens of truth are flower-born:

> The fen had every kind of bloom
> And for every kind there was a face,
> And a voice that has sounded in my room
> Across the sill from the outer gloom.
> Each came singly unto her place.

They come from the primal place "where bird and flower were one and the same," telling the child "why the flower has odor, the bird has song." This is the knowledge of innocence which the poet apprehends. The nightly instruction is really Frost's myth of how poets are made; the flower-maidens are muses. They instruct the youth in philosophy; their voices "sound" all night, harmonizing with the song of the "ringing," reed-filled fen; their garments trail behind them in the appearance of *musae*. The poem alludes to Thalia, the presider of bucolic poetry and known as one of the three Graces inspiring wisdom and love. Because she gives charm and beauty to all nature, she is named after the Greek word meaning "bloom," the exact word Frost uses to describe the face of the maidens.

These muses, or Graces, shape the child's soul with beauty and truth, a genesis that is much the same as Thoreau's account of our spirit's investiture with virtue, poetry, and truth--all of which reside in heaven's vale. This place of soul-making Thoreau describes as "a vale" where "every virtue has its birth/ Ere it descends upon earth," and where "virtue still adventures."[14] The ringing in Frost's vale as well as the instruction in "things of moment" conform to Thoreau's poetic, natal Paradise. A formative Elysium set in a misty vale is a common symbol of the poetic soul's origins.[15] "In a Vale" accounts for the origins of purity, love, and poetry. It is, in sum, Frost's equivalent to the Romantic vale of soul-making.

"THE LAST MOWING"

A profusion of wild flowers marks a momentary stay before confusion in "The Last Mowing," which celebrates a flowering of perfection; its meadow intimates a further range of spirituality and beauty. "The meadow is finished with men," but not with the poet, who intends to revel in the flourishing before the destructive advance of trees and winter. He seeks what Thoreau calls "the true harvest of the year . . . which the reapers have not gathered,"[16] and that is a spiritual apprehension in the real. In earth lies the evidence of heaven for the person of insight, whose moment has come. Having a higher purpose than mowers and plowers, he finds his spirit nourished in flower-time. A passage from Thoreau's meditation on earth's flowery fields as the border to Elysium may clarify the overtones in the blooming Far-away Meadow:

> We live on the verge of another and purer realm. . . .
> The borders of our plot are set with flowers, whose
> seeds were blown from more Elysian fields adjacent.
> They are the potherbs of the gods. Some fairer fruits
> and sweeter fragrances wafted over to us betray
> another realm's vicinity.[17]

Far-away Meadow and its flowers may be such a "border" and adumbrate Elysium, elsewhere described by Frost as "wide fields of asphodel fore'er." Because they are the purest and most sensory objects of beauty, flowers in the poem symbolize an ideal existence. Frost's joy in Far-away Meadow may involve an intuition, arising out of his sensory experience, of the beauty of infinite existence. If Frost apprehends a sublimity in intense sensory experience, he seems to be instructed by Thoreau, who assures us repeatedly that Elysium exists--"There is the field of a wholly new life. . . . There is a place beyond that flaming hill"--[18] and that "we need pray for no higher heaven than the pure senses can furnish, a *purely* sensuous life";

since the eyes were made "to behold beauty, . . .may we not *see* God?"[19] Frost's reveling in the tumult of flowers reflects, for the moment, a vitality of spirit, and involves what Thoreau calls a "finer sort of intercourse than our daily toil permits." It is the flowering "moment": or--literally a time of excellence and distinctness when matter and spirit reach their height.

2. THE ORCHIS: VISIONARY FLOWER

The orchis has royal status among wild flowers in Frost's lexicon. The rose pogonia, purple fringed, coral root, Calypso, and Arethusa orchises are associated with the visionary quest, or are its object. Their flowering heralds the poet's visionary moment, marking some special knowledge or intuition. The orchis not only attends these mysterious moments of the spirit's nourishment but also serves as a beacon for the poet's imaginative meditation. Though "An Encounter" contravenes any visionary moment, the search for the Calypso orchid underscores the seeker's Romantic intention. In "Mowing," the "pale orchises" accompany the mysterious "whispering," the "something" that the poet is on the verge of understanding intuitively. The visionary flower, that is, becomes a part of his insight into truth and the relationship that fact and labor have to dreaming. In "The Tuft of Flowers," "a leaping tongue of bloom"--which might be taken as descriptive of the orchis--occasions "a message from the dawn."[20]

Of all flowers, why does Frost attach such special import to the orchis? He does so because of its rarity, extreme beauty, mysterious aura, and unpredictablity. These qualities also characterize visionary insight, hence the linkage of image and idea. An avid botanizer,[21] Frost was undoubtedly aware of the alternate scarcity and profusion of orchises in different seasons. These flowers may suddenly flourish after years of absence. Furthermore, they resist all attempts at cultivation,[22] growing only, it would seem, for the divine gardener. Their appearance is the evidence of spirit.

Thoreau provides the basis for the orchis's symbolic value; the Journals speak of its scarcity, remoteness, and gorgeous color, blooming where man's spirit is fed and poets grow."[23] It is "a relic from the past"[24] and, presumably, worthy of veneration. In "Woodnotes," Emerson identifies Thoreau as the "seer" of "secret sight," knowing where the orchis grows. Thoreau acknowledges himself as seer-in-residence of the purple-fringed and its domain, the Great Meadow extending from Concord to Lawrence (whose northern reaches Frost himself undoubtedly tramped): "I think that no other but myself in Concord annually finds it. That so queenly flower should annually bloom so rarely and in such withdrawn and secret places as to be rarely seen by man!"[25] These "secret places" are swamps or the fringes of meadows "not quite reached by the mowers"[26] or the silent, damp recesses of thickets or woods. Of the purple-fringed, Thoreau wonders: "Why does it grow there only, far in a swamp, remote from public view?"[27] The purple and Arethusa orchises are "flowers par excellence,"[28] unrivalled in form and color. The latter, "a flower of mark,"[29] is named after a water divinity because it appears in swamps. Because the Calypso orchis gets its name from a sea divinity endowed with prophetic powers, we can understand why it is the object of the quest in "An Encounter." "Some poets must sing in praise of the bulbous Arethusa,"[30] wrote Thoreau. "The Quest of the Purple-Fringed" and "Rose Pogonias" are responses to this invitation.

"THE QUEST OF THE PURPLE-FRINGED"

The discovery of the purple-fringed marks the precise moment of some mysterious understanding that chastens and subdues the quester. That knowledge plus the purpose of the quest are unmistakably tied to the orchis. Emerson's "Woodnotes," commonly taken to be a poetic description of Thoreau as seer, minstrel, and orchis-seeker who plumbs nature's secrets, provides a context for understanding Frost's poem.

> And such I knew, a forest seer,
> A minstrel of the natural year,
> Foreteller of the vernal ides,
> Wise harbinger os spheres and tides,
> . . . . .
> It seemed that Nature could not raise
> A plant in any secret place,
> In quaking bog, or snowy hill,
> Beneath the grass that shades the rill,

> Under the snow, between the rocks,
> In damp fields known to bird and fox.
> But he would come in the very hour
> It opened in its virgin bower,
> As if the sunbeam showed the place,
> And tell its long-descended race.
>
> . . . . .
> It seemed . . .
> As if by secret sight he knew
> Where, in far fields, the orchis grew.
>
> . . . . .
> What others did at distance hear,
> And guessed within the thicket's gloom,
> Was shown to this philosopher,
> And at his bidding seemed to come. (I,ii,1-32)

Every stanza in "The Quest of the Purple-Fringed" is meaningfully informed by this passage. The speaker immediately assumes the role of "minstrel," singing and saying "snatches of verse and song of scenes like this." He has sung of this day before and is clearly a visionary quester, skirting "the margin alders for miles and miles/ In a sweeping line" in search of the orchis, which as Emerson writes, grows in "far" and "damp fields known to bird and fox." Indeed, Frost's quester follows along "the path where the slender fox had come." Note further the unmistakable parallel the fourth stanza has with "Woodnotes:" in following the fox he finds the "far-sought flower" "in the very hour" it richly blooms. Emerson's Thoreau "would come in the very hour/ It [the flower] opened in its virgin bower." Frost's moment of discovery shows the flowers' "color flushed to the petal." It is a moment of perfect stillness and equilibrium in which the spirit is fed:

> There stood the purple spires with no breath of air
> Nor headlong bee
> To disturb their perfect poise the livelong day
> 'Neath the alder tree.

But in the next stanza a curious, baffling transposition occurs at the moment of epiphany: The quester, kneeling and

> putting the boughs aside
> Looked, or at most
> Counted them all to the buds in the copse's depth
> That were pale as a ghost.

This act parallels the Emersonian seer's entrance into the flower's "virgin bower" in the very hour of blooming. Just as Emerson's "philosopher" is rewarded with insight "within the thicket's gloom," so too does Frost's quester find some mysterious understanding in the copse of ghostly pale orchises, after which experience he concludes:

> Then I arose and silently wandered home,
> And I for one
> Said that the fall might come and whirl of leaves,
> For summer was done.

One might remark as Frost did at the end of "Two Look at Two": "and that was all." Is that all to the "vision" which the flowers impart? What does nature say, merely that the fall is come?

Let us go back, for a moment, to the beginning of the poem and see if we can better understand it. There is special significance to the day, the hour, and particularly the moment of discovery, to which the orchis is herald. The poem dramatizes, I think the exact moment of equinox. The change in season from summer to fall occurs at a point of stasis in atmospheric, floral, animal, and human existence. The equinox is that moment of reconciliation (when the world is exactly upright, and day and night are equal). It is the same instant of equilibrium that "Two Tramps in Mud Time" marks in the shift from winter to spring. The quester cryptically remarks, "the day was the day by every flower that blooms." He finds the orchis "in the very hour of its flush of color; the precise moment of flowering marks the equinox. At that time, moreover, the orchises wither as he puts the boughs aside. Frost[31] has come and the seasons dramatically change, upsetting the equilibrium.

The first stanza suggests the immanence of frost, for the seeker feels "the chill of the meadow underfoot,[32]/ But the sun overhead." The weather and season are at delicate balance here, while the last stanzas, marked by a general defloration in the copse, picture the collapse of the momentary stay and the inevitable coming on of leaf decay and increasing darkness. In fact, the concatenation of dramatic, natural events suggests, in a highly oblique way, a condition of spirit that has reached a still point. In Romantic poetry, in astronomical lore, and in the mysteries of astrology, this moment of equinox traditionally represents the state of perfection and harmony between the soul, nature, and God. In man's Paradisiacal state the day and night were of equal length, and this perfection was mirrored in the happy balance of matter and spirit within him, a moral state which, for Donne, "knows neither sharp north nor declining west." Vernal equinox in *Prometheus Unbound* , one of Frost's favorite Romantic poems,[33] occurs at the moment when Prometheus, who represents the creative mind of man, achieves a harmony with himself, the One Mind, Asia, and the cosmos. The equinox, that is, marks the moment of his redemption.

More than an elegy to a dying season, "The Quest of the Purple-Fringed" has colorations of transcendentalism, addressing itself as it does to the uncertain visionary moment when the poles are in perfect alignment, corresponding to man's life in the Golden Age. If Frost considers the world and the human condition as mutable and oscillating between an infinite number of polarities, he still rather wistfully and reverently nods to this passing moment. It is all we know of the perfection that Adam presumably knew. No wonder the quester kneels in prayerful hush at the autumnal moment and then retires in thoughtful silence. Such ideas about the state and position of the spirit in relation to nature, the mind's alignment with reality, and the possibility of achieving an equilibrium--moral or esthetic--are the central themes of several other poems in *A Witness Tree,* namely, "All Revelation," "Happiness Makes Up in Height for What it Lacks in Length," "The Silken Tent," and "Beech."

The moment of insight into the "copse's depth"--and even before--is embroidered with mystical connotation. The quester incants poetry of similar scenes, suggesting that he has not only conjured but also experienced or written previously of these moments. The copse seems the kneeling poet's sanctum, the "secret place" of "Woodnotes," where a hidden truth is harbored in "the thicket's gloom." We are also reminded of the visionary copse of Keats's poet, who "In some delicious ramble . . . found/ A little space with boughs all woven round." It contains a "forlorn flower," unmoved by "Zephyrus," which occasions in the poet a creative, revelatory moment.[34] Frost looks at and counts all the pale orchises, analogized as a "ghost," and therefore linked mysteriously to the spirit world. The flowers announce the coming of the fall, the polar and celestial declination, the collapse of vision, a momentary correspondence with nature, and the consequent lapse into the ordinary world of dualities begun in the primal fall and continuing, days without end, throughout all nature:

> Then I arose and silently wandered home,
> And I for one
> Said that the fall might come and whirl of leaves,
> For summer was done.

A knowledge of the "fall" is the quiet wisdom gained by this latter-day "minstrel of the natural year," "foreteller of the vernal tides," and "harbinger of spheres and tides." The whirl and world of leaves replace the momentary stasis attendant to Frost's visionary orchises, which, as "Woodnotes" suggests, "tell of [their] long descended race" and also man's.

"ROSE POGONIAS"

Written about the same time as "The Quest of the Purple Fringed," "Rose Pogonias" is a closely related orchis poem that echoes the worshipful tone and atmospheric hush evoked by the purple flowers. Stasis and calm attend the delicate and rare pogonia orchises, which stand in individual perfection "sun-shaped and jewel small." They create a larger design of perfect proportion--"a circle scarcely wider/ Than the trees around were tall." Their circularity, stillness, and incense make "a temple of the heat," wherein the beholders partake of "the sun's right worship."[35] The holy rite involves bowing and picking, and raising "a simple prayer" of thanks, with the hope that the circle of a thousand orchises might be spared or, if not, "obtain [a] grace of hours." The religious diction implies a spirit radiating from these delicate, rare, and evanescent flowers, whose "wings of color . . . tinge the atmosphere." Man's best hour of wisdom and reverence is reflected, it would seem, in these mysterious flowers, and man's discerning, indeed Emersonian, eye creates an outline, a pattern, a circular form to frame and contain them.

CHAPTER V
THE DARKER MOOD: FLOWERS AND LEAVES; THE DIMINISHED POET; BIRDS AND BIRDSONG

In several poems of darker mood, Frost questions Romantic assumptions about man's insight into the spirit behind nature. His poetic moods are morphean. Darkness supplants transparency; the condition of life is dissociation, so explained by Emerson:

> The ruin or the blank that we see when we look at nature, is in our own eye. The axis of vision is not coincident with the axis of things, and so they appear not transparent but opaque. The reason why the world lacks unity, and lies broken and in heaps, is because man is disunited with himself.[1]

Joy changes to melancholy with Keatsian swiftness, and no one is more sensitive to to shifting emotions than the poet, whose element is feeling or the lack of it. The stasis and order the poet senses in "Rose Pogonias" and "The Quest of the Purple Fringed" are momentary; now confusion and darkness are the inevitable consequence of Frost's mutable worlds, both inner and outer.

In "The Last Mowing" the speaker fears the trees that will "march into a shadowy claim" of the clearing and annihilate the flowering moment. The line "the trees are all I'm afraid of" indicates a dark nature overtaking the moment of vision and unity, indeed overtaking his spirit. This darkening vision parallels Wordsworth's loss in the great Ode. But Frost is not so sure of recollections and intimations of immortality. He questions, reconsiders, reeconceives, challenges, and even denies the Romantic faith in nature and the mind's power of insight, while at the same time creating artistic order in the very poem that denies order. As Frank Lentricchia argues, Frost's form-making is therapeutic and "redemptive."[2]

The next two chapters discuss poems in which Frost questions

Romantic ideas on permanence, correspondence, benevolence in nature, and the poet's subjective power to perceive essences in nature and then utter his knowledge. Frost's New England world has radically changed from its Transcendental past; and he reveals a darker poetic self in poems that with gathering intensity diminish the role of the Emersonian Romantic. If he regards the poet as subjective, inspired singer, he acutely modifies some Romantic analogues and myths to characterize the modern poet's voice and understanding.

1. FLOWERS AND LEAVES

"LEAVES COMPARED TO FLOWERS"

The rarely discussed "Leaves Compared to Flowers" is representative of Frost's disenchantment with Romanticism. Its contrast of moods is symbolized by flowers and leaves; but its meaning remains obscure.[3] The concluding lines, "petals I may have once pursued,/ Leaves are all my darker mood," summarize a dualism that runs throughout the poem. The flowers and petals refer to the speaker's early visionary quest, but his later days veer from this pursuit to a conviction that life's essence is a sound and melancholy dualism. That the speaker perceives flowers and leaves by a different sense reenforces this dualism. He sees "flowers by day," but he hears and feels "leaves and bark/ To lean against and hear in the dark."[4] This dissociation is intensified, in that leaves are ordinarily identified with death in other poems, such as "In Hardwood Groves," "A Leaf Treader," and "Misgiving."

Here the poet has abandoned his interest in deciduous, flower-bearing trees in favor of fern and lichens--"Late in life I have come on fern/ Now lichens are due to have their turn"--the fern being composed almost totally of fronds, leaf-like structures without blossoms or seeds, and the lichen being a primeval, flowerless, seedless composite of fungi and algae living symbiotically and often growing on bark. Since the lichen is a plant of two members, it is a fitting interest for a philosophical poet who sees the world in dualities. If every thing in nature corresponds to some state of the mind, then

V - The Darker Mood; Flowers and Leaves

Frost's metaphor of the lichen accommodates monistic thought to philosophical dualism. Further, if, as Emerson said, "flowers express to us the delicate affections,"[5] Frost's attention to a quite different phylum of plants, the all-leaved fern, indicates figuratively his later need to express a "darker mood." Leaves and bark, then, are associated with ferns and lichens--as well as large, dark-shading trees--and suggest the darker side of life, as compared to their opposite, the flower-bearing trees of daylight. Those with "wit" find it fair to have "leaves by night and flowers by day," for they are sound dualists.

If the botanical references suggest a duality of attitudes toward life, the poem takes on even wider meaning and sharper clarity when seen in relation to Yeats's "Among School Children" and a passage from Thoreau's Journals.[6] Frost's giant, blooming trees, which he rejects in favor of dualistic leaves and bark, may be related to Yeats's "great rooted blossomer," a chestnut tree, that symbolizes unity of being. Yeats's monistic world view is expressed in the organic unity of "the leaf, the blossom, and the bole." Similarly, the integrity of man's life and labors and moods allows no dualities of body and soul:

> Labor is blossoming, or dancing where
> The body is not bruised to pleasure soul,
> Nor beauty born out of its own despair,
> Nor blear-eyed wisdom out of midnight oil.

In contrast to this Romantic assertion of the inviolable unity in the great blossomer, Frost

> may be one who does not care
> Ever to have tree bloom or bear.
> . . . . .
> Leaves and bark may be tree enough.

Is Frost denying Yeats's premise, even as he adapts the Irish poet's symbolic tree to his own quite different purpose? Stanza 3 may allude to the "great rooted blossomer": "Some giant trees have bloom so small/ They might as well have none at all." For Frost, body and soul were often bruised in a life of toil, doubt, and despair, as

V - The Darker Mood; Flowers and Leaves

Lawrance Thompson makes painfully clear. The poet's "tree" of thought and life yields leaves and bark and very little flower or fruit. His philosophy here is darkly dualistic rather than replendently monistic, In short, Frost's basic moods and intellectual roots do not anchor in a Yeatsian, Romantic substratum, for "unless you put the right thing to its root/ It never will show much flower or fruit." Apparently the soil of Frost's thought, (a metaphor he will develop shortly in "Build Soil") does not nourish a final, flowering unity of being. He stated as much in prose: "to make the final unity. That is the greatest attempt that ever failed."[7] An imperfect world of strain, effort, pain, and sweat is man's condition. For now, the leaves represent his darker mood.

That nocturnal mood is further divided into "Leaves for smooth and bark for rough." Thoreau amplifies the meaning of that darkness and dualism: he knows the "rough" of agony and insanity, and the "smooth" of order and pleasure:

> I can remember that when I was very young I used to
> have a dream night after night, over and over again,
> which might have been named Rough and Smooth.
> All existence, all satisfaction and dissatisfaction, all
> event, was symbolized in this way. Now I seem to be
> lying and tossing, perchance, on a horrible, a fatal
> rough surface, which must soon, indeed, put an end
> to my existence, though even in my dream I knew it
> to be the symbol merely of my misery; and then
> again, suddenly I was lying on a delicious smooth
> surface, as of a summer sea, as of gossamer or
> down or softest plush, and life was such a luxury to
> live. My waking experience *always* has been and is
> an alternate Rough and Smooth. In other words, it is
> Insanity and Sanity.[8]

The passage illuminates the dualities Frost implied, particularly the contrasting mental states. And since Frost's life progressed for many years on a knife-edge between sanity and instability, order and rage, violence and repose, the rough and smooth of Thoreau's dreaming must have jolted the poet with self-recognition. Thoreau was more than a mentor; he was a kindred spirit.

This concern for the dualities of flowers and leaves is foreshadowed in the earlier "Spring Pools."

"SPRING POOLS"

These pools that, though in forests, still reflect
The total sky almost without defect,
And like the flowers beside them, chill and shiver,
Will like the flowers beside them soon be gone,
And yet not out by any brook or river,
But up by roots to bring dark foliage on.

The trees that have it in their pent-up buds
To darken nature and be summer woods--
Let them think twice before they use their powers
To blot out and drink up and sweep away
These flowery water and these watery flowers
From snow that melted only yesterday.

The first poem of *West-Running Brook*, it introduces the polarities of light and dark and of mutability and permanence--organizing themes of the volume. The moment of perfect reflection in spring is, like the flowering zenith of The Last Mowing," almost without defect." The pools mirror heaven and flowers in the brief, watery springtide between snow thaw, when light prevails, and leaf growth, which darken nature. The deft inversion in the line "These flowery waters and these watery flowers" indicates both image and reflection. Nature reflects the infinite and floral beauty--but not for long. A sense of transience, regret, and quirky resentment ("Let them think twice . . .") stems from an awareness of the inevitable demise of cherished flowers and pools and their reflections. This "blot" darkens, cancels, and disgraces; it necessarily destroys his vision of earth and sky unity, and the harmonious doubleness of image and reflection. The speaker clearly has an eye for this kind of abstraction. Why?

Thoreau, who saw watery images as a medium for transcendental "reflection," or meditation, provides some clarification:

V - The Darker Mood; Flowers and Leaves

> These answering reflections--shadow to substance--impress the voyager with a sense of harmony and symmetry . . . a dualism which nature loves. . . . You must be in an abstract mood to see reflections however distinct. . . . When we are enough abstracted . . . we are imaginative, see visions, etc.[9]

Liked the hoped-for "original response" of The Most of It," or the white blur of "A Passing Glimpse" and "For Once, Then, Something," the reflections of the flowery waters imply the speaker's tenuous correspondence with spirit, and a unified vision.

The power that obliterates this loveliness both illustrates and subverts Emerson's claim that "nature always wears the colors of the spirit,"[10] or serves man. If, according to Emerson, "flowers . . . reflected the wisdom fo [man's] best hour,"[11] then, too, "every hour and change corresponds to and authorizes a different state of mind, from breathless noon to grimmest midnight." Likewise, Frost's speaker, in warning the trees, anticipates his darker mood and indicates that he not only would resist nature's inevitable darkening but also is not fully in harmony with the beauty of the scene. He is looking ahead to its passing, instead of reveling in the moment.

This curious defiance suggests that Frost has an argument with the Transcendentalists. "Spring Pools" is tinged with melancholy where we expect joy. However the paradox is explained if we note that although the scene is Romantic, the response is dualistic and ironic. Frost cannot now bring himself to the "exhilaration" of Emerson "crossing a bare common, in snow puddles . . . under a clouded sky."[13] *His* snow-melted spring pools educe melancholy as well as delight. The poem turns upside down the Emersonian oversimplification that "the same scene which yesterday breathed perfume and glittered . . . is overspread with melancholy today."[14] Instead, the poem recalls Emerson's "grimmest midnight."[15]

"Spring Pools" dramatizes the mind's complex relation to the natural world, emphasizing the tenuousness of any correspondence, the inevitable separateness of nature, and the swiftness with which is changes the colors of its spirit--in opposition to man's will for stasis in a flowering moment of beauty. The speaker resists going with the drift of things but knows that all joys all "stays" by definition are momentary.

2. THE DIMINISHED POET

Frost's image of the diminished poet contrasts with its Emersonian counterpart discussed in Chapter Two. The Romantic rider on instinct gives way to the sober, earth-bound poet of gray New England. He is still a guide and a self-reliant soul but in a world severely reduced of the beauty to which Paul Bunyan is wed.

"PAN WITH US"

As the reverse of "Paul's Wife," which characterizes the mythic poet,"Pan With Us" demythologizes the Grecian, Romantic role of the poet. In *A Week on the Concord and Merrimack Rivers* , Thoreau writes of the "glory" of the "ruddy-faced" old gods of "pipe" and "crook." "Pan is not dead. . . . of all the gods of New England . . . I am most constant at his shrine."[16] In contrast, Frost's idle Pan, who has tossed his pipes away, reflects the poet far removed from the days of "pagan mirth" when music and gods haunted every forest bough. His pipes had "less power to stir/ The fruited bough of the juniper." Once Pan's sensuousness and ruddy visage found their mirror in a golden world; but now the gray of "his skin and his hair and his eyes" reflects New England's drabness. Times have indeed changed: "and the world had found new terms of worth." If Thoreau believed that "every people have gods to suit their circumstances,"[17] Frost's Pan reflects a northland diminished in Transcendental pieties. "Pan With Us" revises Thoreau's mythologizing of nature and, through the new figure of Pan, reveals the kind of poetry Frost was writing and would continue to write.

"HANNIBAL"

Frost learned how to accomodate diminishment; indeed, he voiced it as a powerful theme, especially in characterizing the poet. In "Hannibal" he asks how the ambitious, courageous soul handles discouragement and failure.

Was there ever a cause too lost,
Ever a cause that was lost too long,
Or that showed with the lapse of time too vain
For the generous tears of youth and song?

The poem seems to negate the youthful optimism and self-reliance of the Lone Striker's vocational pursuit. Almost any lost cause may be inferred from the poem, but I think it has a biographical meaning related to Frost's poetic ambitions. Hannibal sojourned for years in the Alps, hoping to subdue Rome; Frost spent most of his years in various alpine and farm regions north of Boston. Just as Hannibal's life was a forty-five year study in frustration (he spent seventeen years on the campaign and an entire life of single-minded perseverance against Rome), Frost in his first forty-one years (1874-1915) knew obscurity and frustration in the apparently lost cause of poetic endeavor. Fame and recognition eluded him, though he had surely prepared for poetic laurels as Hannibal did for the crown of military achievement.

Frost may very well have mimicked Wordsworth in identifying Hannibal with a lost poetic cause. One of Wordsworth's prefaces explains that a poet, in shaping taste, has a long, arduous, and almost futile task, like Hannibal's roadbuilding:

> Every author, as far as he is great and. . . *original*,
> has had the task of *creating* the taste by which he is
> to be enjoyed. . . . The predecessors of an original
> Genius of a high order will have smoothed the way
> for all that he has in common with them . . . but, for
> what is peculiarly his own, he will be called upon to
> clear and often to shape his own road:--he will be in
> the condition of Hannibal among the Alps.[18]

If Frost's endeavors in poetry--a poetry he thought to be as radically different in theme and style from the prevailing poetry of his day as *Lyrical Ballads* was in its age--were a lost cause until the 1920's, his identification with Hannibal suggests that he was blazing trails that history would finally have to evaluate. Perhaps he saw in the Carthaginian the image of his own scaling of mountains. Perhaps the title of his last volume, *In the Clearing,* speaks of a Wordsworthian regard for one's own poetic achievement. Frost made his clearing and "shaped his own road."

"REVELATION"

> We make ourselves a place apart
>   Behind light words that tease and flout,
> But oh, the agitated heart
>   Till someone really find us out.
>
> 'Tis pity if the case require
>   (Or so we say) that in the end
> We speak the literal to inspire
>   The understanding of a friend.
>
> But so with all, from babes that play
>   At hide-and-seek to God afar,
> So all who hide too well away
>   Must speak and tell us where they are.

A part of shaping is to establish a voice. Correspondence is all, to be sure, but Frost is uncertain about the manner of expression. The poet's problem with language has universal application. How much does he assert and/or imply? What should be his tone in a bardless, anti-Romantic world? "Revelation" is the disclosure of the soul," wrote Emerson: similarly, the early lyric "Revelation" is about disclosure--that of indirect poetic expression. Poetic revelation is like a child's game of hide-and-seek and God's veiled presence.[19] The "pity" of literalness is that in our desire to be understood we "must speak," halting the game of inference. This is not the nature of the poetic game--or, indeed, of God's game of concealment. Frost's equation of the poet's and God's modes of communication adapts Emerson's idea in "The Over-Soul" that inference is the universal mode of poetic and spiritual communication.

> The action of the soul is oftener in that which is felt
> and left unsaid than in that which is said in any

> conversation. It broods over every society, and they
> unconsciously seek for it in each other. We know
> better than we do. . . . I feel the same truth how often
> in my trivial conversation with my neighbors, that
> somewhat higher in each of us overlooks this by-play,
> and Jove nods to Jove from behind each of us.[20]

Just as an intuited sublimity hovers, aura-like, over all conversation, so too an essence of meaning veils itself in the "by-play" of poetry. Poetry, moving by inference, is the finite representation of the soul's action and is a "heterocosm," like God's creation of the world. This Romantic attitude is so defined by Meyer Abrams: "A poem is a disguised self-revelation, in which its creator, 'visibly invisible,' at the same time expresses and conceals himself."[21]

Frost is not at all sure that a divine presence sanctifies all correspondence. His idea of revelation diminishes Emerson severely: what is "unsaid" is often painful, and the poet eases his solitude by speaking. This balancing act of telling and concealing is both a joy and agitation. There is fun in the play. To the reader who demands of the author the meaning behind a poem, Frost once replied: "'If I had wanted you to know, I should have told you in the poem'" He then quotes Robinson: "The games we play/ To fill the frittered minutes of a day/ Good glasses are to read the spirit through." The anguish of concealing too completely is real; if "correspondence is all," obscurity is nothing, a mute cry of the soul's isolation. If too oblique in tone and figure, "We make ourselves a place apart/ Behind light words that tease and flout." The poet must be understood, finally, or know what Arnold[23] described as the agony of the "buried life": that reservoir of essential feeling, which the individual needs to bring to the surface, but which is obscured by "light words." As in "Revelation," the banter in the "The Buried Life," if not fathomed, brings pain:

> Light flows our war of mocking words, and yet,
> Behold with tears mine eyes are wet!
> I feel a nameless sadness o'er me roll.

Arnold provides us with yet another motive driving the poet, or anyone, to conceal his "inmost soul" through "capricious play:"

Are even lovers powerless to reveal
To one another what indeed they feel?
I knew the mass of men concealed
Their thoughts, for fear that if revealed
They would by other men be met
With blank indifference, or with blame reproved.

Frost needed to mask his Romantic leanings and bardic inclinations. Pound's and Eliot's view of impersonality in modern poetics made it difficult, even risky, to refer to spiritual matters directly. While many of Frost's concealments express his skepticism, they were necessary, lest the poet, as Arnold warned, risk "blank indifference" or be "reproved with blame." Thus, "Revelation" expresses the poet's agitation over the buried life, a life that can only reveal itself through the indirections of "light words that tease and flout." Here, Frost has no faith in Emerson's avowal of a divine sponsor in all correspondence. The poet alone decides what to say and leave unsaid.

"A MISSIVE MISSILE"

Like "Revelation," "A Missive Missile" ponders the difficulties of hidden meanings and symbolic language. The characters on the pebble wheel are like the figures of poetic language; both, in attempting to communicate, may obscure rather than reveal meaning. The poem's impact comes from Frost's linguistic quarrel with Emerson. While it takes up the uncertainty and possible failure of language, the poem also tests Emerson's claim about the primitive origin of language, namely that

> because of [the] radical correspondence between
> visible things and human thoughts, savages . . .
> converse in figures. As we go back in history,
> language becomes more picturesque, until its infancy,
> where it is all poetry. . . . [It] never loses its power to
> affect us.[24]

The "Over-Soul" repeats this claim, using the act of gathering pebbles to represent the ease with which the simple mind communicates in writing, and thus joins the human circle: "The simplest utterances are worthiest to be written; . . . it is like gathering a few pebbles of the ground."[25]   If Emerson thinks "all language is vehicular and transitive,"[26] Frost's paleolithic wheel, which carries no certain meaning, ironically answers this claim. We know nothing before our pre-glacial past; indeed, the boulder-strewing ice itself fragmented our world and language.

Frost not only challenges Emerson's assumptions about linguistics uniting us to our origins, but also reverses any easy assertions of spiritual or cosmological unity. We can only guess at the meaning of past missive missiles--of whatever art or linguistic form.   Their obscurity simply reflects the world's general darkness in language--indeed in all things--and the spadework of archaeology (like the scanning of astronomy) is of little help in unearthing truth.

The second half of the poem implicitly criticizes the Over-Soul concept. The supposed ghost of the prehistoric "petitioner," hovering and "importunate to give a hint" about his sign language on the pebble wheel, fails to communicate to the "slow uncomprehending" speaker. The failure is "enough to make a spirit [*i.e.*, the overseeing ghost] moan" in frustration because the speaker has missed an intended correspondence. Such unsuccess is not possible in an Emersonian view of language, and herein lies the dialectic of the poem. Emerson claims that an Over-Soul overlooks all community, and that language is the supreme expression of spirit: "the soul's communication of truth is the highest event in nature"; indeed, "deep divine thought reduces centuries and milleniums, and makes itself present through all ages."[27] Frost clearly reverses this Transcendental credo, for the spirit in and behind language achieves no correspondence: instead a void suggest a misalignment of souls:

> Far as we often make them reach
> Across the soul-from-soul abyss,
> There is an aeon-limit set
> Beyond which they are doomed to miss.
> Two souls may be too widely met.

Time and distance separate and disunify; Emerson's soul-to-soul unities become "soul-from-soul separations in Frost's universe. The pebble-wheel beach, like the boulder-broken shore in "The Most of It," cannot communicate or find response ("counter-love"):

> That sad-with-distance river beach
> With mortal longing may beseech;
> It cannot speak as far as this.

Far from being an eternal vehicle for the spirit, language slips, slides, and falls away, as does the world. Lacking wholeness, or the grace of faith, man sees the world in pieces. In contrast, Emerson remarks that the soul achieves unity when

> the act of seeing and the thing seen . . . [,] when the subject and the object, are one. . . . Only by the vision of that Wisdom can the horoscope of the ages be read, and by falling back on our better thoughts, by yielding to the spirit of prophecy which is innate in every man, we can know what it saith. Every man's words who speaks from that life must sound vain to those who do not dwell in the same thought on their own part. I dare not speak for it.[28]

Frost's speaker fails to extract meaning and negates this faith in eternal correspondences and wholeness. Skeptical about outmoded Romantic theories of language and having the advantage of modern anthropology and linguistics to indicate that words are more than primitive symbolism, Frost avoids errors of the past.

The use of language once again is the subject of Frost's reflections on the character of the soul, and in particular the poet's soul.

"THE FEAR OF GOD"

> If you should rise from Nowhere up to Somewhere,
> From being No one up to being Someone,
> Be sure to keep repeating to yourself
> You owe it to an arbitrary god

72

V - The Darker Mood: Birds and Birdsong

> Whose mercy to you rather than to others
> Won't bear too critical examination.
> Stay unassuming. If for lack of license
> To wear the uniform of who you are,
> You should be tempted to make up for it
> In a subordinating look or tone
> Beware of coming too much to the surface,
> And using for apparel what was meant
> To be the curtain of the inmost soul.

"The Fear of God" says each soul reveals itself in its actions, "the tone" it takes, and the "apparel" it shows. Likewise, Emerson holds that each soul creates an image by which it is judged; and that the proper "tone the man takes" is in "being deferential to a higher spirit than his own": "If he have not found his home in God, his manners, his forms of speech, the turn of his sentences, the build shall I say, of all his opinions will involuntarily confess it."[29] In the community of men, in the worship of God, and in the craft of poetry, the soul must "Beware of coming too much to the surface." A poet's true "apparel" is not in obvious show, or literalness, but in the subtlety of his language. In discussing great poets, Emerson also said that grace and wisdom come to those who put off arrogance and pride, whereas "the vain traveller attempts to embellish his life by quoting my lord and the prince. . . . The ambitious vulgar show you their . . . brooches."[30] To put off pride and to "stay unassuming" are two tenets of Emersonian integrity that Frost follows. His fanciest apparel is metaphor or synechdoche. To be unassuming is to be subtle, literally to be under "under the surface."

3. BIRDS AND BIRDSONG

Birds and birdsong traditionally represent the poet and his poetry. For the Romantics, the nightingale, skylark, and thrush correspond to the blithe poetic spirit filling the night air with strains of unpremeditated art. The song of Keats's "viewless" nightingale is the aural symbol of beauty, permanence, and the ideal to which the visionary poet aspires. Thoreau characterizes the intensity of the imagination as dependent on "the different moods or degrees of wildness and poetry of which the song of birds is the keynote."[31] What the flower is to the eye, the bird's song is to the ear. Thoreau remarks, "The meeting with a rare and beautiful bird like this is like meeting with some rare and beautiful flower, which you may never find again, perchance, like the great purple fringed orchis, at least."[32]

Frost's poetry often plays ironically on this attitude. Like his Pan, birds and their songs accentuate the theme of diminution. Whereas the flight or perch of Romantic songbirds is transcendent, Frost's birds are local, resident, generally shrill or low-keyed, and sober. The sawing strain of the oven bird mimics Frost's tone and echoes his attitude towards nature. The phoebes in "The Need of Being Versed in Country Things" may weep pathetically (to a Romantic observer); but Frost knows better, dismissing the fallacy even as he ends the poem on a bird note. Similarly, he disclaims any special value or intelligence in the small bird in "The Woodpile." Self-preservation, rather than any spirit of nocturnal carolling, guides the bird of "Acceptance"; it is not nature's herald but a part of the darkened universe: "No voice in nature is heard to cry aloud/ At what happened. Birds, at least, must know/ It is the change to darkness in the sky." In Frost, bird or poet assumes a radically diminished role from Shelley's luminous poet-skylark. In contrast to the skylark, the oven bird is Frost's symbol of the poetic spirit.

"THE OVEN BIRD"

There is a singer everyone has heard,
Loud, a mid-summer and a mid-wood bird,
Who makes the solid tree trunks sound again.
He says that leaves are old and that for flowers
Mid-summer is to spring as one to ten.
He says the early petal fall is past
When pear and cherry bloom went down in showers
On sunny days a moment overcast;
And comes that other fall we name the fall.
He says the highway dust is over all.
The bird would cease and be as other birds
But that he knows in singing not to sing.

V - The Darker Mood: Birds and Birdsong

The question that he frames in all but words
Is what to make of a diminished thing.

Like Shelley's skylark, the oven bird is a herald and teaches the poet how to see and sing.[33] Commonly known as the teacher bird,[34] the oven bird instructs in the tradition of Wordsworth's throstle, who "is no mean preacher" but Nature's "teacher." In all other repects, however, Frost's oven bird contrasts with the Romantic ideal of blithe, spontaneous song. It perches low in its oven house of mud, countering Shelley's skylark, who resides "like a high-born maiden/ In palace-tower." Nor does it fly, unlike Shelley's lark that goes "sailing to heaven." Drab, not at all a "glow worm golden," it is associated with a dry, leafy, flowerless time, rather than a colorful, scented spring of "vernal showers";

Most tellingly, the oven bird's song is discordant, not harmonious. In singing of old leaves, a past petal-fall, and dust over all, the bird represents the poet questioning Romantic assumptions--a reversal of the Transcendentalist who augments nature. Like other Frost poems, this one ends in surmise.

The tone of the oven bird corresponds with Frost's own poetic voice, dramatizing just how closely the poem follows Thoreau's idea that "the poet . . . should speak in harmony with nature The tone and pitch of his voice is the main thing."[35] The Journals repeatedly describe the "hollow-sounding note of the oven-bird . . . from the depth of the wood . . . [a] note loud and unmistakable, making the hollow woods ring."[36] Frost's mid-wood bird similarly "makes the solid tree trunks sound again." The "d's," "s's," and "t's" echo the harsh, shuttling dissonance that Thoreau describes as the "thrum" of "his sawyer-like strain."[37] He notes that the oven bird is unmelodious, and "does not fly at all";[33] moreover, its dome-like nest is on the ground, out of sight and cunningly constructed. All of these facts suggest how appropriately the bird conforms to Frost's image of the poet; he too is close to earth, retiring, protective, and singing the discordant sound of sense. Grounded, he observes things as they are, seeing at first hand that "the highway dust is over all." A reliable spokesman, the bird indicates that midsummer flowers are ten times diminished compared to those of spring. Thoreau describes August's diminution in similar proportions: "Methinks there are few new flowers of late. . . .

Summer gets to be an old story. Birds leave off singing, as flowers blossoming, *i.e.*, perhaps in the same proportion. . . .About [this] time did not the . . . oven-bird cease?"[39] No wonder Frost's "bird would cease and be as other birds"; it is simply following the seasonal declination described by his mentor, here an arithmentician of natural phenomena.

In ceasing to sing, the oven bird is like other birds in midsummer; but as the figure of the poet, its muteness is appropriate.[40] The difficult line--"But that he knows in singing not to sing"--has two implicatons: first, it refers to the natural reticence of the oven bird, who says much in "singing not." Second, it suggest that his thrumming does not "sing"; that is, does not say, poetically, what do the glorious birds of springtide. Instead, the silent poet/bird heralds "the fall." The paradox of the reticent dissonant "song" is an artfully framed (i.e., contrived) question "in all but words."

Frost must have received instruction from Thoreau who, when he did not hear the oven bird in August, made the following remarks:

> Has not the year grown old? Methinks we do ourselves, at any rate, somewhat tire of the season and observe less attentively and with less interest the opening of new flowers and the song of birds. It is the signs of the fall that affect us most It is hard to live in the summer content with it. . . . How different the feeble twittering of the birds here at sunrise from the full quire of the spring!!![41]

"HYLA BROOK"

Frost's use of seasonal characteristics to reflect the modern poet's mood also appears in "Hyla Brook," a companion piece to "The Oven Bird" in *Mountain Interval*. Like the birds of spring, Hyla tree frogs sing in a spring mist and faded snow. Their night-long ghostly, sleigh-bell lyric haunts the memory, marking a time when nature awakes. The vanishing of water and song, like the petal-fall of "The Oven Bird," depicts not only natural change, but also lyric or poetic change, from Romantic overflow to abatement to a hard, dry realism characteristic of Frost's verse. "Our brook" in midsummer (or an advanced season of poetic song) "is other far/ Than with brooks taken otherwhere in song." That "otherwhere" may be Tennyson's babbler,"[42] but probably closer to home.

Like the oven bird's song, theirs originates in Thoreau's Journal, which describes the peeper as "lord of sound." In choir, "the sounds of peeping frogs (*Hylodes*) and dreaming toads are mingled in a sort of indistinct universal evening lullaby to creation."[43] Thoreau links the frogs' song with the beginnings of life and a vernal past that

> leaves such a lasting trace on the ear's memory that often I think I hear their peeping when I do not. It is a singularly emphatic and ear-piercing proclamation of animal life . . . not so much of the earth earthy as of the air airy. It rises at once on the wind and is at home there, and we are incapable of tracing it further back.[44]

The hylas' song is like "A brook to none but who remember long" and that is the "otherwhere" of Thoreau's Romantic remembrances. The faded song like the vanished stream are now ditties of no tone, "like ghost of sleigh-bells in a ghost of snow."

"A MINOR BIRD"; "NOW CLOSE THE WINDOWS"

Like the tone of "The Oven Bird," the lesser key of a "minor bird" is yet another way of suggesting diminished nature. Though we should "love the things we love for what they are," the key sufficiently annoys the speaker that he wishes the bird away ("it seemed as if I could bear no more"). But the "fault" lies in the listener "in wanting to silence any song, for his reaction dramatizes the failure of correspondence. The speaker prefers what is absent, that is, the dominant keys of caroling "major" birds, who are consonant with nature. Augmenting the key of the minor bird would put the speaker back in the harmonic springtide of skylark and nightingale.

This same attitude prevails in "Now Close the Windows"; the speaker desires a birdless silence and withdrawal. Between the time of the oven bird's last autumnal song and the spring strains of the "earliest bird," the hibernating poet shuts his windows against the wintry blast. the distant spring rain of "To the Thawing Wind" will "bring the singer" and "nester," bathe his window, "melt the glass," and turn him out of doors once more.

Anti-Romantic, or untraditional birds also teach us the virtue of silence or restraint. "On a Bird Singing in Its Sleep" intimates that an instinctual protectiveness counters too much pouring forth of soul:

"ON A BIRD SINGING IN ITS SLEEP"
A bird half wakened in the lunar noon
Sang halfway through its little inborn tune.
Partly because it sang but once all night
And that from no especial bush's height;
Partly because it sang ventriloquist
And had the inspiriation to desist
Almost before the prick of hostile ears,
It ventured less in peril than appears.
It could not have come down to us so far
Through the interstices of things ajar
On the long bead chain of repeated birth
To be a bird while we are men on earth
If singing out of sleep and dream that way
Had made it much more easily a prey.

In the evolutionary process the survival of a fragile, vulnerable creature depends on its controlling its voice, and can serve as a model for the poet. A midnight dream may once have inspired ecstatic song in a Romantic nightingale and invited thoughts of suicide in the Keatsian listener, but singing "in the lunar noon" of Frost's real world might assure a singer's quick end.   Thus an innate ventriloquism in bird and poet provides necessary protection. Any singing has its perils. The "hostile ears" may belong to birds' natural enemies, or, symbolically taken, those presences threatening to poets--rivals and critics, against whom the poet must be on guard.[45]

The example of this bird, like the oven bird, tells the poet that, paradoxically, it takes "inspiration to desist" in singing. Otherwise, the poet may imperil himself by singing with Romantic abandon instead of vocal restraint. A poetry of maskless faith cannot effectively be sung in a time hostile to such lyrics. Neither bird nor poet could "have come down to us so far/ Through the interstices of things ajar." He must ventriloquize the "little inborn tune" infrequently and from "no especial . . . height," lest he be a prey. This ability is the singer's power and security, like protective coloration, a part of his nature to play hide-and-seek. Thoreau remarks that ventriloquism is at the heart of the thrush's beauty and mystery: "I go in search of him. He sounds no nearer. On a low bough" he sings, "as it were ventriloquizing; for though I am scarcely more than a rod off, he seems further off than ever."[46] As a poet, Frost would also throw his voice.

CHAPTER VI
THE VISIONARY QUEST

I paused and said, 'I will turn back from here.
No, I will go on farther--and we shall see.'

> A man that looks on glass,
>   On it may stay his eye,
> Or, if he pleaseth, through it pass
>   And the heavens espy.
> (Herbert, quoted by Thoreau)

The quest for an unknown power, or ultimate truth, whose ephemeral grail is nature is a central Romantic endeavor, and one Frost undertakes (as we have see in "The Quest of the Purple Fringed"), energized by a cloud of other poets. The process of his pursuit and the uncertain insights attendant to it are the concerns of this chapter. I have grouped poems in an order going from those of qualified, tentative affirmation to those of increasing negation about the possibility of insight, the mind's visionary potentiality, and the reward of questing. The poet is subtle and various in his responses to these themes and those Romantic writers to whom he is indebted.

Frost is foremost a poet of feeling and not a philosopher with a consistent, coherent regard for the mind's relation to nature.[1] His characteristic (and often ironic) uncertainty of vision in most of these poems is summarized in a favorite word, "something," which defines his fleeting intuition of the sublime and the imagination's cloudy encounter with an infinite, inscrutable presence. Thus, "Something or someone watching made that gust" igniting the bonfire; "Something [efficient or final] there is that doesn't love a wall"; "a something white, uncertain" ghosts from the depths of an Apollonian well. Unlike Frost, Thoreau is clear in his use of the same transcendent word: "I see, smell, taste, hear, feel, that everlasting Something to which we are all allied, at once our maker, our abode, our destiny, our very selves."[2]

Though Frost's encounters with nature usually end in a highly qualified tentativeness, yearning uncertainty, scepticism, or denial, they are at least attempts to examine some possible unity between poet and nature. He hopes for a Romantic correspondence of mind and matter, leading to the perception of a higher truth. And while "all revelation has been ours" for a cloud of other poets, it rarely is for the diminished, post-Emersonian, even when the quester has fleeting correspondence with nature, as in "Two Look at Two." Poem after poem tests Romantic assumptions. "To a Moth seen in Winter" and "The Wood Pile," for example, question the Romantic supposition that nature mediates and symbolizes spirit. The expectation of vision in "The Wood Pile"--I will go farther--and we shall see"--ends not in correspondence or insight but in the matter-of-fact perception that order--a cord of maple--lies in man's labor. Likewise, no correspondence exists between poet and moth; rather the hand extending with love "across the gulf of well nigh everything" measures separation from nature.[3]

Frost's inability to wed himself to the "one life within us and abroad," whether through the psychic mode of "wise-passiveness," noble interchange, or active creation, stems from a deficiency of "generosity" of heart. In Romanticism this generous love allows the imagination to spiritualize reality.[4] Frost does not let go with his heart, strain as he will to perceive essence in nature. The will is there, but not the spirit. The cosmic isolation expressed by Frost, results from being unable to accept or replace the doctrine of monistic nature. But therein lies Frost's poetic strength, for in resisting the doctrine--in having an ingrained defensiveness--he does not fictionalize nature but shows it realistically, as the chaos it often is. (This regard for nature is common to all "dejected" Romantics.) Frost has the faintest hints of spirituality in his quests, but he never affirms the kind of creative, visionary joy known to Thoreau, who wrote: "If these gates of golden willows affect me, they correspond to the beauty and promise of some experience on which I am entering. If I am overflowing with life, am rich in experience for which I lack expression, then nature will be my language full of poetry,--all nature will fable and every natural phenomenon be a myth. . . . I pray for such inward experience as will make nature significant.[5]

Frost's resistance to the Romantic impulse to "build up greatest things/ From least suggestion," characterizes the tone, tension, and theme of many poems. Resistance and controlled uncertainty become the stuff of poetry: "Anything you do to the facts falsifies them, but anything the facts do to you--yet, even against your will; yes, resist them with all your strength--transforms them into poetry."[6] Receptivity uncontaminated by doctrine can generate the best poetry: "Never larrup an emotion. Set yourself against the moon. Resist the moon. If the moon's going to do anything to you, it's up to the moon."[7] Nor can the imagination be "requisitioned": "The curse of our poetry," he says, "is that we lay it on things."[8]

Though nature is no certain guide, the imagination is still creative, establishing boundaries between the known and unknown, as "Beech" demonstrates. So the unity Frost commonly asserts is aesthetic (as we have seen), not spiritual. A poem's artistic perfection is consolation for the lost correspondence with nature. Yet "Two Look at Two" and "Unharvested" and even "For Once, Then, Something" show that Frost never totally rejects this Romantic belief in correspondence. This quest for a vision of unity continues throughout the poetry; however its fulfillment is either so tentative or so subtle as to be almost unrecognizable, especially in his orchis poems.

1. THE TENTATIVE "SOMETHING"

"TWO LOOK AT TWO"

The quest in "Two Look at Two" results in a moment of grace, "one unlooked for favor": a brief, probable correspondence between the couple and nature. Generally identified as a Wordsworthian moment, the idealism of Emerson more appropriately describes nature's "gift" as the instant when "the animals, the mountains, reflected the wisdom of [a man's] best hour, as much as they had delighted the simplicity of his childhood."[9] These rare times depend on the state of one's spirit while perceiving.[10] Indeed, the couple prepare for the correspondence. They are man and wife, and their quest is impelled by "love," an important sign word that begins and ends the poem. As the alpha and omega, the love relationship between man and woman is a prerequisite to the natural correspondence and counter love with the paired buck and doe. Frost states that human "correspondence is all": the genial mind alone establishes unity and relationship with another:

> Mind must convince mind that it can uncurl and wave the same filaments of subtlety, soul convince soul that it can give off the same shimmers of eternity. At no point would anyone but a brute fool want to break off this correspondence. It is all there is to satisfaction; and it is salutory to live in the fear of its being broken off.[11]

The bond of love between man and woman provides the emotional charge for any further correspondences in nature, it would seem. The souls achieve this interchange in rare moments of feeling. The title "Two Look at Two" suggests that in natural pairings, love can occasion--even impell--a visionary marriage with nature. In this respect Frost significantly modifies the Wordsworthian and Thoreauvian image of the visionary as a solitary, or a bachelor of nature. Frost acknowledges human, married love as antecedent to any "marriage" with nature. Perception, when informed by generous human love produces the triumphant correspondence:

> Two had seen two. . . .
> . . . . .
> A great wave from it going over them
> As if the earth in one unlooked for favor
> Had made them certain earth returned their love.

Love alone makes perception more than just mechanical; through the heart we radiate value into the thing seen. It is as much man and wife's generous feeling as nature's "favor" that creates the moment of "counter-love" and "original response." We are, says Frost, most spiritualized and spiritualizing when in love with another of the opposite sex.

Implicit in the poem is the testing of Emerson's claim about the power of love:

the blank that we see when we look at nature, is in
our own eye. . . . The world lacks unity . . . because
man is disunited with himself. He cannot be a
naturalist until he satisfies all the demands of the
spirit. Love is as much its demand as perception.
Indeed, neither can be perfect without the other. In
the uttermost meaning of the words, thought is
devout, and devotion is thought. Deep calls unto
deep. But in actual life, the marriage is not
celebrated.[12]

As in "To a Moth Seen in Winter," where the stretching of a hand is
an act of love bridging, for the moment, the gap between nature, "Two
Look at Two" celebrates unity.

The exact definition of the man and wife's puzzling search is not
clear. They repeat "'This is all. . . . This, then is all. . . . This must be
all.'" Apparently they labor upward toward fulfilment, dominated by an
idea demanding factual proof. They have undoubtedly questioned the
possibility of correspondence or vision in nature. Frost dramatizes
but also qualifies Emerson's claim that "the faithful thinker" must "work
on the world" with his understanding, devotion, and "holiest affections,
then will God go forth anew into the creation" and achieve the
marriage with nature: "When the fact is seen under the light of an
idea . . . we behold the real higher law."[13] For Frost, the strong
thinking couple are saying nothing definitive about correspondence--or
interchange (the most critical of Romantic assumptions)--until they see
for themselves.

At the end of Nature, Emerson assures us that nature will provide
concrete objects as evidence for the mind laboring under an idea.
Conversely, "each phenomenon has its roots in the faculties and
affections of the mind."[14] In the poem this fluid interchange of mind
and nature is so described as "A great wave from it [nature] going
over them." The certainty that "earth returned their love," (though
hedged by "as if") strongly echoes Emerson's description of
correspondence as a liquid surge and reflux--Frost's "great wave":

Nature is not fixed but fluid. Spirit alters, moulds,
makes it. The immobility or bruteness of nature is

the absence of spirit; to pure spirit it is fluid, it is
volatile, it is obedient. . . . Know then that the world
exists for you.   for you is the phenomenon
perfect. . . . As fast as you conform your life to the
pure idea in your mind, that will unfold its great
proportions. A correspondent revolution in things will
attend the influx of the spirit.[15]

Man and woman's correspondence with buck and doe symbolizes
what remains of the Emersonian moment in a fragmented world of
"rock and washout," earthslide and rough paths, tumbled walls and
split boulders. No apocalypse attends the great wave, but for a
triumphant instant, as doe and buck pass, a sense of unity flows
between creatures (though a wall intervenes). This is Frost's most
Emersonian moment.

"BIRCHES"

Similar to "Unharvested" in its metaphorical contemplation of the
ideal, or essence, "Birches" explores the possibility of visionary
experience, counterpointing Shelley's idealism against a more modest
claim about man's climb toward heaven. Related to this theme are
Frost's ideas on imagination, contrarieties of spirit and matter and of
thought and action, and the reconciliation involved in a fulfilled life.
The white birches stand in contrast to dark woods. They describe
arcs "left and right/ Across the lines of straighter, darker trees."
Nature's only heaven-pointing tree is bowed to earth in ice storms.
These opposites of white and dark, arc and line, heaven and earth
bespeak dualism. Frost early establishes the trees as mediators:

> Often you must have seen them
> Loaded with ice a sunny winter morning
> After a rain. They click upon themselves
> As the breeze rises, and turn many-colored
> As the stir cracks and crazes their enamel.
> Soon the sun's warmth makes them shed crystal shells
> Shattering and avalanching on the snow-crust--
> Such heaps of broken glass to sweep away

VI - The Visionary Quest: "Something"

You'd think the inner dome of heaven had fallen.
They are dragged to the withered bracken by the load.

Such description is precise, brilliant.
Key words in the passage--"many-colored," "shattering," "dome of heaven"--point to Shelley's celebrated stanza in "Adonais" on Platonic dualism:

The One remains, the many change and pass;
Heaven's light forever shines, Earth's shadows fly;
Life, like a dome of many-colored glass,
Stains the white radiance of Eternity,
Until Death tramples it to fragments.

Shelley's contrarieties of mutable and immutable worlds, expressed in the imagery of light and dark, whiteness and coloration, eternal radiance and fragmentation, inform "Birches." As the white avenue toward heaven, the birch parallels the "white radiance of Eternity." Subtly associated with the realms of spirit and matter, it is both a member of the darker trees of earth (it has black branches) and distinguished from them by its axial whiteness. Dragged to earth, their arcs of many colored glass confirm Shelley's image of earthly existence being a prismatic stain of eternity's white light. As they spring back heavenward after a storm, their crystal shells fragment and their natural and symbolic whiteness reappears.
(Storms and clearings express the duality of the earthly condition, as "Happiness Makes Up in Height for What It Lacks in Length" and other poems show.) Like the birch, man must bow to storms; yet he aspires to the white radiance of eternity.
These dualities, suggested in the weighty description of the ice storm (which requires twenty lines), are vital to an understanding of the speaker's desire to be a swinger of birches. Preceding the lengthy description of the boy's art, Frost states, "But I was going to say when Truth broke in/ With all her matter-of-fact about the ice storm/ (Now am I free to be poetical?)"[17] The "Truth" is that ice storms, rather than boys, bend birches, and that the dualities of ice-storm and the sun's radiance (Shelley's "Heaven's light forever shin[ing]") are the matter-of-fact conditions of life; yet however literal

Frost may be, the allusions to Shelley suggest symbolic meaning.

Like Zaccheus, the speaker would "climb black branches up a snow-white trunk/ Toward heaven." Contrasts in colors and shapes, emphasizing a unity of opposites, follows Thoreau's description of birches, "their perpendicularity contrasting with the direction of the branches, geometry mixed with nature."[18] The italicized "toward" (rather than "to") suggests that Frost intends no Romantic abandonment of the real for the ideal. Climbing implies effort rather than spontaneous flight, though he "dream[s] of going back" to be a swinger of birches--

> when I'm weary of considerations,
> And life is too much like a pathless woods
> Where your face burns and tickles with the cobwebs
> Broken across it, and one eye is weeping
> From a twig's having lashed across it open.

Earthly affliction and confusion descend on the forest-bound seekers of "The Woodpile" and "An Encounter." But here the world-weary speaker would "throw a line of purpose" across a boyhood experience; that purpose is a heavenward climb.

Frustration haunts the mutable worlds of "Birches" and "Adonais," described in the latter as a realm of "sorrow," "mourning," "tears and gall," from which Shelley advises we seek shelter through death and consequent union in "Heaven's light." Frost acknowledges the need for relief by a withdrawal "toward" heaven, but makes no Romantic commitment to an unknown empyrean realm. Shelley urges, "Die,/ If thou wouldst be with that which thou dost seek! . . . / Why linger, why turn back, why shrink my heart?/ . . . No more let Life divide what Death can join together" (464 ff).

Frost counters with a calculating, sane diminishment of such Romantic extremity:

> I'd like to get away from earth awhile
> And then come back to it and begin over.
> May no fate willfully misunderstand me
> And half grant what I wish and snatch me away
> Not to return. Earth's the right place for love:

VI - The Visionary Quest: "Something"

I don't know where it's likely to go better.

To be sure, the references to fate and love have their Shelleyan context, being necessary parts of the empyreal light which constitutes creation:

> That sustaining Love
> Which through the web of being blindly wove
> By man and beast and earth and air and sea,
> Burns bright or dim, as each are mirrors of
> The fire for which all thirst. (481-85)

Uncertain of such empyrean love and the consequence of any fate plucking him from earth, Frost will only flirt with Platonic notions, climbing the limber but firmly rooted birch. The act involves delicate balancing of spirit and matter, in which the poised, white-dark tree tests Frost's suppositions. Dualistic, the poet contemplates spirit but does not abandon earth. Frost can have it both ways: "That would be good both going and coming back"; he could do worse by being totally unconcerned with the life of the spirit or imagination, like those of Shelley's "Trembling throng/ Whose sails were never to the tempest [of inspiration] given." He could do worse by letting go--climbing or flying with abandon. The birch provides just enough support for Frost's intellectual and imaginative ascension, yet it restrains him from Shelleyan excess.

Swinging on birches suggests control, skill, balance, reconciliation, and a sure denouement. The play is similar to Frost's description of poetry-making:

> No one can really hold that the ecstasy should be
> static and stand still in one place. It begins in delight,
> it inclines to the impulse, it assumes direction with the
> first line laid down, it runs a course of lucky events,
> and ends in a clarification of life . . . in a momentary
> stay against confusion. It has denouement. It has an
> outcome.[19]

The act of writing poetry, like the swinging of birches is an arc of

88

motion, ascent, and denouement. It is "play."

Of the many contrasts made in "Birches," that of youthful play and sober maturity have received scant critical attention. The recollection of a time of glad animal movements provides a Wordsworthian "tranquil restoration" of soul, for the boyhood experience is, in a way, "life and food/ For future years" and a basis for interior strength. "Birches" dramatizes the idea that though the glory and the dream of childhood are gone, the remembrance, as Wordsworth writes, "doth breed perpetual benediction." Frost's speaker himself was once a swinger of birches and "dream[s] of going back to be"; would not this restore in him the spirit which life, just as the ice-storm stunts the trees, has subdued? The weariness, confusion, and pain are clearly a Wordsworthian inheritance--of the boy grown into man in the "Intimations" ode:

> Full soon thy Soul shall have her earthly freight
> And custom lie upon thee with a weight
> Heavy as frost, and deep almost as life.

That weight of frost, Frost relieves by the dream recollection of swinging on birches; that childhood joy offers strength. Indeed, memory of that early time issues in "years that bring the philosophic mind." The child is the father to the man in "Birches."

"FOR ONCE, THEN, SOMETHING"

While "Birches" aspires upward, "For Once, Then, Something" gazes downward to a mysterious essence. This quest ends in greater uncertainty than in any other poem treated so far. Is the momentary "something" "beyond" and "through" the clear reflection the glimmer of "truth" or merely a white pebble of quartz? Like the sea gazers of "Neither Out Far Nor In Deep," the rebuked, straining beholder accepts a mere reflection but also has a slight, penetrating insight into nature.

The poem's Romantic background helps us fathom its central symbol, well-gazing. The well is both the mirror of man's mind and, traditionally, the day's telescope wherein the stars can be seen at noon. The purpose in Thoreau's habitual investigations of well bottoms is to gain a visionary insight--heaven's truth--which he does in his inspection of John Field's well.[20] Similarly, Walden Pond is "well" and "mirror," "into which the beholder measures measures the depth of his own nature."[21] "Water betrays the spirit that is in the air."[22] In A Week . . . , wells reveal the stars, the traditional symbol of truth and of spirit: "For lore that's deep must deeply studied be,/ As from deep wells men read star-poetry."[23]

Frost seeks such "star-poetry," but the light is wrong. Nature itself interferes with vision; "a wreath of fern and cloud puffs," a drop of water, and as his own face obstruct the downward vision that is also upward. The star of truth (or is it a quartz pebble?) cannot be clearly seen. Whatever lay there "at bottom"--i.e., "fundamentally" or "essentially" and not merely "at the well floor"--remains uncertain. He sees only his laureate self, the pictured center and source of all things,[24] and it may be that, in part, his own Romantic posturings blur vision.

The white pebble originates most likely from one of Frost's earliest unpublished poems which associates whiteness and white stones with Platonic thought and visionary apprehension. His high school valedictory speech refers to misty dreams and bending boughs as "white as pure thought";[25] the poet-dreamer

> gathers many a snow-white stone;
> He weighs them . . .
> Divining each one's silvery tone.
> He drops them! When the stream makes music.
> Fair visions with its vault-voice swell:
> And so, for us, the future rises,
> As thought stones stir our heart's 'Farewell!'[26]

These white thought-stones, associated with poetry, music, prophetic insight, and Platonic thought, anticipate the white quartz pebble. The poetic visions, swelling with the water's "vault-voice" (and originating in the white stones) appear to be in "For Once, Then, Something" the well's watery promise for the speaker as he gazes downward. But unlike the time of believing youth, adult days of quest roil with darkness and uncertainty.

VI - The Visionary Quest: "Something"

"A BOUNDLESS MOMENT"

"A Boundless Moment" records an instant of infinite possibility when a flower is discovered out of season. If the Paradise-in-bloom is unbounded by time and season, the receptive speaker is "ready to believe the most" of such a phenomenon, taking the bloom as a revelation of a transcendent principle. "Bringing March against his thought," the speaker guards against his fondest hopes of encountering the extraordinary, a white June lily, Paradisea Liliastrum, so named as being worthy of Paradise. The flower connotes the possibility of Edenic glory--in short, a boundless moment in a world circumstanced by dark and doubt.

It is first seen as "pale, but not a ghost," suggesting a kinship with the world of spirit. For the moment boundaries are lifted; the world appears "strange," to the transfixed beholders. But claims must be supported by fact; "pretense deceives." As Frost writes in "Mowing," "Anything more than the truth would have seemed too weak." The truth (which is the real concern of this poem) is established and borne out. (The point of view is like that from the beech Witness Tree, which observes the boundary between the known and unknown and stands as proof of man's "being not unbounded.") The truth (expressed aptly in a fragment) is: "A young beech clinging to its last year's leaves." It is the appropriate tree on the known side of the wild, fronting the boundless unknown. Though the speaker and his companion flirt with the infinite, or the possibly Paradisaical, it is not "in us to assume . . . for ours" anything not seen and rooted in fact. He will not assume any "luxuriance"--that is, any overabundance, either floral or, by implication, trascendental. It is solely the recognizable and factual which he affirms as "truth" as the observers "move on," bounded by time and circumstance but nonetheless receptive to evidence of the timeless and limitless in nature.

The experience in "A Boundless Moment" reiterates a remakably similar drama of mistaken identity recorded in Thoreau's Journal. He takes the white seeds of the virgin's bower for a "shad bush in full bloom" in autumn, remarking, after his excitement: "I thought at first I had made a discovery more interesting than the blossoming of apple trees in the fall. . . . It carried me round to spring again."[27] For both writers the white petals are the hoped-for evidence of the miraculous.

In artfully naming his flower "Paradise-in-bloom," Frost embellishes on the factual precision of Thoreau's entry and deftly conveys his transcendental inclination.

"A PASSING GLIMPSE"

Like the indistinct glimmer of white in Frost's visionary well, an unknown flower provides the briefest flash of insight in "A Passing Glimpse." But the iron rails of necessity never allow a second, extended glance. Frost apprehends a unique "something" mysterious in the flower which corresponds to an intuition: "Was something brushed across my mind/ That no one on earth will ever find?" Is the experience the most of a glimpse of eternity Frost can know? These apprehensions are no less evanescent than those expressed by the Romantic poets. Intellectual beauty "visits with inconstant glance." Shelley's "glance" is Frost's "glimpse" falling dart-like on men in "uncertain moments." "Heaven gives its glimpses only to those/ Not in position to look too close."

The mysterious, visionary flower invites a typically Romantic reception of truth in "wise passiveness," but this one floral impulse from a vernal wood is so momentary that its meaning is uncertain. Indeed, moving with speed and a new angle of vision inspires new thoughts, as Emerson remarks in a passage from Nature : "What new thoughts are suggested by seeing a face [i.e., "view"] of country quite familiar, in the rapid movement of the railroad car!"[28] "A Passing Glimpse," whose perspective is from a moving train, poetically expresses the passage. The rushing train blurs reality, the uncertain flower being the image of an uncertain thought.

While Frost is not assenting to Emerson's idealism, he is playing with it. If nature is "ideal" to Emerson "so long as [he] cannot try the accuracy of [his] senses,"[29] Frost, being unable to get off his speeding train, assents to the uncertainty of intuition. If "Nature is made to conspire with spirit to emancipate us,"[30] the poem acknowledges some interchange, but no deep revelation. Frost is in some agreement with Emerson's claim that from a speeding train, which changes one's ordinary angle of vision, "a low degree of the sublime is felt, from the fact probably that man is hereby apprized that whilst the world is a spectacle, something in himself is stable."[31] Frost's blurred flowers are the evidence of his vague intimation of the sublime; they attest that the mind has the power of dim insight, if not the high wattage ascribed to it by Emerson.

2. DARK ENCOUNTERS

We now come to those quest poems that are predominantly negative about even a fleeting truth.

"THE MOST OF IT"

Like "Two Look at Two," "The Most of It" tests the Romantic doctrine of correspondence and the possibility of visionary understanding. Lawrance Thompson has identified the solitary quester as the neo-Romantic poet Wade Van Dore, with whom Frost grew impatient for asking of nature something it could not give. "The Most of It" is Frost's answer to Van Dore's poems that call to nature for reply, according to Thompson.[32] However, I see the poem as a response to more potent writers than Van Dore, and agree with Richard Poirier that Frost had a long background of reading and thinking and that Wordsworth's echo poems were also an incentive to Frost.[33]

The ambiguous response to the cries of Frost's solitary is a diminishment of what Wordsworth's boy of Winander would expect of nature, but it is not necessarily "despairing" in showing man's isolation.[34] The poem dramatizes the rift between the human world and the universe the echo and the buck restrict the Romantic assumption of our reciprocity with nature. It is reasonable to think that the poem resists the Emersonian notions that the mind creates what it seeks, projects value into what it perceives, and so finds congruence of inner and outer reality.[35] In one sense, however, Frost is heir to Emerson in making the most of a natural phenomenon, but the "most" proves to be a severe restriction of Emersonian idealism.

A number of Romantic references provide a context in which to read Frost's poem. Wordsworth's "Yes, It was the Mountain Echo" affirms the congruence of the human and divine; "sound for sound" we receive "unsolicited reply": "yes, we have/ Answers, and we know not whence;/ Echoes from beyond the grave,/ Recognized Intelligence.

93

That an echo is a sign of such an Intelligence is also Thoreau's expectation as he listens from Walden's shore (which has many a "tree-hidden cliff across the lake" and a "boulder-broken beach").[36] Echoes are nature's idealizations of distant sounds, inducing in us an awareness of Higher Laws. For Thoreau, then, "the echo is, to some extent, an original sound, and therein is the magic and charm of it. It is not merely a repetition . . . but partly the voice of the wood [or] wood-nymph."[37]

"Original response" and "counter love" are what Thoreau expects in a generous, sportive interchange with nature. His own echo brings "novelty," and is "a profounder Socratic method of suggesting thoughts unutterable to me the speaker.[38] Preferring "kindred voices" of echoes to his companions' conversation, Thoreau would "form a community" based on counter-love.[39] But Frost's quester receives only "copy speech" and presumably remains isolated. "Nothing ever came of what he cried," Frost says, except for the tentative embodiment of dissonant, brute nature.

What, then, is the quester's failure? It is a defect of the soul, though he ardently wills to believe. Nature fails to respond to the psyche, not simply because these are days too far removed from happy Romantic pieties. More to the point, the split between faith and will within the quester subverts the visionary moment, and provides the dramatic tension of "The Most of It." Frost tests Emerson's assertion that "he cannot be a naturalist until he satisifes all the demands of the spirit. Love is as much its demand as perception."[40] It is precisely Van Dore's "troubled heart" over the loneliness of wilderness life that annoyed Frost and, in part, moved him to write his poem.[41] Unfortunately, his "cry" is not the profoundly sympathetic love of Emerson; it produces only a "mocking echo." For this unqualified naturalist, the poem denies the doctrine of correspondence.

Its tone suggests that the quester is self-deceived. The first line--"He thought he kept the universe alone"--and the "mocking echo" of his own voice, which is suggestive of the Demiurge's laugh, initiate an ironic tenor, almost as if Frost is twitting the idealism of Emerson's exhortation, "Know then that the world exists for you. . . . Nature is not fixed but fluid. Spirit alters, moulds, makes it."[42] In Frost's "The Most of It," nature is brutal, stark, and forceful--something dark and instinctual that mind and words cannot control.

VI - The Visionary Quest: Dark Encounters

The title itself is ironic, referring to the Romantic predisposition for making the most of a natural phenomenon. In a foreword to the poem, Frost remarks that the title is related to the phrase "making the most of things,"[43] that is, building the greatest things (value) from least suggestion (fact). Thoreau uses this saying when he describes how the imagination yields a truth after musing on an unfortunate fact. Meditating on the purpose behind a forest fire he accidentally started, Thoreau says, "I . . . attended to the phenomenon before me, determined to make the most of it."[44] He concludes that from this apparently chance happening he served as an "agent of the Director of the woods," helping clear and beautify them so that people might have walking room and space for berry bushes. In short, Thoreau has taken a disaster and made the most of it philosophically and theologically.

The title, then, is the meaning of the poem, which severely reduces the meaning of Thoreau's phrase. The mocking echo and brute response to the quester's cry are the most that Frost makes of a Romantic expectation of unity. The quester gives emotionally and hopefully, but receives minimally from nature; indeed, "nothing ever came of what he cried,/ *Unless*" that "nothing" was incarnated as brute, soulless, purely physical nature. The Frostian response is put in a simile, "*As* a great buck"; the figure is important, fitting into the conditional mode of the second half of the poem beginning with the word "Unless."

The buck illustrates Emerson's asssertion that the "bruteness of nature is the absence of spirit"; in ironic reply to Emerson's claim, "Know then that the world exists for you,"[45] Frost's universe reciprocates with brute sound and stark power. The buck's presence, like the Demiurge's, announces the unmistakable reality of the dirt and wallow of earthly existence, unglossed by the mind.

The "response" comes unexpectedly in the form of "a great buck," whose impressive presence also serves as a tenuous sign of the sublimity which the protagonist seeks. For Frost is never completely reductive, always allowing for a mysterious "something" in nature. He believed that unexpected natural wonder was the purpose of seeking the solitude of wilderness.[46] The buck is cousin to Thoreau's great buck moose, "God's own horses" of *The Maine Woods*, lustily crashing through the forest in answer to Indian Joe's buck horn.[47]

Like the orchises of Thoreau's Journals, the buck is a rare "gift," an ambiguous sign of an unknown presence; he sees the animals as "the true denizens of the forest, filling a vacuum which now first I had discovered had not been filled for me."[48] With these words Thoreau makes the most of his unexpected sighting of this awesome animal which had fired his imagination during the hunt. Its mysterious presence seems an "echoing, or creeping from afar" or a "dull, dry rushing sound" in the "primeval woods."[49] It is the sound of "tree fall" and calls to mind Frost's uncertain "embodiment that crashed/ In the cliff's talus." Later Thoreau inspects and measures the slain moose, seeing it as a sign of a higher reality.

It is against this Transcendental heritage that Frost's great buck can be meaningfully regarded. While it is typical of Frost to go no further than to say "and that was all," echoes of Thoreau ring throughout the poem. As Poirier notes about the last words, "to be told that 'that was all' does not, needless to say, mean that 'all' is nothing."[50] For the buck is the embodiment of "nothing." In effect, the poem leaves us with an attitude that in the midst of this mountain, lake, and forest scene, radiates raw, inhuman, untameable Nature, much like the awesome, alien wilderness of *The Maine Woods.*

In "Two Look at Two" and "Directive," the world is largely fragmented despite moments of intuited unity; the boulder-broken beach" and talus-cliffed world of "The Most of It" repeat the rock-strewn, boulder-split upland where two look at two and where the quester in "Directive" seeks a broken goblet. This ruin reflects a Non-Platonic world. The original philosopher of the One, Emerson's Plato, is "the mountain from which all these drift boulders were detached."[51] The buck and the aspiring quester of "The Most of It" live in the drift boulders of a world that has broken away from its original unity. This image of fragmentation reflects modern chaos. The figure and the attitude are pure Emerson: "The reason why the world lacks unity, and lies broken and in heaps, is because man is disunited with himself."[52] Frost would agree. The world mirrors us and we mirror the world; it is this fact which Frost's quester must accept before he begins projecting himself and cries onto nature. "Counter-love" assumes a perfect alignment between man and nature, but as his dark encounters show, Frost cannot believe it or allow it.

"AN ENCOUNTER"

This seldom discussed quest poem is somewhat more ironical than "The Most of It" in undercutting a potential visionary experience. A "resurrected tree" comes unexpectedly before the eyes of the speaker and, like the man-made woodpile, invites contemplation. The telegraph pole gives Frost a chance to play with Romantic notions of the communication--via nature--between an eternal power and humankind.

The encounter is clothed in religious imagery: the "tree" is compared to Christ, the divine mediator and incarnation of spirit. Against "heaven" is seen a "resurrected tree/ . . . that had been down and raised again," a "spectre"; "the strange position of his hands--/ Up at his shoulders" suggests the crucifixion. Once vital (but now dead) nature is raised by man, "barkless" and trilling with news, but of a wholly human horizontal interchange, "from men to men." Nature does not work mysteriously to communicate with man; rather man raises (literally) nature, and the only correspondence Frost allows is the human, not the divine working through nature's ministry. Nature is not, in Emerson's term, a "mute gospel," and cannot be identified with Christ's role as bringer of "news" (*i.e.*, "gospel").

While Frost dramatizes this diminishment of nature's power, he nonetheless uses Romantic traditions. In asking "What's the news you carry--if you know?" the speaker, certainly, has a humorous, almost absurd soliloquy; nonetheless, he also--in a disguised, almost off-handed manner--attempts a Romantic correspondence with the tree in order to extract some "news." The "news" may be taken merely as telegraphic messages; however, in the context of Romantic poetry, it subtly suggests revelation--or, in Christian terms, tidings of life, death, God, and salvation.

But Frost only entertains the thought of spiritual unity and vision, just as he only plays with and then rejects the possibility of any correspondence with the small, fearful bird of "The Wood-Pile": ("Who was so foolish as to think what *he* thought"). The parenthetical "if you know" reveals Frost's ambivalence toward nature's power to illuminate. It leaves unanswered whether or not nature is mediant, correspondent, and value-filled. Indeed, the problem underlying the poem is whether natural fact is a sign of spiritual truth, allowing the questing, questioning speaker an insight that might relieve him of his toil and confusion in the cedar swamp. He hopes for an understanding akin to Wordsworth's vision "into the life of things," described as "that serene and blessed mood,/ In which the burthen of the mystery,/ In which the heavy and the weary weight/ Of all this unintellegible world,/ Is lightened." However, the encounter leads to no such vision. Instead, the speaker finds amusement in talking to himself. The line, "Me? I'm not off for anywhere at all," may be read as another casual, humorous response to a question that the speaker pretends the tree to be making. His answer suggests that he is simply lost; but it also is an ironical answer to the typical Frostian questions of whether correspondence and vision are possible in nature, and whether man can be resurrected through them.

The unexpected encounter with the tree is typical of Romantic moments of discovery. Nature guides the speaker to a discovery by hooking and arresting him, making him "look up to heaven." This gift (or is it chance?) is Frost's diminished, if not ironical, equivalent to the grace of the Romantic visionary moment. The poem's setting also has Romantic echoes. Leaving the familiar road for the wild swamp is risk-taking, an imaginative act, an example of the will braving alien entanglements. It corresponds to Thoreau's metaphor of leaving the road, so that he can think anew: "Did he ever get out of the road which all men and fools travel? You call yourself a great traveller, perhaps, but can you get beyond the influence of a certain class of ideas?"[53] The swamp in "An Encounter," like the setting in "The Wood-Pile," is visionary ground, the boundary between the natural and supernatural, the spot where life and greenness are perpetually nourished.[54] Thoreau himself "enter[s] a swamp as a sacred place, a *sanctum sanctorum*. There is the strength, the marrow, of Nature" where he "would recreate" himself.[55] The Journals set many such moments of tranquil restoration in the temple of the swamp,[56] a meeting place for human and divine. These entries provide a meaningful reference for Frost's swamp settings, which, after the example of Thoreau, occasion a new life in the speaker's soul and define the spiritual character of his quest and encounter. While the Thoreauvian source is suggestive of Frost's Romantic, visionary concerns, his tone undercuts and masks the spiritual dimensions of the poem.

The applied science of electricity, rather than Romantic nature, provides man with messages; everywhere the telegraph replaces the faded Wordsworthian spirit: "'You here' I said. 'Where aren't you nowadays?'" Replacing the living tree of nature and the cruciform of Christianity is the "resurrected" telegraph cross. Thoreau's Journals often identify the ubiquitous telegraph "harp"[57] as a symbol of creative interchange between human soul, nature, and divinity.[58] The telegraph harp, for both writers, projects our ideas; scientific invention animates and enriches mute nature. For Frost the "one life within us and abroad" is the electrical impulse of human-made sound--not a Coleridgean confluence of spirit and animated nature, as "The Eolean Harp" proposes.

Industrious man resurrects the swamp "tree" for his science. How different from Thoreau's discovery of "immortal wood" in Concord's swamp and its "translation" for holy purpose:

> That big swamp white oak . . . which I found prostrate in the swamp. . . . Immortal wood! that had begun to live again. . . . These old stumps stand like anchorites and yogees, putting off their earthly garments, more and more sublimed from year to year, ready to be translated, and then they ripe for my fire. . . . I administer the last sacrament and purification.[59]

The only "immortal" wood Frost administers to is the treated telegraph pole, used not to "translate" spiritually but transfer man's word. Thoreau's "sublime anchorite" has become the drudge of technology. It's knowing what to do with things that count.

The uncomfortable weather suits both the ironic tenor and failure of correspondence in the encounter. It is a day of complete stillness, in which the growing haze and heat render all nature lifeless. This is a "weather breeder," a term also used by Thoreau to describe a day "very warm, without perceptible wind, with a comparatively lifeless [air] . . . with . . . an invisible mist sobering down every surface; and the water . . . was perfectly smooth all day. This was a weather-breeder."[60] The haze in "An Encounter" likewise sobers down every surface; a neutralized nature seems appropriate to the poem's negative vision. Indeed, the atmospheric conditions are similar to those in a famous "weather-wise" Romantic poem, "Dejection: An Ode," in which the inertness mirrors the soul's blankness. There, both soul and nature are in the condition of a weather breeder, whose oppressive lull presages foulness. If Coleridge gazes on nature "with how blank an eye!" so does Frost's sceptical quester who will not directly admit the purpose of his search and finally dismisses it lightly. He won't acknowledge being "off for anywhere at all" because he realizes how out-of-date is his goal. This reticence indicates a tentativeness and disengagement that finds its fit analogue in the neutral weather that hangs over the speaker.

The last two lines of the poem, wherein the speaker remarks that he sometimes "wander[s] out of beaten ways/ Half looking for the orchid Calypso," are of inestimable importance in indicating the visionary character of the quest; for the orchid, as we saw in Chapter III, is a sign of some special, mysterious presence attending deep thought or culminating a quest. The nonchalance of the last line should not beguile us; the type of orchid particularized refers to godhood and matters metaphysical, but hidden; for Calypso means in Greek "she who conceals." She is a semi-divinity in the Odyssey who promises Ulysses immortality and eternal youth. Her divine office should not be overlooked in probing the meaning of the speaker's quest, his desiring the encounter, and its ultimate failure.

"FRAGMENTARY BLUE"

Why make so much of fragmentary blue
In here and there a bird, or butterfly,
Or flower, or wearing-stone, or open eye,
When heaven presents in sheets the solid hue?

Since earth is earth, perhaps, not heaven (as yet)--
Though some savants make earth include the sky;
And blue so far above us comes so high,
It only gives our wish for blue a whet.

"Fragmentary Blue" also inquires heavenward, posing a question that Frost asks often: are nature's fragments of blue the evidence of heaven? The poem is in the tradition of contemplating the each in all; Frost's catalogue, however, is sportive: he refers to all the categories of created nature--animal (bird and butterfly), vegetable ("flower"), mineral ("wearing-stone"), and human or animal ("open eye").

"Savants," or cheerful monists, make "earth include the sky"; Frost, however, in the voice of a tentative but not melancholy dualist, is not "as yet" prepared to claim that matter and spirit are a unity. The foremost "savant" who sees earth as heaven, identifies the color blue as a symbol of spirit, and treats the clear blue of water as an "open eye" is Thoreau. (The French word "savant" may obliquely refer to him, our foremost transcendentalist of French ancestry.) "Fragmentary Blue" resonates with the language and thought of *Walden* , whose pond is a chief symbol of the each in all.

The "prevailing blue" of Walden Pond "is the color of its iris. . . . It is earth's eye; looking into which the beholder measures the depth of his own nature."[61] In Thoreau's monistic universe, blue is "the evidence of . . . purity" of spirit,[62] and the color mirrors the mind's perfection. Frost's "blue so far above us" is, for Thoreau, immanent in nature. Thoreau "makes earth include the sky" in asserting, "I cannot come nearer to God and Heaven/ Than I lived to Walden even"; in winter "Heaven is under our feet as well as over our heads."[63]

Because Frost's blue is "so far above us" (a heaven unknowable and unattainable), it "gives our wish for blue a whet." Frost will not see traces of the color as evidence that heaven is one with earth. Earth may be shot through with glimmers of heaven, but it remains separate from it--fragmented. Frost may be referring subtly to Walden Pond's essence in that it whets our spiritual appetite but literally "wets" (Frost enjoys such puns) the senses if we, as Thoreau, immerse ourselves in it.

"NEITHER OUT FAR NOR IN DEEP"

A calmer search for vision seems to be the crux of the problematic "Neither Out Far Nor In Deep." Does the poem reflect Frost's scepticism about man's spiritual aspirations, or does it, like "Sand Dunes," "The Trial by Existence" and "Riders," admire, if guardedly, the dignity of man's perseverance to know and his will to believe? The poem may express religious affirmation and the Emersonian idea that nature mirrors the eternal. It may conversely measure the emptiness of a "terrifying universe," as Lionel Trilling remarked at the famous "cultural episode" celebrating Frost's eighty-fifth birthday.[64] In sum, since the poem is so chary, no interpretation is certain and final.

We can be assisted, however, by examining a passage in *A Week on the Concord and Merrimack Rivers*, which instructs in how to behold the infinite in watery surfaces:

> The shallowest still water is unfathomable. Wherever the tree and skies are reflected, there is more than Atlantic depth, and no danger of fancy running aground. We notice that it required a separate intention of the eye, a more free and abstracted vision, to see the reflected trees and the sky, than to see the river bottom merely; and so are there manifold visions in the direction of every object, and even the most opaque reflect the heavens from their surface. Some men have their eyes naturally intend to the one and some to the other object.
>
> > 'A man that looks on glass,
> > On it may stay his eye,
> > Or, if he pleaseth, through it pass,
> > And the heavens espy.'[65]

The passage helps illuminate the Romantic heritage of the poem, though Frost claims nothing about the fulfillment of man's visionary aspirations. Whereas Thoreau sees the infinite reflected in all objects, Frost remains uncommitted, although his people doggedly look at the sea all day, hoping to see beyond opaque reality. Frost's shoreside pilgrims stand along "the wetter ground like glass" and it "stay[s]" their "eye," but they have not the capacity to "through it pass,/ And the heavens espy." Failing to look out far or in deep, they see only the nearest reflections of "a standing gull" or ship that raises it hull, but "wherever the truth may be" they patiently gaze, imaginations aground.

Frost is unwilling to allow "a separate intention of the eye" see heaven in watery reflections. He remembers Ishmael's warning the masthead philosophers lost in transcendental attitudinizing. Though visionless, the people along the sand never find their limitations to be a "bar," (*i.e.*, an obstruction) to their imagination, to their gazings into the real or reflected depths, or to any watch they keep. But Frost is well aware of the sand-bars that prevent outward passages of the soul from reaching the depths.[66]

The form of the poem provides further evidence of its organic ties to Thoreau's lyric. The stanza form, rhyme scheme, and trimeter, which includes an anapest within the iambic line, are the same as those of Thoreau's quatrain. However, the constraints of the people's vision is reinforced by the short, clipped lines 2, 3, 13, and 14. "Neither Out Far Nor In Deep" is unique in that it is related in form and meaning to a poem of Thoreau; but in Frost's mentor, the vigil really is directed out far and in deep.

"THE DEMIURGE'S LAUGH"

In this subtle poem the visionary quest is halted by a demon's mockery of the pursuit of a false god. The laughter announces the quester's loss of illusion and subsequent aimlessness. Using as evidence Frost's gloss in the first edition of *A Boy's Will* , Thompson reads the poem as a pursuit of science, or, more specifically, creative evolution,[67] which is "no true god." This reading gains strength in the context of other glosses in the volume; these commentaries show a thematic concern for an understanding of the self, the soul, love, fellowship, death, and art, and imply that "The Demiurge's Laugh" concerns the quest for truth or knowledge.

But any meaning attached to the quest must account for the Demiurge, whose "trail" takes us to Plato's *Timaeus*, a dialogue dramatizing the lengths to which man uses his imagination in trying to understand the mysteries of the universe. The Demiurge is Plato's subordinate god who created the world by copying the ideal plan of the Creator. But the Demiurge's material world, by definition, is its model's inferior. Thus, any quest for the ideal originating from the Demiurge's visible creation must fail. In short, if nature cannot be the locus of truth, the hunt for the "Demon," who is "no true god," must

VI - The Visionary Quest: Dark Encounters

therefore result in his mocking of man. However we choose to identify the Demiurge--as science, evolution, a possible mediator between man and god, the source of knowledge or truth--he performs the role accorded to him in myth: he scorns our spiritual searchings and derides our hope for understanding.[68]

Frost's parable rejects the notion that we receive ultimate truth through our inductive faculty operating on material reality; also, the possibility of knowing absolutes--based on the Romantic view that nature and a Supreme Intelligence are one--is discarded. Plato's Demiurge acts as the voice and symbol of Frost's implicit dualism.

The mythic Demiurge may further act as author of evil,[69] turning the quester from his pursuit and instilling a fearful awareness "that lasted many and many a year." Out of the quest for knowledge and truth (vested, presumably, in the ambiguous Demiurge) comes an awareness of evil. This apparently ironic reversal of the Romantic quest dramatizes "the evil of good born,"[70] which Frost charged Emerson and "the great tradition of monists" to be unaware of.

"Hymn to Intellectual Beauty" also provides a reference[71] for understanding the Romantic character and ironies of the quest. Shelley seeks the ideal, an "unseen," uncertain power that poets call "Demon, Ghost, and Heaven" (27). This bounding, youthful pursuit is punctuated by fleeting intuitions of an immortal presence, culminating in a triumphant, momentary vision, in which he "shrieked, and clasped [his] hands in ecstasy" (60). The lines leading up to this fulfillment are similar to Frost's joyful hunt through the woods. Shelley writes:

> While yet a boy I sought for ghosts, and sped
> Through many a listening chamber, cave and ruin,
> And starlight wood, with fearful steps pursuing
> Hopes of high talk with the departed dead.
> . . . . .
> I was not heard--I saw them not--
> When musing deeply on the lot
> Of life . . .
> Sudden, thy shadow fell on me;
> I shrieked, and clasped my hands in ecstasy! (49 ff.)

He is chasing demons, whose sublime "voices" (25) not only can provide "responses" (26) to his deepest questionings but also speak as the souls of the dead.

Just as the shadow of Intellectual Beauty falls on Shelley's quester, proving to be the formative vision of his life, Frost's aural experience befalls him in shadows, "just as the light was beginning to fail"; the sound "has lasted me many and many a year." In Shelley the shadow of the ideal "descend[s]" (80), impelling him to love and worship "every form containing" it. Shadowy Beauty, the fair demon of forms, binds Shelley to love, hope, and self-esteem; for it is a protective spirit of good. In ironic contrast, Frost's Demon arises "from his wallow" to mock the quester's headlong pursuit. The demon represents more than brute fact; he is "one who utterly couldn't care" about man's quest, and stands as an inversion of Shelleyan Beauty (which poets call "Demon") addressed as "Thou that to human thought are nourishment . . . / Thou messenger of sympathies" (44, 42).

Frost's demon departs, "brushing his eye as he went"; he is anything but "dear, and yet dearer for its mystery" (12), for he abandons the stunned speaker without purpose or illusion. As the negating demon of evil and death, he leaves the soul in an abyss. Shelley's cry--

Depart not as thy shadow came!
Depart not--lest the grave should be,
Like life and fear, a dark reality (46-48)--

is precisely the dark knowledge contained in the admission: "And well I knew what the demon meant." In Frost's quest for vision he has chased ahead and is caught like a fool in an Alastorian wood, where "sameness" breeds perplexity rather than lucidity.

Although in this early work the Frostian quester is fooled by the Romantic hunt, future poems record the defenses he erects against such embarrassments, and the strategic retreats he makes from such indulgences. Indeed, the Demiurge's resounding laughter may be a projection of Frost's own compulsive self-mockery and skepticism over mystical experiences. Thompson tells of Frost hearing voices deriding mystical experiences which were recounted by his mother. At other times "he clearly heard the voice repeating something he himself had said a few minutes earlier, repeating and yet endowing his own words with tones so different from his that the effect seemed to be one of mockery.[72]

Laughter attends Frost's states of border-line sanity and is a projection of a self divided between belief and skepticism. He writes in a letter:

> I was cast for gloom. . . . I have heard laughter by daylight when I thought it was my own because at that moment when it broke I had parted my lips to take food. Just so I have been afraid of myself and caught at my throat when I thought I was making some terrible din of a mill whistle that happened to come on the same instant with the opening of my mouth to yawn. But I have not laughed. No man can tell you the sound of the way of my laughter. I have neighed at night in the woods behind a house like vampires. But there are no vampires, there are no ghouls, there are no demons, there is nothing but me.[73]

If, as Frost suggests, there are no demons, the Demiurge's laughter must originate from the self, which mocks the quest and its goal.

CHAPTER VII
POEMS OF DIALECTIC

Nature within her inmost self divides
To trouble men with having to take sides.

In Emerson's "Uriel" Frost finds the image of his poetic self, a versifying angel "of piercing eye," twitting precept and orthodoxy in poetry of wit, paradox, antithesis, allusion, and irony. Frost's argumentative self is guided by wisdom and "counter-wisdom"[1] that take alternate sides on any philosophical question. Thriving on dialectic or dialogue, Frost's poetic argumentation counterattacks prevailing Romantic (and other) fictions. Just as the voice of Uriel may appear Satanic to those who do not undersand the two-sidedness to reality ("Evil will bless and ice will burn"), Frost's ironic skepticism may seem difficult--even perverse--if it is not understood as an attempt to counterbalance established Romanticism and thus arrive at more rounded truths.

Because Frost finds it strategically inappropriate to speak out directly on important matters, he often assumes masks, like Yeats, so as not to be found out.[2] The ironist's mask is the best defense against the powerful voices of past literature which threaten to overwhelm the contemporary poet. Temperamentally suited to the challenge, Frost's quick, defensive mind is able to thrive (and survive) in dialectic.[3]

His talent for rejoinder takes the poetic form of a studied irony that incorporates the language and ideas of the Romantic writers which he debates. As Frost remarks about assimilating other poets: "You steal them to new uses."[4] If "he wanted poetry to play pranks on prevailing fictions,"[5] it was his theft of still current Romantic beliefs by which he initiated a dialectic. Romantic literature even determines the verbal form and direction his poems will take. Frost's arguments are not simply statements of "rational observation re-enforced by meditation,"[6] nor are they necessarily dialogues in which the two speakers are always Frost himself;[7] rather, they are often pointed dialogues with

107

specific Romantic works which presume a theory about the natural and moral world. His favorite targets are those beliefs avowed by the most noteworthy Romantic writers: Shelley on death and spiritual rebirth; Emerson on the primacy of instinct, revelation, love, and the expanding soul; Thoreau on wildness, nature's changes in colors, and the void; Coleridge on charity; Keats on oblivion. The purpose of this chapter is to note how Frost's answering poems counter or resist these famous Romantic writers' themes; Frost's dialectical poems leave us with the impression of a speaker separated from earlier idealism. In effect these poems elaborate the lines, "Petals I may have once pursued./ Leaves are all my darker mood." This darker mood of scepticism is generally more pronounced in these dialectical poems than in the quest poems already discussed. Frost's skepticism and anti-Romanticism reach a nadir in "Come In," "Design," and "Desert Places," the last poems in this chapter.

"A LEAF TREADER"

We begin with the Shelleyan context of "A Leaf Treader." Every line centers on the leaves. Fearful, The speaker wants to overcome them rather than be swept along with them to death. He hears them threatening; they speak to him, appealing to the "fugitive" in his heart, tapping, touching, and inviting him to "grief." Resisting the call to become one with the leaves contrasts with Shelley's ecstatic plea to become a part of autumnal dispersion, decay, and death, voiced in "Ode to the West Wind." While Frost uses Shelley's leaves, which are identified with the human soul, every line of "A Leaf Treader" counters the aerial flights of idealism, apocalypse, suicide, and rebirth depicted by the Ode.

If Shelley is the sun-treader, as Browning describes him, Frost is a leaf-treader exhausting himself among "all the color and form of leaves" which "God knows." They are the "Pestilence-stricken multitudes . . . / Yellow and black, and pale, and hectic red" that flee before the divine blast. The remark, "Perhaps I have put forth too much strength and been too fierce from fear," echoes Shelley's address to the all-powerful wind that it be one with his spirit in courage and strength: "Be thou, spirit fierce,/ My spirit. . . . If I . . . [could] share/ The impulses of thy strength." Frost's first stanza attributes all power, will, and purposefulness not to the Shelleyan apocalyptical spirit in the wind, but the human speaker who puts the leaves to bed. He alone is the animating force in this universe, not the Romantic "wild spirit." He has "safely trodden underfoot the leaves" in an exhausting, fearful ritual that attempts to dispell any destructive force or death-wish intimated in the falling leaves.

The speaker's fear of the leaves is clarified in stanza two. They hang over him all summer, threatening: "And when they came it seemed with a will to carry me with them to death." Likewise, in "Ode to the West Wind" the fall will turn earth into a "vast sepulchre." In desiring to become a part of the dead leaves Shelley would be destroyed to be reborn. It is this escapist, suicidal appeal of the leaves which Frost finds dangerously attractive: "They spoke of the fugitive in my heart as if it were leaf to leaf/ They tapped at my eyelids and touched my lips with an invitation to grief." This is the closest the leaf treader comes to the following Shelleyan identification with leaves:

> Oh, lift me as a . . . leaf. . . .
> I fall upon the thorns of life! I bleed!
> . . . . .
> What if my leaves are falling like its own!
> . . . . .
>   Be thou me, impetuous one!
>
> Drive my dead thoughts over the universe
> Like withered leaves to quicken a new birth!

The treader resists these Shelleyan flights, however appealing they might seem. The last lines counter the Romantic impulse to identify man's fate with natural processes. Frost includes death--certainly--but no assured rebirth, spiritual or otherwise, of which Shelley is so confident. His faith, subtly affirmed in "God knows," sustains him. Therefore, the self-command "Now up my knee on top of another year of snow," suggests that through his will, man dominates nature where he can and subdues the desire to scatter himself with it. Such treading is the proper rejoinder to Romantic abandonment and the measure of Frost's quarrel with Shelley's sun-treading.

"MISGIVING"

In "Misgiving," the same anti-Shelleyan argumentation obtains. The foliage cries, "We will go with you, O Wind!" but "his summoning blast" only creates "vaguer and vaguer stir," a feeble "reluctant stir," finally dropping the leaves "no further than where they were." Like Shelley, Frost identifies himself (in the last stanza) with the leaves, but he does not believe in the wind's power to lift him and "Drive my dead thoughts over the universe/ Like withered leaves to quicken a new birth." Frost's wind is surely the destroyer but not the preserver of new life and visionary understanding. Rather phlegmatically he concludes,

> I only hope that when I am free
> As they are free to go in quest
> Of the knowledge beyond the bounds of life
> It may not seem better to me to rest.

The knowledge here is the Shelleyan resurrection and revelation hoped for beyond the autumnal blast. Frost seems indifferent to this "quest," ironically answering Shelley's expectation that the wind, after putting to flight and destroying the old leaves, "Be through my lips to unawakened earth/ The trumpet of a prophecy!" Frost believes in the "rest" that comes with Shelley's winter, but as for a spring of the spirit being far behind---*i.e* ., "beyond the bounds of life"--he is uncertain. Sleep, the fall, and rest are all.

"WILLFUL HOMING"

Equally ironic as "Misgiving" but tougher in stance, this retaliatory poem quarrels with Emerson's Shelley-like exhortation that man follow his impulse rather than judgment. Emerson claims that "an emotion communicates to the intellect the power to sap and upheave nature" and free us from its bondage:

> There is good reason why we should prize this
> liberation. The fate of the poor shepherd, who,
> blinded and lost in the snow-storm, perishes in a drift

within a few feet of his cottage door, is an emblem of
the state of man. On the brink of the waters of life
and truth, we are miserably dying.[8]

Frost will have none of this, and by way of reply uses Emerson's
analogy of the shepherd as the dramatic core. The blinded, lost
speaker, like his counterpart in Emerson, does not "sap and upheave"
nature; rather, it is on top of him, pushing forcefully down on him. He
is not "carried away by his thought"; no dream "holds him like an
insanity."[9] Instead, he "calmly consider[s] a course./ He peers out
shrewdly." The emphasis on calculation rather than emotional
response answers the fiction that impulse and intuition serve as the
agents of man's salvation. When the compass of spirit is unreadable,
we, unaided, save ourselves by deliberation and willfulness. "Since
he means to come to a door he will come to a door."

Frost's representative man, the "shrewd" homecomer, stands in
contrast to Emerson's emblematic shepherd dying "within a few feet
of his . . . door." Calm deliberation brings Frost's man home "wide of
the knob a yard or more"; a compromised "aim and rate" results in a
near miss and some fumbling, but not disaster. Emerson's shepherd
is the rare exception to the ordinary human state of affairs. Frost's
man relies on reasoning will, not Emersonian instinct, to sustain
himself.

"THE COW IN APPLE TIME;" "THE RUNAWAY"

Frost has more to say about instinct in these two poems, arguing
that man has a practical need to control animal nature. These poems
show how far Frost departs from the Transcendental doctrine of the
virtue of wildness. The indirect argument of these two poems is that
in man's ordered farmyard, control rather than instinctual freedom is
preferred, a point which provides the corrective to Thoreau's assertion
that

> I love even to see the domestic animals reassert their
> native rights,--any evidence that they have not wholly
> lost their original wild habits and vigor; as when my
> neighbor's cow breaks out of her pasture early in the

> spring and boldly swims the river. . . . I rejoice that
> horses and steers have to be broken before they can
> be made the slaves of men, and that men themselves
> have some wild oats still left to sow before they
> become submissive members of society.[10]

The "Something" that impels Frost's cow over the wall needs to be subdued for the benefit of man and animal; its well-being guarantees milk and beef. Thoreau could never be so mindful of commodity as is Frost, who here is more farmer than sage, more jokester than philosopher. What is that "something" that inspires her to take off, disregard boundaries, spurn authority, and bellow? That something refers to hard cider--liquor. The cow is drunk from the fermentation of cider in her stomachs. This fact is common knowledge among Vermont farmers; one has to be versed in country things to catch the humor here, and, as well, the truth that instinctive animal nature is fallible. We need to guard against downward comparisons. In this regard the poem is linked to "The White-Tailed Hornet."

Wild nature also needs to be checked and tamed in "The Runaway." Mindful of the first traces of snow flakes and a horse outdoors, the poet remarks, "Whoever it is that leaves him out so late . . . / Ought to be told to come and take him in." Frost's prudence seems a response to Thoreau's admiration of instinct expressed in a Journal passage at the time of first snow:

> Cattle and horses . . . retain many of their wild
> habits or instincts wonderfully. . . . I have heard of a
> horse which his master could not catch in his pasture
> when the first snowflakes were falling, who persisted
> in wintering out. As he persisted in keeping out of his
> reach, his master finally left him. When the snow had
> covered the ground three or four inches deep, the
> horse pawed it away to come at the grass. . . . By the
> next day he had had enough of free life and pined for
> his stable, and so suffered himself to be caught.[11]

The image of the horse may correspond to the speaker, but it is wildness, not fear,[12] that dominates this poem. In Frost's world, man

112

saves animal nature from destroying itself. Just as he improves chaotic nature in "The Aim Was Song," he controls and sustains an otherwise untamed cow and colt. Frost sees with husbandman's eyes, distrusting the pure goodness of wildness in nature, whereas Thoreau sees with the eye of a philosopher searching for ultimate sources in phenomena. Animal domesticity speaks only of man's influence; wild nature speaks of a "something" mysterious and much more significant. However, Frost is here not concerned with ultimates but the order man imposes.

"TRIPLE BRONZE"

In the same way that Frost doubts the rightness of instinct and impulse, he resists fictions about the soul's relation to the infinite. He reverses Emerson's monistic advice to yield to, dilate, absorb, and embrace the All. "Triple Bronze," "Devotion," "The Secret Sits," and "The Lockless Door" tell us that containment, resistance, and withdrawal are the true leanings of the soul; in every instance in making his point, Frost uses Emerson against himself to intensify his anti-Romantic responses.

"Triple Bronze" outlines the defenses "Between too much and me," and sets up a tripartite, strategic retreat from the Infinite, crime, and foreign nations. This shrinking from the world and the cosmos is one man's hermitic reaction to our century's impingements on the individual, but the poem also has an Emersonian context that once again defines Frost's quarrel with Romantic idealism. To Emerson, the dilating soul encompasses the universe, reducing all facts to a unity under a "higher law" and bringing all events to understanding. The mind alone restores the universe, altering, molding, and making it into his kingdom. Man becomes its master. The following passage from *Nature* summarizing these claims of idealism provides a reference for Frost's attack:

> Every spirit builds itself a house, and beyond its house a world, and beyond its world a heaven. Know then that the world exists for you. For you is the phenomenon perfect. What we are, that only can we see. All that Adam had, all that Caesar could, you

> have and can do. Adam called his house, heaven
> and earth; Caesar called his house Rome; you
> perhaps call yours . . . a hundred acres of ploughed
> land; or a scholar's garret. . . . . Build therefore your
> own world.[13]

Frost's rational soul, like a drumlin woodchuck, relies on defenses to survive in a sometimes threatening world, which can hardly be said to "exist for" him perfectly. His soul cannot dilate to contain the universe. Containment, protectiveness, and diminishment--a retreat from the All--therefore define the character of the soul. The movement of "Triple Bronze reverses Emerson's assurances that the spirit builds a house, a world, and a heaven in a kind of accruing dilation and absorption of the universe--an advance toward the All.

Barriers defend the self from "too much." Man's first "house" is his "hide"; his second, a wall; his third, a national boundary. "I'm in favor of a skin, and fences and tariff walls," Frost writes just before the poem's publication.[14] He conceives his world not on great expectations that it exists ideally for man. His Yankee mettle is bronzed to such notions. What Thoreau says of stoical strength of character--"Only he can be trusted with gifts who can present a face of bronze to expectations"[15]--applies as well to Frost's disposition. "Triple Bronze" shows such a fact to the world, and defenses that are instinctively thorough.

"DEVOTION"

> The heart can think of no devotion
> Greater than being shore to the ocean--
> Holding the curve of one position,
> Counting an endless repetition.

This poem is a rhymed corrective to Emerson's monism, which assumes a bond of love uniting all men with god and circulating universally. The pervading holiness of the heart's affections is so expressed in a devotional passage in "The Over-Soul":

Every friend whom not thy fantastic will but the great

114

and tender heart in thee craveth, shall lock thee in his embrace. And this because the heart in thee is the heart of all; not a valve, not a wall, not an intersection is there anywhere in nature, but one blood rolls uninterruptedly an endless circulation through all men, as the water of the globe is all one sea, and, truly seen its tide is one.[16]

Using Emerson's metaphors, Frost argues a finiteness of man's heart (a traditional term for the soul), which borders on infinitude but does not necessarily assume a oneness with it. The heart goes neither out far nor in deep but is the material barrier fronting the infinite, and the container of life and spirit--put poetically, "the shore to the ocean" of infinity. It is a "wall," a "valve" counting an "endless repetition" of heartbeats (or waves) that mark finite time. Frost disavows a transcendental blood flowing in "endless circulation" through all men and all nature. The heart is a borderer, barrier, and container "Holding the curve of one position" much as the shore defines edges and fronts the sea. Instead of flowing out into all nature, it resists it while defining it. Such is the nature of man's mind or soul here and in "Sand Dunes."

"THE SECRET SITS"

We dance round in a ring and suppose,
But the Secret sits in the middle and knows.

Like "Triple Bronze" and "Devotion," this couplet reasserts, but with even more skeptical zeal, the separation between the self and the infinite, and corrects and recasts the relation between man's mind and the One Mind made in Emerson's "The World-Soul." Puzzlement and supposition characterize man's circling pursuit of God, or truth--the ultimate "Secret," which is, finally, unknowable to Frost. He plays with these lines describing the World-Soul: "Still, still the secret presses;/ The nearing clouds draw down;/ . . . ./ Stars weave eternal rings;/ . . . / Yet there in the parlor sits/ Some figure of noble guise,--/. . . ./ That's writ upon our cell;/
. . . ./ The sage, till he hit the secret,/ Would hang his head in shame,/

Our brothers have not read it,/ Not one has found the key."

The World-Soul sits passively at the center of things, rather than pressing actively on us for interpretation. Frost does not believe that the human mind and the One Mind are in correspondence; an unmistakable separation and dualism reigns here. However, in one of his earliest poems, written in high school, he accepts the Romantic doctrine of the mind's marriage to nature and the dream vision that attends it:

> All nature seems to weave a circle of
> Enchantment round the mind, and give full sway
> To flitting thoughts and dreams of bygone years.[17]

The language echoes the famous last lines of "Kubla Khan"[18] celebrating the Platonic poet of whom mortals stand in awe as they "Weave a circle round him thrice/. . ./ For he on honey dew hath fed,/ And drunk the milk of Paradise." Just as "Kubla Khan" and "A Dream of Julius Caesar" apprehend a mysterious knowledge at the center of the circle man and nature form, "The Secret Sits," with its allusions to Coleridge and Emerson, places an inscrutable but knowing God, or mind, or secret, in the middle of man's ring of dancing. For man is not at the still point but on the circumference of truth, ever uncertain in his dance of life. If Emerson monistically regarded his eye and mind at the center of all things, Frost sees man wheeling like the stars around the focal, unknown "Secret," which holds all moving things in place and at a distance.

"THE LOCKLESS DOOR"

Lawrance Thompson's account of the origins of this poem show that Frost's terrors of a night in 1895 haunted him sufficiently that he wrote the poem as an act of exorcism; it contains dream symbolism that suggests the influence of "the prophetic Daniel."[19] The poem has, indeed, a profound spiritual fear and despair arising out of a possible confrontation with the almighty; the reference is more to Emerson than Daniel, however.

The mysterious presence and knock at the door occasion the speaker's fearful retreat. This is clearly an act of choice, though he has the power, if not the courage, to open the lockless door and face the one who knocks, apparently someone expected for many years. The speaker prays between the knockings but then climbs through the window, emptying his "cage" and hiding in the world.

The general meaning sharpens if we read it as a reversal of the moment of revelation, described in "The Over-Soul" as the grace of knowing the self and God simultaneously. Awe, emotion, and delight attend "the announcements of the soul": "In these communications the power to see is not separated from the will to do, but the insight proceeds from obedience, and the obedience procedes from a joyful perception."[20] No barriers stand against the soul when it "mingles with the universal soul."[21] The living presence of God, the universal soul, or Revelation, is always available if, as Emerson says, man opens himself to experience--stated metaphorically, if he "unlock[s], at all risks, his human doors."[22] But "we must pick no locks"; that is, we must not extort truth but "let the tide of being . . . float us into the secret of nature."[23]

"The Lockless Door" carries the speaker to the threshold of Emersonian revelation, but as is so typical of Frost's poetry, man makes a fearful, strategic retreat from a divine presence that bodes something terrifying rather than comforting. If the moments of Revelation are "perceptions of the absolute law" and "solutions of the soul's own questions,"[24] the mind's apocalypses may be spectral, created out of fear, despair, and terror, rather than the benevolent calm which Emerson presumes. Frost would rather flee than endure a dark response to the soul's questionings. His retreat dramatizes what Emerson said about the man who is deferential to a higher spirit than his own: "If he have not found his home in God . . . let him brave it out how he will."[25]

The speaker's "cage" is presumably the soul's house. Emerson writes of "the chambers and magazines of the soul" unsearched by philosophy.[26] "Fate" asserts that "every spirit makes its house; but afterwards the house confines the spirit."[27] Emptying his "cage/ To hide in the world" implies that the speaker abandons the soul's inquiries. Flight shows his fear, and a cowardice that Emerson predicts: "But if he would know what the great god speaketh he must 'go into his closet and shut the door.'. . . God will not make himself manifest to cowards."[28] Frost's runaway is not willing to open the door

117

and see what Revelation stands outside. Rather than dwell in the soul and risk the terrors of self-examination, he chooses the world to hide in. A spiritual fugitive and masker, he would "alter with age."

Christ said, "Knock, and it shall be opened unto you,"[29] but for Frost the knocking brings terror and flight. It is understandable that the speaker "raised both hands/ In prayer to the door," whether out of fear or supplication. He is apparently conforming to Matthew's injunction (adapted by Emerson in "The Over-Soul"), "when thou prayest, enter into thy closet, and when thou hast shut thy door, pray to thy Father which is in secret; and Thy Father which seeth in secret shall reward thee openly."[30] This closet and door are the setting wherein Emerson warns men not to inquire into the future and question the immortality of the soul. It is also the soul's sanctum and dramatizes Frost's terror in confronting some possibly unbearable revelation. He understandably hides in a more comfortable place--his home that is the world. How he "alter[s] with age" in it is anyone's guess; but it seems that the spiritual void here leads to the utter hopelessness of the speaker's soul in "Desert Places."

"LOVE AND A QUESTION"

A confrontation at an open door tests another spiritual principle in "Love and a Question." This ballad, in so many ways a sequel to "The Rime of the Ancient Mariner," puts Coleridge's moral vision of fellowship and charity to the question. Frost's familiarity with the poem is well documented; he taught and parodied it a year before writing "Love and a Question."[31] He apparently pondered the Mariner's exclusion from the wedding company. The Mariner, an outcast, cursed man whose presence would taint the joyful marriage feast, stands at the door and tells his woeful tale to the Wedding Guest who is stunned and chastened by its moral impact and who becomes a sadder, wiser man the following morning. The powerful message is that love for all things is man's first obligation and leads to his salvation. "Love and a Question" treats this Christian moral by having a forlorn "Stranger" confront a bridegroom at the doorway, or "porch." Frost's bridegroom acts similarly to Coleridge's Wedding Guest. (Or is he Frost's projection of the groom in the "Ancient Mariner"?) The bridegroom continues the moral questioning implicit in the drama unfolding before the feast hall and in the narrative proper, and ponders whether or not to practice what Coleridge's Mariner has preached.

Frost's bridegroom does as much as he feels obligated to do under the circumstances. He gives bread, money, and a "heartfelt prayer," enacting the Mariner's injunction of charity: "He prayeth well, who loveth well/ Both man and bird and beast." But Frost's bridegroom understands the limits to Christian fellowship, for complete hospitality might "mar" the newly sanctified love relationship. Coleridge's unqualified, universal charity has its bounds in Frost's world. Men may live and work together, but they also live and love apart.

The last stanza summarizes the moral quandry of choosing between the private, marital love that he hopes to protect and the Christian charity that is the duty of all men.

> But whether or not a man was asked
> To mar the love of two
> By harboring woe in the bridal house,
> The bridegroom wished he knew.

The Stranger is presumably no victim of ordinary misery; his "woe" must be special if it is able to endanger new love. Seen in the moral light of the Ancient Mariner's cosmic "woeful agony" (578), the Stranger's affliction implies deep suffering and calamity, impelled, presumably, by impiety, accursedness, and despair. The convulsions of the hermit, the pilot, and the pilot's boy indicate the seriousness of exposure to the Mariner. Nonetheless, his purpose is highly moral. Telling his story to others is both evangelical and penitential. If, then, the Stranger is a type of the Ancinet Mariner, no wonder the bridegroom questions whether fellowship is the way and the light. The Stranger must remain outside the door, as did the Mariner, lest the marriage chamber be violated. A kind of epithalamion in its "welcoming," "Love and a Question," like many other poems by Frost, defines the limits of moral idealism, which is not unbounded.

Other parallels with Coleridge's poem support this interpretation. Like the Mariner, the Stranger is immediately introduced, asking the bridegroom for shelter "with the eyes more than the lips." These

119

compelling eyes derive from the Mariner's "glittering" and "bright" eye which holds the wedding guest and suggests special knowledge and intent:

> He holds him with his glittering eye--
> The wedding Guest stood still
> And listens like a three years' child
> The mariner hath his will. (12-15)

The stranger's "burden" of "care," anticipating the "woe" of the penultimate line, reminds us of the Mariner's albatross hanging as a curse of spiritual isolation, despair, and suffering.

Desiring "shelter for the night" implies, in part, the Stranger's need for soothing sleep. Similarly, the Mariner knows its care-removing blessedness: "O sleep! it is a gentle thing/ Beloved from pole to pole" (292-93). But the Stranger does not enter the house, just as the Ancient Mariner does not go into the feast hall. In the tradition of an epithalamion, no "doleful dreriment" or taint of evil should darken the nuptial feast and bridal chamber. Innocence and purity must be protected, and it is most likely for this that both poems give the barest glimpse of the brides, who stand far within feast-hall and house. The similar descriptions of the brides further link the poems: In the "Ancient Mariner" she is "red as a rose," (34) and in the later poem, "Her face [is] rose-red with the glowing coal" as she bends over the fire.

The protectiveness of Frost's bridegroom is apparent in his "wish[ing] her heart in a case of gold/ And pinned with a silver pin." After all, marriage is an exclusive relationship, but he is also apprehensive as is the Wedding Guest, who at one point cries, "I fear thee, ancient Mariner" (345). No wonder Frost's bridegroom wishes his beloved's heart in a case of gold, inviolable to all woes associated with the Stranger. The question of moral responsibility and charity has easy answers for Frost's bridegroom, who holds to the primacy of marriage. Coleridge's injunction to love all things suggests the preeminence of charity, but Frost questions its priority. Woven into "Love and a Question" is an implicit awareness of the Mariner's moral universe and the cursed loneliness of the soul that, while it should be accomodated, cannot intrude upon the higher sanctity of the bridal house.

"COME IN"

We reach the extent of Frost's anti-Romanticism in "Come In," "Design," and "Desert Places." These poems show, respectively, a willful resistance to the soul's dissolving into nature; a skepticism in which he sees signs of indifferent, "other," malevolent nature; and a despair that stems from the void within the spirit and throughout nature. The negativism and skepticism in these three poems are the antithesis of Romantic convictions and bring to a conclusion our discussion of Frost's dialectics.

As a would-be Romantic listener, Frost is cautious in pursuing the deceptive thrush beckoning him in "Come In." The attraction and resistance to the thrush's song measure Frost's ambivalence about Romantic promise.[32] The "call to come in" echoes the "invitation to grief" which the Shelleyan leaves evoke in the speaker of "A Leaf Treader." Frost may have assented to Romantic pieties in the "temple of the heat" of "Rose Pogonias," but will not here enter the sanctum of "the pillared dark." By standing in the dusk outside, Frost resists identification with some transfixed Keatsian listener ready to abandon the world almost suicidally: "Darkling I listen; and for many a time/ I have been half in love with easeful death." Frost's thrush and dark forest invite surrender and oblivion, prompting a desire to

leave the world unseen
And with thee fade away into the forest dim:

Fade far away, dissolve, and quite forget
What thou among the leaves hast never known,
The weariness, the fever, and the fret.

However attractive the song is to Keats, Frost will not pursue it; the music is "*Almost* like a call to come in." He will not imagine more than the loveliness that he hears. For every song of invitation to "the dark and lament," the law of compensation provides the light of stars.[33]

The bird is the American wood thrush, for Thoreau the most melodious and provocative song bird, whose effects it has on the fancy he records in his Journals. It invites abandonment, wildness, and vision, tendencies Thoreau notes:

> The thrush alone declares the immortal wealth and vigor that is in the forest. . . . Wherever a man hears it . . . the gates of heaven are not shut against him. . . . This bird never fails to speak to me out of an ether purer than that I breathe, immortal beauty and vigor. . . . He sings to make men take higher and truer views of things.[34]

"Come In" resists these Romantic indulgences, Frost being wary of ideas his Romantic self relishes but at the same time keeps under control.[35]

Frost is fascinated by the unknown locale of the thrush's song, but will not let go with the heart and fancy to cross the border between light and dark as did Thoreau after hearing the bird:

> There is a sweet wild world which lies along the strain of a wood thrush--the rich intervales which border the stream of its song--more thoroughly genial to my nature than any other.[36]

Those "intervales" are the cleared, fertile stretches on which Frost would presumably regard Hor Mountain or survey the stars, and, like an astronomer or navigator, know where he is. He can admire the dark beauty of the thrush's song but prefers starlight. That border area is what is most genial to his poetic nature.

The poem concerns that dusky margin between transport and control, wildness and rationality, ascent heavenward and tug earthward. Although aware of Thoreau's paean to the thrush: "This is the only bird whose note affects . . . my . . . imagination. . . . I long for wildness, a nature which I cannot put my foot through, woods where the thrush forever sings . . . where I might have a fertile unknown for a soil about me,"[37] Frost halts at the edge of these Thoreauvian woods, defining the boundaries between the known and unknown, control and release. In "Come In," Frost toes the line between truth and illusion that enables him to make a coherent life. His quest poems were never more resistant to the possibility of vision, nor more staunch in sustaining his integrity by not yielding to illusion.

"DESIGN"

This poem is Frost's darkest flowering moment, measuring just how negative and skeptical his vision could be. In "Design," a flower is a sign of spirit--but for an unexpected, totally ironic inversion of meaning we have commonly attributed to it. It is a subverted cosmic flower. The white heal-all is part of the design of "death and blight," rather than the evidence, as we witness in other flower poems, of some beneficent spirit. The question, "What had that flower to do with being white,/ The wayside blue and innocent heal-all?" accentuates the white spider and moth's mystery. There may be a relation among all things, transcendentally considered, but the pattern of this morning rite does not betoken a principle of good. The extraordinary color of the usually blue and medicinally useful heal-all, and its relation to the other white objects in the design, viewed in the light of morning, provide a basis for Frost's metaphysical speculations on the night's appalling design of darkness. His thoughts are remarkably like one of Thoreau's meditations on color relationships in nature. He sees "condition," or hue as a sign of "being":

> It is remarkable that animals are often obviously manifestly related to the plants which they feed upon or live among,--as caterpillars, butterflies. . . . I noticed a yellow spider on a golden rod, as if every condition might have its expression in some form of animated being.[38]

From evidence of every "lily pad floating on the river . . . riddled by insects," Thoreau asks, "Is not disease the rule of existence?[39]

Thoreau singles out the prunella, or heal-all, in its autumnal change of color as an indication of some deeper "revolution of spirit, possibly presaging tragedy"--of the sort alluded to in the Macbeth-like "witches broth" of "Design:" "The prunella leaves have turned a delicate claret or lake color by the roadside. I am interested in these revolutions as much as in those of kingdoms. Is there not tragedy enough in the autumn?"[40] Thoreau infers cosmic meaning in small things--the "roadside" prunella is the fateful "wayside" heal-all of "Design"--but, anticipating Frost, he does not presume to know their specific import. Possibly the prunella's radical change of color indicates some "tragedy." The essence of tragedy is a mysterious, often appalling fate, or dark design, that governs all things great and small; Frost's innocent heal-all contains these Thoreauvian depths of meaning, and more.

"DESERT PLACES"

"Desert Places" is a spiritual low point in Frost's poetry; of all the poems in *A Further Range* "taken singly" it is singular in its apathy and lack of tentativeness that characterizes most of Frost's work. It expresses the poet's frozen psychic state, which contrasts with the creative thaw and flow of "A Hillside Thaw" and "To the Thawing Wind." The cold, lifeless world mirrors the speaker's soul: "I am too absent-spirited to count;/ The loneliness includes me unawares." Because the speaker cannot project passion and life into it and thereby transform it imaginatively, nature is dead and valueless. What an inert soul sees is vacant nature--triply whited: "A blanker whiteness of benighted snow/ With no expression, nothing to express." An inner void, objectified in the field of snow, suggests the sterility of dejected Romantics. The "benighted" snow reflects spiritual darkness and echoes Wordsworth, who, without the light of faith, "in heart and mind/ Benighted" ranges "the field of human life" in quest for knowledge.[41] Frost knows only the soul's night that "Will be more lonely ere it will be less." "A few weeds and stubble" and dormant animals are the shrunken nature that suggests the minimal life of the speaker.

Thoreau often uses these same images--but to describe a correspondence. Speaking of drifts of field-snow, he likens man's constricting winter life to a hibernating marmot;[42] such dormancy of spirit is frequently put in seasonal and climatic analogues. To him, thaw and spring represent creativity and the correspondence of mind and nature. Seasonal growth and its opposite, weeds and stubble, express various relationships between mind and nature; for example, although natural barrenness reflects spiritual poverty, it is "the marriage of the soul with nature that makes the intellect fruitful, that gives birth to imagination. When we were dead and dry as the highway, some sense which has been healthily fed will put us in relation with Nature."[43]

The shift in Frost's last stanza to interstellar spaces expands cosmic loneliness, inverting dramatically the transcendental notion that the universe reflects the soul. Frost's vast desert places echo not Thoreau's spirit and faith but, instead his "awareness of the "desert" and "waste-land" of astronomers' "star territory." Thoreau says:

> [The astronomer's] skies are shoal, and imagination, like a thirsty traveler, pants to be through their desert. The roving mind . . . launches itself to where distance fails to follow [*i.e.*, infinity, God]. I know that there are many stars, I know that they are far enough off, bright enough, steady enough in their orbits--but what are they all worth? They are more waste land in the West,--star territory. . . . I have interest but for six feet of star.[44]

Frost's interest in his six feet is its spiritual relation to the universal void, which he has so much nearer home, in himself. In this poem he uses Thoreau's personal narrative, but erases its faith, leaving, of course, the desert.

Frost's dialectics toughly respond to cherished Romantic beliefs. We have noted in other chapters that his pursuit of truth, insight, and correspondence with nature do not come easily or cheaply, or often--sometimes, in fact, do not come at all, as these last poems indicate. Nature is "other" and indifferent to the speaker's needs. This argumentative, skeptical, resistant Frost has been our concern in recent chapters, characterizing him as a tough, disenchanted poet in dialectic with the cloud of Romantic poets, for the most part. This negative, combative stance here does not mean that the poet has been unable to unify his life and find a center, however.

If Romantic ideals invite repeated negative responses in the poet, ending in the spiritual void of "Desert Places," the following chapters will indicate the positive legacy of Romanticism. The strength and integrity of the poet's spirit are the rewards of a lifetime of reading, absorbing, and living the principles of Thoreau, who was an unending passion for Frost, not simply because he found Thoreau's exquisite naturalistic wriitng a context for poetic argumentation and dialectic, but because he provided Frost with a practical program for spiritual unification of the self through labor. The poems that are the issue of this positive influence are his Thoreauvian heritage--his abundant cloud--and they are among his greatest verses.

CHAPTER VIII
LABOR, ART, AND IMAGINATION

Hard and steady and engrossing labor with the hands, especially out of doors, is invaluable to the literary man and serves him directly (Thoreau, Journal).

> My object in living is to unite
> My avocation and my vocation
> As my two eyes make one in sight.

Frost learns from Thoreau that the true poet does not idly play at correspondences and wait for a natural fact to flower spontaneously into a truth. No, the true poet works, and in his labor he finds solace, involvement, and profit. The wisdom of the Preacher rings true here for everyone sensing the void: "He who watches the wind will never sow, and he who keeps an eye on the clouds will never reap. . . . In the morning sow your seed betimes, and do not stop work until evening, for you do not know whether this or that sowing will be successful, or whether both alike will do well" (Eccles. 4, 6). The pursuit of unity does not always involve just the mind, actively pursuing or passively receiving or engaging in a "noble interchange" with nature. It can involve active, physical labor--working on and with facts. The poet picks apples to have his dream. He must earn his vision. The interplay of mind and fact must have this strongly physical basis; without it, the vision is cheap or simply delusive.

The fact is the sweetest dream that labor knows. We labor; we work on a fact with our hands, not merely our mind, to know it. Indeed, experience is sensate knowing. This is Frost's Thoreauvian inheritance. Thoreau also teaches him to focus on the common and to sense the object fully. If we use all our senses in knowing, one day--as Thoreau promises in his doctrine of Romantic naturalism--the fact will flower into a truth.

127

VIII - Labor, Art, and Imagination

What is more, Frost sees in Thoreau that a man's highest obligation is to refine his unique self. As a poet, philosopher, and laborer, Thoreau does not minimize any part of his nature or any activity. The whole person is to be improved, not merely one part. Ideally a person works manually and intellectually with equal intensity to bring about self-reformation and perfection.[1] One should live a unified life whose labor is at once spiritual and physical. To labor for mere commodity would be life without principle. Labor, if it is truly creative--that is, if it contributes to individual self-perfection--supports the body and soul simultaneously.

For Thoreau and also for Frost, his heir, certain manual labor is critical to perfecting the poet. Engaging in the entire process of getting a living or making an object or providing one's necessities helps develop the mind to its fullest extent; it must think, anticipate, and foresee the process from beginning to end. And the hand must execute what the mind conceives; thus, labor is an integral part of creative living and self-perfection. There must be this unity between hand and sensibility, the physical process and the poetic account.

Thoreau teaches Frost to see how the spiritual state grows out of the physical and mundane. John Farmer's experience ("Higher Laws," *Walden*) is exemplary; his vision begins in thoughts of the day's physical activities.[2] He hears a flute, whose harmonies instill in him an intuition of beauty and of higher laws. "All that he could think of was to practise some new austerity, to let his mind descend into his body and redeem it, and treat himself with ever increasing respect."[3] The assertions are that John Farmer--everyman in his highest spiritual state--can rely on labor to initiate new visions, and that redemption and grace and self-respect grow out of one's working closely with the physical and immediate. Unsatisfactory are Romantic withdrawal, visionary quest that involves merely eye or ear in cooperation with nature, and passive reception. The true higher law is in the real world which the hands work on steadily.

Many of Frost's poems describe the poet's task as like that of woodchopping, planting, cording, mowing, plowing, building, and surveying. These are acts of subduing and shaping nature; similarly, the making of poetry is an arduous reducing of facts, words and sounds into a coherent whole. This process brings the whole soul of man into activity. Just as the farmer achieves order (and commodity) through physical labor--a pasture, after all, is nature cleared and ordered--the poet achieves form through an exercise of imagination on nature. These organizing metaphors are native to Thoreau's views of the poet, *poesis*, and the integrity of the soul, and are Frost's Transcendental heritage. When read in relationship to their sources, the labor poems show the deep-rooted allegiances which Frost has with his mentor, Thoreau.

1. UNITING WORK AND PLAY, LOVE AND NEED: "TWO TRAMPS IN MUD TIME"

In idea and symbol many of Frost's labor poems reveal his affirmative ties to Transcendentalism. One of his most accomplished poems linked to this tradition, "Two Tramps in Mud Time" is about the poet and the sources of poetry. It accounts for the origins of a poet's imagination, and delineates how his mind and art are shaped by the relationship among his experiences, labors, and knowledge. It dramatizes a poet's role as striving to unite action and knowledge, work and play, vocation and avocation. Ideally, for the poet a poem achieves that final integration; Frost would describe the process.[4]

The all-important act of chopping wood is an exercise of the spirit:

> The blows that a life of self control
> Spares to strike for the common good
> That day, giving a loose to my soul,
> I spent on the unimportant wood.

Channeling one's energies (or rage) in a productive, physical act creates a life of self-control. It is also a positive, integrating act, for, as he states later, the task has mortal and providential consequences. The labor is made of love, but just what kind of integration of soul and how it is achieved are not fully revealed. Somehow the chopping (his avocation) is vitally bound with intellectual activity (his vocation) and is highly attractive:

> The weight of an ax-head poised aloft,
> The grip on earth of outspread feet.
> The life of muscles rocking soft

And smooth and moist in vernal heat.

The labor is performed when both nature and its season are at a precarious balance. Warmth and chill, thaw and frost, and buds at bloom correspond to the speaker's need for equilibrium and also to the moment of imagination when opposites are reconcilled. This delicate balance is always threatened with disintegration. Thus, "the lurking frost in the earth beneath/ That will steal forth after the sun is set/ And show on the water its crystal teeth" represents relapse and chaos, the other side of the speaker--that is, the disunified, darker, subterranean part of his nature, whose capability for rage or loss of self-control is presently being checked by labor. Indeed, that "lurking frost" may be a pun of the poet's own name,[6] suggestive of an icy hate threatening to break down the soul's order, a ruin which applies also to Frost's poetry-making and, as Thompson makes clear, to his sanity.

The two tramps are an immediate threat to the speaker's attempt to achieve integration. They interfere with the speaker's purpose: "One of them put me off my aim." A crude order of humanity, they are like Murphy and his lumberjacks in "Paul's Wife," who attempt by word and deed to disrupt Paul's marriage to Beauty. Singular in their aim, and representatives of "need," the tramps follow a purely physical vocation that fulfills only a bodily need. Coming out of the mud, they seem almost savages. These woodcutters symbolize dissociation and the anti-poetic, for they exclude love and spirit in their work.

Frost more than likely developed this symbol from Thoreau's woodchopper who represents an extreme contrast to the poet:

> Now that the Indian is gone, he [the woodcutter] stands nearest to nature. . . . How far still is the writer of books from the man . . . who chops in the woods! There are ages between them. . . . The contrast itself always attracts the civilized poet to what is rudest and most primitive in his contemporaries, all this rather proves a certain interval between the poet and the chopper whose labor he refers to, than an unusual nearness to him, on the principle that familiarity breeds contempt.[7]

130

VIII - Labor, Art, and Imagination: "Two Tramps in Mud Time"

It is just this interval between the physical-primitive and the intellectual-artistic that Thoreau and Frost want to bridge; for in this reconciliation lies wholeness and the creative moment. (Thoreau, as we shall see, provides Frost with passages identifying the chopper's labor with the poet's, but the contrast made here is between the singularity of the woodcutter's occupation and the multiplicity-within-unity characterizing the poet.)

To summarize, the tensions in nature, the instability of the season, and the tramps' potentiality to upset the speaker's inner balance all symbolically suggest the creative moment which, as Frost describes it, exists in precarious equipoise when opposites come together: "Life sways perilously at the confluence of opposing forces. Poetry in general plays perilously in the same wild place."[8] The poet's motif of natural balances has just this special significance, expressing figuratively the moment of reconciliation and poetry-making.

The idea that nature's phenomena reflect the mind derives from Thoreau, who states, "The poet's creative moment is when the frost is coming out in the spring."[9] "Two Tramps in Mud Time" subtly plays on the context surrounding this passage. Thoreau identifies the fluid, creative processes of earth at mud-time with the poetic spirit. Like nature's balance at the moment between frost and mud, the tension of opposites within the poet occasions the imaginative moment. If the conditions for equipoise are unfavorable, the creative moment collapses, like nature's liquifactions. Thoreau illustrates: "As in the case of some too easy poets, if the weather is too warm and rainy of long continues it [the creative moment] becomes more diarrhoea, mud and clay relaxed."[10] For Frost, Mud Time is the time for imagination or chaos, that is, for the poet or the tramps. It is, like the instant of thaw, a tenuous, rare, peak point, a vernal and spiritual equinox that man and nature achieve after a long and often arduous progress. Thus, in "Two Tramps in Mud Time" outer weather relects the inner spirit--imagination.

And now the questions: How does woodchopping pertain to the speaker's vocation, and why is it so important to the integration that he hopes for? If the chopping is done out of love, how is it also a "need"? The labor has some unique relationship, I think, to the making of poetry. The line "The work is play for mortal stakes" suggests this special meaning, for Frost throughout his prose writing refers to poetry as "play"; the "deed" is the integrating act of imagination. Thoreau also regards vigorous labor as "play" and a vital part of writing. *A Week on the Concord and Merrimack Rivers* explains the relationship between woodchopping and poetry-making:

> Learn to split wood, at least. The necessity of labor and conversation with many men and things to the scholar is rarely well remembered; steady labor with the hands, which engrosses the attention also, is unquestionably the best method of removing palaver and sentimentality out of one's style, both of speaking and writing. If he has worked hard from morning till night, though he may have grieved that he could not be watching the train of his thoughts during that time, yet the few hasty lines which at evening record his day's experience will be more musical and true than his freest but idle fancy could have furnished. . . . He will not idly dance at his work who has wood to cut and cord before nightfall in the short days of winter; but every stroke will be husbanded, and ring soberly through the wood; and so will the strokes of that scholar's pen, which at evening record the story of the day, ring soberly, yet cheerily, on the ear of the reader, long after the echoes of his axe have died away. The scholar may be sure that he writes the tougher truth for the calluses on his palms. They give firmness to the sentence. Indeed, the mind never makes a great and successful effort, without a corresponding energy of the body. . . . Plainness and vigor and sincerity, the ornaments of style, were better learned on the farm and in the workshop than in the schools.[11]

Thoreau's (and Frost's) union of vocation and avocation is based on these principles. Labor is the germ of art, the initiator of the poetic process, which, in a Romantic view , brings the whole soul of man into activity.[12] No wonder chopping is important in the poem.

The unity of vision the speaker desires is expressed in a beautiful

132

metaphor, derived from Thoreau, which exactly describes how, in an act of love and labor, vocation and avocation meld. The speaker's "two eyes make one in sight." Just so, Thoreau receives the materials for his poetry by pursing some activity not directly related to his vocation of writing--seeing, as it were, with peripheral vision:

> Again, as so many times, I [am] reminded of the advantage to the poet, and philosopher, and naturalist, and whomsoever, of pursuing from time to time some other business than his chosen one,--seeing with the side of the eye. The poet will so get visions which no deliberate abandonment can secure. The philosopher is so forced to recognize principles which long study might not detect. And the naturalist even will stumble upon some new and unexpected flower or animal.[13]

Thoreau's conviction that a poet's diversions are finally unified in a wholeness of vision expresses a concept of imagination so close to Frost's idea of the mind being a recording, projecting integrating "giant" that we are persuaded once again of his dominance on Frost. The celebrated remark on poetry-making seems fully inspired by Thoreau:

> The impressions most useful to my purposes [*i.e* ., poetry-making] seem always those I was unaware of and so made no note of at the time when taken, and the conclusion is come to that like giants we are always hurling experience ahead of us to pave the future with against the day when we may want to strike a line of purpose across it for somewhere.[14]

In Frost's poem, woodchopping is the germ of experience which the poet will some day use in a creative act and is therefore the "deed" for "the future's sake."

We can understand why Frost refuses to defer his "love" to the tramps' "need." His high object in life would then be obstructed. Frost's aim transcends any Christian, golden-rule morality; one's first obligation is to himself. He learned this determined individualism from Thoreau, who remarks, "Absolutely speaking, Do unto others as you would that they should do unto you is by no means a golden rule," because such an ethic separates the individual from his pursuit of self-perfection and accomplishment. He continues:

> Christ . . . taught mankind but imperfectly how to live; his thoughts were all directed toward another world. There is another kind of success than his. Even here we have a sort of living to get, and must buffet it somewhat longer. . . . We must make shift to live, betwixt spirit and matter, such a human life as we can.[15]

Poetry, as the vocation alluded to in the poem's last stanza, is created out of love and need, work and play. The "deed" in the penultimate line is the poetic, integrating act, which involves "mortal stakes"--that is, human gain or reward. At the same time, the deed is done "For Heaven and the future's sakes," suggesting that poetry partakes of the eternal. These last lines of the poem refer to poetry as "God-belief" (as well as "love-belief" and "self-belief"); somehow through imagination the future is believed into existence. And a poem's esthetic wholeness also fashions a unified spiritual belief. Art is a mode of faith, as Frost states, a "believing the thing [poem] into existence, saying as you go more than you ever hoped you were going to be able to say, and coming with surprise to an end that you foreknew only with some sort of emotion."[16] The "deed" done "for Heaven and the future's sakes" involves "the relationship we enter into with God to believe the future in--to Believe the hereafter in."[17] Seen in this light, one can understand why Frost defines poetry as no less than "everything."

2. MAKING HAY: "MOWING"

There was never a sound beside the wood but one,
And that was my long scythe whispering to the ground.
What was it it whispered? I knew not well myself;
Perhaps it was something about the heat of the sun,

Something, perhaps, about the lack of sound--
And that was why it whispered and did not speak.
It was no dream of the gift of idle hours,
Or easy gold at the hand of fay or elf:
Anything more than the truth would have seemed too weak
To the earnest love that laid the swale in rows,
Not without feeble-pointed spikes of flowers
(Pale orchises), and scared a bright green snake.
The fact is the sweetest dream that labor knows.
My long scythe whispered and left the hay to make.

The act of mowing is, of course, the central metaphor in this poem, and its focal line celebrates the consequence of that labor. "The fact is the sweetest dream that labor knows" has several levels of meaning tied to the denotations of "fact."[18] The "fact" is physical actuality, or practical experience (as distinguished from dream or fanciful speculation). It is also that which is done or made--a deed. In rendering nature into form and commodity, the mower achieves the sweetest vision or fanciful creation (that is, "dream") that labor can know. The making of hay is the *factum* [19] (that which is made into form) that previously was not, until desire and earnest love created it. Likewise, the labor of ordering words is a making of poetry, also a *factum* realized by work, desire, and dream. The poem and the hay are fact (that which is made).

The relationship between mowing (the metaphor grows out of Frost's experiences as a farmer) and imagnative labor has a parallel in *Walden*, where mowing is a figure for the mind's reduction of facts to order, meaning, and value. To live deep is "to cut a broad swath and shave close . . . and reduce [life] to its lowest terms."[20] Thoreau's "fronting" the "essential facts of life" is the intent of artist and thinker, for it involves an ordering process in which cutting, shaving, and reducing life to its lowest terms are the highest learning experiences. In so doing, the writer can give a true account of the actual. The truth taught in the process may be mean or sublime; but the focus of the poet-laborer's effort is always reality--the fact--in which value (if any) lies. "The fact is the sweetest dream that labor knows" is the source of wisdom because all poetry, all "departure," and all significance start in it. Thoreau states in his Journal,

135

VIII - Labor, Art and Imagination: "Mowing"

> How indispensable to a correct study of Nature is a
> perception of her true meaning. The fact will one day
> flower out into a truth. The season will mature and
> fructify what the understanding had cultivated.[21]

From a fact the understanding harvests a truth and the imagination
yields value. "Mowing" is much more noncommital than Thoreau
about such a flowering. A poem is such a ripening of thought, and if
it comes the effort is, therefore, the sweetest dream that labor knows.
In the metaphor of mowing, Frost, like Thoreau, properly investigates
that harvest and form-making.

From beginning to end of the poem, one sound, a mysterious
whispering, emanates not from nature alone, but from the interaction
of scythe and swale. Sound is the product of human labor, but
whatever its message, it is clearly not animistic nature offering a
Romantic afflatus. "There was never a sound beside the wood but
one"--"something" indefinite, as speech without voice. Whatever
scythe and grass say, nature provides no magical Aeolian harmony,
no gratuitous visionary utterances, no romantic winds of inspiration.
If nature has a message, it comes from man's creative effort. A
mysterious "something" that pervades the swale is not independent
from sweat and scythe. Emerson would ask, "What was it that nature
would say?" sensing a "repose" and "mute music" within withered
flowers.[22] Frost senses "something" in the whispering among the
"feeble-pointed spikes of orchises" (his visionary flower) but *only* as
the scythe cuts through them. In "Mowing," nature's music is
diminished to a whisper, but the sound derives from fact, not from an
inaudible Emersonian harmony.

The whispering may be understood if we remember Wordsworth's
concept of interaction: the mind half-hearing and half-creating in vital
cooperation with nature. Thence comes deeper awareness and
sometimes visionary understanding of the "one life within us and
abroad." In Frost's view of the interaction of soul and nature, as
dramatized in "Mowing," the whisperings generate not from "wise
passiveness" but from man's active labor, though he cannot know the
"truth" which inheres in the sound. Since man is both creator and
perceiver of the whispering, Frost suggests that man is the locus of
all things; but he is not a Romantic, a receiver of visionary experience.

136

VIII - Labor, Art and Imagination: "Mowing"

In "Mowing," nature is a partial correspondent, issuing effluences only as man exercises labor on it. The speaker's laborious "making," however, allows for the hay "to make"--*i.e* ., dry out; this making suggests a cooperation and reliance between man and nature. But this concept of correspondence is a severe qualification of the Romantic doctrine. Underlying Frost's seeming simplicity is a sophisticated understanding of Romantic theory. *Mowing itself* produces the *factum* of hay; thus, "It was no dream of the gift of idle hours." The fact at hand and the occult whisperings are made in labor, not in passive dreaming.

Furthermore, the whispering is no "easy gold at the hand of fay or elf." Keats may travel in the realms of gold and derive inspiration from such radiance; but Frost's realm is the *factum* of labor, not a fairy land. It is the muscle-impelled scythe, not a fanciful elf, which produces (one could say "inspires") the whisperings, the real "music" made by man ordering for fodder the matted chaos of nature. Therefore, "Anything more than the truth would seem too weak/ To the earnest love that laid the swale in rows." Man first cuts down nature with earnest, or serious, love, not with facile, emotional regard for nature. He opposes and reduces nature so that, in curing hay, it works for him. Truth and the matter of poetry reside in the physical world of work and fact; anything more than these certainties as to the basis of the whispering would involve metaphysical truth, about which the speaker does not make guesses. He accepts the actual sounds produced in labor; they are the audible reminder of the matter-of-fact heat of the sun for the sweating mower. Yes, the earnest love expressed in labor is enough for him. Anything else would indeed be weak. In *Walden* Thoreau remarks that the facts of nature may be mean or sublime and that the truth is rooted in experience, sensation, and the observation of facts. For Frost a vision may "perhaps" come well after labor, as in "After Apple Picking," or not at all. In his labor poems, he resists immediate dreaming, remaining content with fronting the facts.

3. CLEANING UP NATURE: "THE PASTURE"

I'm going out to clean the pasture spring;
I'll only stop to rake the leaves away

(And wait to watch the water clear, I may)
I sha'n't be gone long.--you come too.

I'm going out to fetch the little calf
That's standing by the mother. It's so young
It totters when she licks it with her tongue,
I sha'n't be gone long.--You come too.

"The Pasture" introduces Frost's collected poems not only because it is typical of how he celebrates natural beauty, but also because it illustrates that a poet's primary task is to order nature. The work of mowing keeps a pasture. Just as "Directive" guides the reader back to the spring and source of all things, "The Pasture" invites him to the domain of the farmer-poet, wherein spring, pasture, and calf may be regarded not only as setting and subject, but also as source of his poetry.[23]

The speaker intends to clean up nature, a task that Frost considers primary to the poet: "The thing that art does for life is to clean it up, to strip it to form."[24] Raking the leaves away from the pasture spring achieves a literal clarification, and though the act is casual, the implication is that asserting order--however slight--on nature is satisfying. The speaker says, "I'll only . . . wait to watch the water clear." The farmer's task is the poet's: to clarify and achieve a momentary stay. New leaves will surely confuse that order and will have to be cleaned away too. Such is the task of anyone attempting to achieve form. Here again Frost sees a unity and identity in avocational labor and his poetic vocation; his organizing figure is husbandry. But nature also cooperates in the clearing process. With the help of the farmer, the water clears itself. (He now watches, just as the mower leaves "the hay to make.") This cooperation suggests something of Frost's theory of poetry: a poem begins as a deliberate act of will and subsequently involves a natural, spontaneous organization of materials, much like the spring's progress from confusion to clarity.

Frost says of "The Pasture": "There is a poem about love that's new in treatment and effect. You won't find anything in the whole of English poetry just like that."[25] Many kinds of love are implied, but mainly the speaker's strong affection for his tasks of clearing the pasture and retrieving the calf. The latter is paralleled in the second stanza by the dam's cleaning her calf; the licking of the calf further suggests that nature cleans itself (even a new-born is dirty and "disordered"). In this detail and in the fetching, Frost is again reminding us of both the split and the kinship between man and nature.

The pasture is nature's arena of love, like the silken tent, which is held by ties of love to "everything on earth the compass round." It is "earnest love" that describes the pasture mowing. Love is the origin of all things: life, labor, and poetry, all of which are found in the pasture in the spring. Perhaps Frost is subtly inviting us to the sources of inspiration-- symbolized here, as in "Directive," in the water spring. The focal point of any pasture, its spring, is the setting and source of life and of Frost's poetry. His task is with love, which is the power behind his concept of poetry and the vital impulse in the making of poems.

It is no wonder that the third line, "I sha'n't be gone long--you come too," is used as the epigraph to the last volume of Frost's poetry, *In the Clearing*; for the poet, from beginning to end, invites us to know what poetry is--a cleaning and clearing of nature and clarification of life. But the invitation also suggests Frost's repeated warnings about getting too lost in nature. The very last poem in his works, "In Winter in the Woods Alone," a precise counterpart to "The Pasture," depicts a brief foray into nature, where after a maple is cut down, there's a four o'clock retreat home. The speaker there is also not gone long. Like "The Pasture," Frost's last poem is a little parable of the poet's role to subdue and clear nature and of his relation to it.

4. CULTIVATING THOUGHT: "THE STRONG ARE SAYING NOTHING," "THE INVESTMENT," "A MOOD APART"

"The Strong Are Saying Nothing" is concerned with another form of earnest love--putting in the seed. People work alone in the uncertain spring weather, which, as in "Two Tramps in Mud Time," hovers between warmth and frost. The speaker labors in the midst of white, rounded plum blossoms and black squares of mold. In addition to these contrasts of tones and climatic conditions, the poem establishes the oppositions of wind and soil (soil being "the grave").

To the strong, wind and soil may hold little or much beyond the grave, but as in "Too Anxious For Rivers," teleological matters remain unresolvable. And similar to the arguments in "Mowing," labor is the only profitable activity, and fact the only certainty; any metaphysical resolutions would be merely "dream[s] of the gift of idle hours." Nor does the wind, as we shall note, offer any traditional Romantic apocalypse. Anything more than the truth of labor and fact would be too weak. The strong exist and even thrive unquestioningly in the contrarieties that surround them. These are frost and warmth, wind and soil, black and white, spirit and matter, life and grave, future and past, hope and uncertainty. These opposites suggest that a healthy dualism is life's essence and necessary condition.

Like "Putting in the Seed," this poem concerns imposing form on nature, specifically the making of a garden. A garden--like a basket, a letter, a room, an idea, a picture, or a poem--is an "individual enterprise" whereby "nature reaches its height in form and through us exceeds itself." It is a "small man-made figure of order and concentration." In imposing form, the strong establish a "stay" that is "engrossing, gratifying, and comforting";[26] but beyond an implicit faith in form-making and labor, they can say nothing about metaphysical truth. The strong live out Voltaire's injunction that we turn from philosophizing and tend our own gardens.

While the garden is a general figure, plowing, planting, and sowing in neat rows symbolize the creative effort of the poet setting his thoughts in precise order. We may read this poem and "Putting in the Seed" in relation to Thoreau's grand "trope" of planting and cultivating his bean field. He states, "Some must work in fields if only for the sake of tropes and expression, to serve a parable-maker one day."[27] This is the poem's intent: to allow the avocation of farming to analogize the vocation of poetry. Thoreau, like Frost, cultivates his garden as a work of art, weeding it of imperfection. Frost's bed of a few selected seeds is his labor of love, a sowing of thought like Thoreau's proud labor that precisely orders his bean rows, the beans being seeds of "sincerity, truth, simplicity, faith [and] innocence." This figurative sowing by both poets is done "alone." The squares of mold made by the "final flat of the hoe's approval stamp" formally demark each seed and, along with the plowing and sowing, betoken a final imposition of order on the garden. The labored-over plot of ground

140

represents a neat, ordered, and controlled writing style, after the examples of Thoreau, who writes:

> I want to see a sentence run clear through to the end, as deep and fertile as a well-drawn furrow which shows that the plow was pressed down to the beam. If our scholars would lead more earnest lives, we should not witness those lame conclusions to their ill-sown discourses, but their sentences would pass over the ground like loaded rollers, and not mere hollow and wooden ones, to press the seed and make it germinate.[28]

Thoreau notes how laboring men attain a "force and precision of style," and he asserts that sincerity and plainness are best acquired in fields, not schools. Once again husbandry analogizes the writer's cultivation of mind and craft (both are demanding and difficult); the neat, fertile field is correlative to his mind and the processes of self-perfection.

The first three stanzas of the poem focus closely on the farmer's isolated labor; their particularity contrasts with the last stanza's startling generalization. If there is uncertain hope and little faith in matters beyond the grave (either the human burial site or the seedbed), then are germination, growth, and man's cultivating power all that we can know and see? Why should matters about the grave, hope, and faith enter abruptly? Frost's use of wind, a common Romantic symbol of Biblical origin, is illuminating.

In Romantic poetry the wind acts as the breath of God, inspiration, and revelation quickening man's spirit. It attunes him to the universal mind. We think immediately of Shelley's West Wind sweeping through the poet and inspiring him to new knowledge and poetic power. The wind serves the same purpose in Wordsworth's opening lines of *The Prelude*, being a "correspondent breeze" to the imagination's stirrings.[29] A "redundant [literally, *unda*: "waves"] energy," it anticipates Frost's wind coming "wave on wave."[30] Wordsworth's heaven-sent wind inspires hope and "harmonious verse" in days of sweet leisure."[31]

To Frost these are delusive "dreams of the gift of idle hours," the "easy gold" of fairy winds. He rejects such indulgences for the real imaginative experiences: labor and immersion in fact, which are the core and substance of poetry. He may entertain Romantic assumptions and, in the instance of the wind, even play on its traditional symbolism--but he does so for ironic purpose. The cry of what is hoped to be is not carried in his wind. It breathes no radiant, soul-stirring truth. The wind, moreover, says nothing about matters beyond the grave; simply, man, God, nature, and wind are out of tune. Typically, if anything poetic or visionary comes, it will arise not from the wind or in the "Sweet leisure" of passiveness, but out of labor. Once again, Frost uses the language and symbolism of Romanticism while denying its doctrines. As one of the "strong"--working, fully concscious, and unillusioned--he is saying nothing till he *sees*.

Need of ocular proof shows a stubborn negativism, which Wordsworth and Coleridge call the "despotism of the eye"[32] over the other senses, the heart, and the intellect:

> the bodily eye, in every stage of life
> The most despotic of our senses, gained
> Such strength in *me* as often held my mind
> In absolute dominion.[33]

Saying that this lack of organic interaction is the "impairment of imagination," Wordsworth cannot achieve a noble interchange with the "Soul of Nature" that manifests itself in "winds"

> And roaring water, and in lights and shades
> That marched and countermarched about the hills
> In glorious apparition, Powers on whom
> I daily waited, now all eye and now
> All ear; but never long without the heart
> Employed, and man's unfolding intellect.[34]

Frost's restraint of the heart, his single vision, and his aural dissociation allow no generous intuition, such as a "glorious apparition" in nature's wind--"no cry of what is hoped to be"; sight, sound, and soul do not meld, as in the Wordsworthian moment of vision. Frost's poetry, however, feeds on that lamentable failure, creating a poetry of denial.

Though the idle Romantic may believe in winds carrying a divine intelligence, the laboring speaker of Frost's poem finds his task compelling enough and needs no emotional or fanciful self-indulgence. He refuses to construct a message from airy suggestions. The poem, on one level of meaning, then, dramatizes the imagination's resistance to quicken in the presence of nature and engage in a noble interchange. If, as Wordsworth says, "visionary power attends the motions of the viewless winds," that rare power--for the "strong" of Frost's world--must be accompanied by actual sight and a concrete image. Without ocular proof the winds are viewless and valueless. To exercise the eye's tyranny on reality--*i.e.*, to insist on seeing--is Frost's way of maintaining balance and sanity in his poetry, while at the same time wistfully and obliquely touching on the possibility of vision.

Nature will speak in due time for the laborer. If the winds are arid, the earth will say "beans" soon enough. The proper focus is earthward--to the cultivated, stamped "grave." This is indeed diminishment, the sane negativism of a poet who refuses to allow the eye to color the heart and intellect. A skeptical Frost is saying nothing positive till he sees; that is the limit, here, of the poet's visionary power.

"THE INVESTMENT"

Over back where they speak of life as staying
(You couldn't call it living, for it ain't'),
There was an old, old house renewed with paint,
And in it a piano loudly playing.

Out in the plowed ground in the cold a digger,
Among unearthed potatoes standing still,
Was counting winter dinners, one a hill,
With half an ear to the piano's vigor.

All that piano and new paint back there,
Was it some money suddenly come into?
Or some extravagance young love had been to?
Or old love on an impulse not to care--

Not to sink under being man and wife,
But get some color and music out of life?

"The Investment" pictures the laborer, once again, standing in his potato field, this time listening to a piano. Its music gives him pause from digging, but again there is no soaring; no large Romantic claims of divine harmony, inspiration, or enchantment are made for the music. Soberly the speaker, who knows the drabness and poverty of "over back," speculates about the music and all that yellow paint. It is Frost's manner, as we have seen, to allude subtly to the Romantic tradition; he refers to a Romantic regard for music, whose harmonies provide the impulse for dreaming, visionary fulfillment, and the glorious life that would resolve the poverty and commonness of backwoods existence. The poem offers a no-nonsense corrective to the transcendental musings of Thoreau, who recorded the following imaginative response, in picture and color, upon hearing "the sound of a distant piano":

> I am affected. What coloring variously fair and intense our life admits of! How a thought will mould and paint it! . . . . At length the melody steals into my being. . . . I am attuned to the universe, I am fitted to hear, my being moves in a sphere of melody, my fancy and imagination are excited to an inconceivable degree. This is no longer the dull earth on which I stood. It is possible to live a grander life here; . . . already our thoughts bid a proud farewell to the so-called actual life and its humble glories. Now this is the verdict of a soul in health.[35]

"The Investment" answers Thoreau's enthusiasms, is as much as Frost will concede about the degree of "coloring" our life admits of--that is, actual yellow paint to brighten an old house, but not a Thoreauvian coloring of imagination that makes an ideal world out of the real. Real paint rather than painted thoughts. Thus is Thoreau cleverly reproved. The earth need not be "dull"; but wishful illusion cannot falsely glorify it. "The grander life" lies not in an imaginative leap to heaven but in an investment or indulgence in color and music to keep man and woman from sinking under. That is all of "the grander life" that Frost admits to in the potato-farm world of "over back," whose digger in the field never abandons counting his potatoes while listening with half an ear to the piano.

"A MOOD APART"

Once down on my knees to growing plants
I prodded the earth with a lazy tool
In time with a medley of sotto chants;
But becoming aware of some boys from school
Who had stopped outside the fence to spy,
I stopped my song and almost heart,
For any eye is an evil eye
That looks in on to a mood apart.

The farming scene of "A Mood Apart" is like that of "Putting in the Seed" and "The Investment." But here the labors of gardening and cultivation are correlative to singing; work and song exist as a unity. Kneeling as if in prayer "to growing plants," the speaker prods the earth while at the same time keeping "in time with a medley of sotto chants." The word "chants" carries liturgical connotations, thereby reinforcing the prayerful role of the kneeling speaker. His medley comes rhythmically, as a part of and perhaps induced by, the regular motion of prodding. Labor and song occur spontaneously. Singing *sotto voce* suggests a privateness of purpose and pleasure in creativity. Here his form-making is "engrossing, gratifying," and an "individual enterprise."[36] "We haven't to get a team together before we can play," according to Frost.

The cultivating and chanting cease as the speaker senses boys of "evil eye." These spies violate the gardener's poetic rite and his "mood apart." Appropriately, the intruders are schoolboys, unformed products of laid-on education, whose learning, though necessary, comes from "the devil."[37] The speaker exemplifies spontaneity, while the schoolboys stand for something quite different. In "The Figure a Poem Makes" Frost distinguishes two ways of coming to knowledge: the wild free ways of imagination, and the school boy's institutionalized methodology. "A school boy may be defined as one

145

who can tell you what he knows in the order in which he learned it."[38] In the poem, these opposites are implied in the schoolboys and the poet, their moods being two disparate attitudes--the one loving and worshipful, the other furtive and mocking.

"A Mood Apart" may have been influenced by Emerson, who in *Nature* likens the poet's spiritual dependency on God to "a plant upon the earth." He draws his power from nature, the "face" of God, and needs isolation to admire beauty. But because of their different mood, laborers in the field disrupt the reverie of the poet: "You cannot freely admire a noble landscape," says Emerson, "if laborers are digging in the field hard by. The poet finds something ridiculous in his delight until he is out of the sight of men."[39] Whereas Emerson divorces labor from imaginative perception, Frost joins them. The chanting farmer-poet thrives out of men's sight but is arrested by mocking boys. They, like the tramps who put the poet off his aim, represent a discordant force, for the kneeling laborer strives for order--agricultural, esthetic, and spiritual.

5. THE ECONOMY OF THE MIND: "BUILD SOIL"

Figures of cultivation and other farm labors also appear in "Build Soil: A Political Pastoral," and carry Frost's ideas on economic matters and also on the poet's role. A writer's first responsibility is to develop his thought and imagination, which, like fertile soil, need continual enrichment.

The subtitle, "A Political Pastoral," is important. The pastoral mode involves not only a critique of political and social life from the perspective of country simplicity[40] but also the poet's role in relation to the times (or to his personal life). "Lycidas" is the standard example of the shepherd-poet appraising the purpose and relevance of poetry and facing adversity. Vergil's first Eclogue, from which the form and characters of "Build Soil" derive, concerns adversity, expropriation, poverty, and loss of liberty, and how all these affect poetry. *Canam nulla carmina,* "I may sing no songs," remarks Melibaeus. The pastoral mode is as much about establishing a poetic voice and tone--usually ironic--as it is criticizing city life and civilization. "Build Soil" disapproves of the pseudo-sophistication and aberrant intentions of poets writing on social and political matters; at

146

the same time it offers a directive as to where wisdom and self-perfection can be found: in reclusion and meditation, figured as pastoral labor.

The word "political" also has a complex of meanings, referring not only to government and the political occasion at which the poem was first read, but also to polity, a society's form of government determined by the theory on which it stands, its aims, and its relation to the individual's rights, liberties, and needs for his fulfillment. And, in another sense, the poem is about Frost's politics, his constructing a personal policy to orient his life and poetic endeavors. His politics--to define the term as the total complex of relations between people in society--is to "keep off each other and keep each other off," so as to effect a "one-man revolution"; then, meditation, isolation, and imaginative porductivity will cuminate in the bringing of poetry to market. It is a politics of governing oneself and maintaining absolute autonomy over one's mind. His is the *Libertas* that Vergil's Tityrus yearns for, and the freedom from restraint and "social conspiracy" that underlies Emerson's concept of self-reliance. "Build Soil" is radically Emersonian in its politics, endorsing ideas about government from the essay "Politics": "The only interest for the consideration of the State is persons. . . . Hence the less government we have the better,--the fewer laws, and the less confided power. The antidote to this abuse of formal government is the influence of private character, the growth of the Individual. . . . The wise man is the State."[41]

It would seem odd that Frost, who avoided politics, government problems, and economics in his poetry, would want to limit his meaning in "Build Soil" to a condemnation of overextension in our economy, but that is the extent to date of critical interpretation of the poem. That "Build Soil" has not been discusses beyond its political and social themes is surprising indeed when we consider that the speakers are poets and the subject of poetry permeates the work.[42] It is more than a work that twits the poets of the thirties who chided him for avoiding the day's problems; it is a manifesto for the true poet of imagination. The subjects of politics, socialism, and social responsibility are integral to Frost's central concern in the poem: how the poet avoids overextending or compromising his imagination and achieves self-reliance and freedom from doctrine in order to fulfill his high role. In speaking of political freedom, Frost typically refers to the freedom of the poet; similarly, in speaking of farming and shepherding, he refers to the poet's avocation and the ordering of his mind. His intention is to sing not of topical, temporal, and specific matters of immediate importance to the nation, but

> Of types, composite and imagined people:
> To affirm there is such a thing as evil
> Personified, but ask to be excused
> From saying on a jury 'Here's the guilty.'

The only revolution to which Tityrus is committed is a "one-man revolution," whose soil and substance lie in isolation, thought, and eventually, poetry. Every new poem, by Frost's own definition, is "a revolution of the spirit."[43]

The revolution is in imagination, not politics and polemics. The poet's task is not to "name names and tell you who by name is wicked"; that sort of literalness is for Congress and newspapers. Nor are sounding alarms and focussing on immediate matters of government and law the true province of the poet. Indeed, Frost states three years after publishing "Build Soil" that the poet should not be the legislator of the world.[44]

The poet's inalienable right is not only political freedom (which guarantees his choice to be a poet) but also imaginative freedom--the freedom of departure and of his materials. These guarantees of expression and integrity of mind are Frost's interests and cannot be channelled by political doctrine or social theory. Socialism does not foster these liberties, for, according to Frost, it demands interaction of poets and people, and "intermental" dependencies which erode the privacy of imaginative endeavor. Poetry would be impoverished--like run-out farm soil, pale and metallic--if it becomes the instrument of political or social orthodoxy. Poetry of purpose or propaganda, such as Sandburg's or MacLeish's poems in that decade of depression when "Build Soil" was written, are often thinly literal, weak because brought to market without full concentration of thought and craft--in a word, premature. Like a crop, poetry must have a proper germination, growth, and cultivation before it is reaped and offered. That process, as Frost suggests, involves withdrawal, reflection, concentration, and intellectual effort--what Richard Poirier has called

"the work of knowing."
A fertilized soil best nourishes the seeds of thought that eventually
burst forth in rich poetry:

> Plant, breed, produce,
> But what you raise or grow, why feed it out,
> Eat it or plow it under where it stands
> To build the soil. For what is more accursed
> Than an impoverished soil . . .
> . . . . .
> Build soil. Turn the farm in upon itself
> Until it can contain itself no more,
> But sweating-full, drips wine and oil a little.
> I will go to my run-out social mind
> And be unsocial with it as I can.
> The thought I have, and my first impulse is
> To take to market--I will turn it under . . .
> And so on to the limit of my nature.

This is a parable on carefully and completely preparing for the
creative moment. Poets turn their thoughts over to the limit of
concentration so as to produce a full, ripe harvest, bursting with poetic
craft, thought, and wisdom.

The figure of "build soil" derives from Thoreau, who describes the
writer's harvest as dependent on "making a soil":

> It is a great art in the writer to improve from day to
> day just that soil and fertility which he had, to harvest
> that crop which his life yields, whatever it may be. . . .
> He should be digging, not soaring. Just as earnest
> as your life is, so deep is your soil. If strong and
> deep, you will sow wheat and raise bread of life in
> it.[45]

Meliboeus' early comment on Tityrus' occupation also makes a slyly
exact identification of farming and poetry-making: "You live by writing/
Your poems on a farm and call that farming."[46] Building one's own
inner soil, like husbandry, takes self-knowledge, patience, labor, and

timing; that is, the philosopher-poet best prepares "to the limit of [his] nature."

A writer, like a crafty plower, knows the limits of his capabilities, the depth of this thought, and what he can and cannot achieve by cultivation. Thoreau remarks, "mighty themes, like immortality," requires "manuring highly," waiting patiently, and plowing deeply; but the hasty writer "turns up nothing but yellow sand."[47] Daily improvement of mind can guarantee, as a product of thought, rich art. In stating that

> we both know poets
> Who fall all over each other to bring soil
> And even subsoil and hardpan to market,

Frost ridicules those poets who sell their sole resource--their mind--for lucre, allowing somebody else the purchase and use of it. This is surely a prostitution.

Truth, virtue, and wisdom are the poetic products of meditation and study. The soil and garden of the mind say, finally, "wine and oil," or in Thoreau's term "beans," because of the poet-farmer's cultivation. "Build Soil" uses Thoreau's trope of the bean field in *Walden*, which equates cultivation with an enrichment of the mind that will yield through the years its harvest of "sincerity, truth, simplicity, faith, innocence."[48] Using the beans as an analogy, Thoreau goes on to say that we should grow truth and justice: "Our ambassadors should be instructed to send home such seeds as these, and Congress help to distribute them over the land." However, Frost's Congress has no such implemental role, for virtue is finally left for the individual to grow within himself. Frost keeps his "eye on Congress," which can be trusted to give alarms but not to distribute Thoreau's "kernels of worth and friendliness," his seeds of truth and justice.

Thoreau, like Frost, withdraws from society to tend his soil and earn a double harvest of beans and truth, simplicity and sincerity, leading to artistic order. Both dramatize that "runout" social minds are "driven in" and enriched by such a withdrawal. True revolutions of the spirit are clearly individual and not congressional. No wonder that the witty yet serious Tityrus thinks a ten-year five year plan of withdrawal and "self-restraint" an admirable one-man conspiracy. He and Frost could say with Thoreau: "I went to the woods to front the essential facts of life" and nitrify the mind. The issue is finally the marketable poem:

> we . . .
> must bring to the meeting the maturest
> The longest-saved-up, raciest, localest
> We have strength of reserve in us to bring.

These lines may well describe Frost's own poetry, especially *A Boy's Will*, which took some twenty years to get to market.

The themes of withdrawal, revolution, and utter self-reliance lead back to the always-influential Emerson, who pleaded for separateness as the way to sanity and good sense. Frost's shunning of "intermental" and "interpersonal" relationships between poet, men, or nations stems from Emerson's principle of self-reliance. Dependence on others muddles the imagination. Poems then become mixed, a hodge-podge of thought and art. The consequence of dependencies, according to Emerson, is that "the sinew and heart of man seem to be drawn out"; men and poets, because extended, lean on each other, "becom[ing] timorous, desponding, whimperers. . . . We are . . . afraid of each other."[49] Similarly Frost remarks, "We congregate, embracing from distrust." Emerson singles out ambition as the great destructive force to those who would "renovate life and our social state."[50] Frost, a true son of Emerson, also sees the restraint of ambition, like the self-restraint of the poet building soil, as the key to order. Poet, chemist, or politician must limit his freedom and ingenuity, or risk disorder:

> None shall be as ambitious as he can.
> None should be as ingenious as he could,
> Not if I had my say. Bounds should be set
> To ingenuity for being so cruel
> In bringing change unheralded on the unready.

How pertinent is Emersonian thought to Frost's beleaguered thirties--and to our day.

While qualifying our ideas of freedom, Emerson also condemns the untoward restraints of custom, conformity, and the conspiracy of society against the individual. "Build Soil" echoes these ideas, viewing socialism in the thirties as akin to Emerson's "joint-stock company, in which the members agree, for the better securing of his bread to each shareholder, to surrender the liberty and culture of the eater. The virtue in most request is conformity. . . . It loves not realities and creators, but names and customs. . . . Nothing is at last sacred but the integrity of your own mind."[51] Similarly, in "Build Soil" conformist poets, like conformist citizens, are not truly creative, but simply "name names" and sing the customs.

To ensure his integrity, Frost steals away from poets and philosophers who may interrupt his "thought-flow":

> Suppose someone comes near me who in rate
> Of speech and thinking is so much my better
> I am imposed on, silenced and discouraged.
> Do I submit to being supplied by him
> As the more economical producer,
> More wonderful, more beautiful producer?
> No. I unostentatiously move off
> Far enough for my thought-flow to resume.
> Thought product and food product are to me
> Nothing compared to the producing of them.

The process itself is the important concern here. He most values the condition and quality of the mind's *flow*, rather than its *yield*. (The "product" is as inessential as the "unimportant wood" of "Two Tramps in Mud Time.") Nourished in isolation, the creative process unifies Frost, whose "soil" is enriched by Vergil, Thoreau, and Emerson. It is an exercise of poetic faith, attended by wonder and fulfillment, that leads to the soul's "momentary stay. "Build Soil" exemplifies the kind of poem Frost would bring to market.

6. THE REWARDS OF LABOR: "AFTER APPLE-PICKING"

"After Apple-Picking" dramatizes the effects of fact and labor upon the spirit and can be read along with other poems probing these subjects, namely, "Two Tramps in Mud Time," "Mowing," "Beech." and

VIII - Labor, Art and Imagination: "After Apple Picking"

"Build Soil." The origins of its complex symbolic meaning are in Emerson, Thoreau, Milton, and Keats, whose ideas Frost has turned under to the limit of his nature, producing a work as rich in craft and meaning as any he ever writes.

In examining man's creative, dreaming psyche after labor, the poem speaks symbolically of human fulfillment, grace, salvation, and heaven. We have already discussed Frost's metaphor of farm labor as a unifying, formative experience on creative imagination. In this poem the picking of apples is the sweetest dream that labor knows.[52] Truth and beauty created in dreams and imagination are directly dependent on the facts of intense experience. Frost's dream-reward, proportionally intense, stems from the ardor of his labor.

The poem lyrically dramatizes Thoreau's observation on the relationship between labor and art:

Hard and steady and engrossing labor with the hands, especially out of doors, is invaluable to the literary man, and serves him directly. . . . When I get home at evening, somewhat weary, I find myself more susceptible than usual to the finest influences, as music and poetry. The very air can intoxicate me, or the least sight or sound, as if my finer senses had acquired an appetite by their fast.[53]

Labor not only primes creativity, but also flashes pictures on the inward eye. This phenomenon results from what Thoreau describes as relaxed but sharp attention. The woodchopper "really forgets himself, forgets to observe, and at night he *dreams* of the swamp." He is able to dream with precise and gorgeous detail because of his powerful, unconscious receptivity in the woods. Thoreau makes a contrast: "Not so the naturalist; enough of his unconscious life does not pass there. A man can hardly be said to be *there*, if he knows that he is there, or to go there if he knows where he is going."[54] Frost also asserts that the poet, unlike the scientist or scholar, while going about his business randomly, cavalierly, is unwittingly preparing for the creative or dream moment.

This visionary moment flows organically out of factual experience and labor, from which poetry feeds, as we have seen. Emerson's essay "Intellect" exactly describes the psychic results of the interaction of fact, labor, and imagination:

> If you gather apples in the sunshine . . . and then retire within doors and shut your eyes and press them with your hand, you shall still see apples hanging in the bright light with boughs and leaves thereto. . . . There lie the impressions on the retentive organ, though you knew it not. So lies the whole series of natural images with which your life has made you acquainted, in your memory, though you know it not.[55]

Impelled by the "active power" of mind, "the fit image" wells up spontaneously, according to Emerson, not as a mirror of diminished nature but as a radiant magnification of nature, as in Frost's apples. They are no easy dream, but earned.

The essence of "After Apple-Picking" is not only "winter sleep" but also the relation between matter and spirit, or fact and value, which Emerson elaborates on in *Nature*. The facts of nature point to a "higher law": they are "the end or last issue of spirit," and "the terminus . . . of the invisible world," existing as "the substantial thoughts of the creator"; the moral law is the "marrow" of "every process." Just so, Thoreau would know beans through his labors. But the difference between Frost and his Romantic forebears is that, while he understands and approaches their idealism, he does not commit himself to its claims. This evasive strategy is the center of the poem's ambiguity and complexity.

The opening lines suggest the transcendental faith that factual nature leads to higher laws, to spirit, to heaven. Thus, "my long two-pointed ladder's sticking through a tree/ Toward heaven still" intimates that the visible creation (apples) and laboring for it *may* lead one toward heaven or spirit or the ideal. "Essence of winter sleep" is the dream-vision (the ultimate nature of sleep) and is curiously equated with "the scent of apples." Apparently Frost identifies the real ("scent") with the ideal ("essence") as does Emerson. In *Nature* "moral sentiment . . . scents the air" and "sinks" into man's soul,[57] informing him of higher laws. So too do Frost's apples sink into his soul, vitalizing imagination. But no higher realm parades before him; while what he sees approaches vision, it stops well short of any revelation. "Thus Frost has both Emerson's world of spirit and the old Romantic equivocation, or doubt, about what he sees. It it an Emersonian-Romantic vision or just some waking dream--"just some human sleep"?

Frost's "essence" remains ambiguous. It refers partly to idealized nature envisioned in dream (dream being one of the essences of winter sleep) and to ultimates--God, heaven, vision, mind. The mind knows through nature and the senses, creating essences out of the real; understandably, then, Frost meticulously accounts for the feel, smell, sight, and sound of apples in reliving the experience. Emerson states that "essence" reveals itself through man's intellect working on nature; we envision essence in the "coarse" and "distant phenomena of matter."[58] Frost's dream-apples are real nature made ideal by the imagination. The progress of the poem suggests that the physical world and sense experience are a ladder leading to the metaphysical world, to the creator, to heaven, which are apprehended by the idealizing imagination. The last lines, however, temper Emerson's confidence and enthusiasm, as is typical of Frost, but the idealism, though muted, unmistakably remains.

Dream, imagination, and intellect are therefore graces by which the higher world is darkly known, a means of restoring the fallen world--if not a way to salvation. The poem traces, on one level, the restorative, creative process, beginning with the early morning strangeness of vision and extending to the "long sleep." The vision begins in and is enveloped by unaccountable mystery and perplexity:

> I cannot rub the strangeness from my sight
> I got from looking through a pane of glass
> I skimmed this morning from the drinking trough
> And held against the world of hoary grass.
> It melted, and I let it fall and break.

A distorted and extraordinary "world of hoary grass" (a world, that is, of Frost) seen through a pane of ice introduces the speaker to the dream, or ideal, world.

Apple-picking is a unifying act, much like woodchopping in "Two

155

Tramps in Mud Time," for love and need are one to the picker. He cherishes each apple for itself and as a commodity. Because his reward is both provision and a vision of the spiritual world, the deed is "really done/ For Heaven and the future's sakes." Labor leads to dream; matter involves spirit; the ladder pointing toward heaven suggests these reconciliations of the real and ideal. In labor and its consequences in dream lies the speaker's unification of self and redemption of soul. This unifying process is suggested in the strangeness seen in the morning world of hoary grass and its subsequent dream counterpart, the evening vision after labor.

This achieved integration, with its clarity of vision at the end, dramatizes Emerson's idea that man restores eternal beauty to the world "by the redemption of his soul." He asserts:

> The ruin or the blank that we see when we look at nature, is in our own eye. The axis of vision is not coincident with the axis of things, and so they appear not transparent but opaque. The reason why the world lacks unity, and lies broken and in heaps, is because man is disunited with himself. He cannot be a naturalist until he satisfies all the demands of the spirit. Love is as much its demand as perception. Indeed, neither can be perfect without the other.[59]

Perception fused with feeling reintegrates man with nature, allowing him insight, "transparent" vision into the life of things. Such is the dream of apples, Frost's Emersonian equivalent of the inward eye's clear illumination in which the fruit is "cherished" or regarded with love. This illumination not only derives from the real world but is an idealization of the "world of hoary grass," a distorted or opaque view by an eye which sees through a glass if not darkly, at most translucently. The morning pane of ice is man's ordinary window on the world. In contrast, the imagination's inward eye sees more clearly and profoundly. Breaking the pane of ice is one of the steps to a higher vision which the dream symbolizes.

The poem's shimmers of transcendental thought are muted and qualified by Frost's view of our inherent disunity with ourselves and with the broken world, a view that stems from Emerson's own estimation of the human condition, as the above passage shows. A basically Christian view tempers the poem's idealism, in which there is a deeper kinship with Milton's Adam than with the Emersonian voice. Many critics have noted that "After Apple-Picking" alludes to "after the fall," when man is condemned to a life of sweat, labor, and the painful sense of his mortality.[60] Adam remarks in *Paradise Lost*, "With labor I must earn/ My bread . . . my labor will sustain me" (X,1054-56). Because labor and pain are the consequence of eating the apple, the fall is, for Frost, and for Emerson in "Experience," the central fact of our condition. However, criticism on Frost's Edenic conscience has not adequately focussed on the consequences of the fall for human imagination.

If by eating the apple we lose our innocence and "right reason," it is also the beginning of knowledge of evil. Life becomes, as a result, a heroic test to regain what we have lost, and imagination and dream, tied to our moral sense, are the instruments of our hope and salvation. As Milton and Frost avow, we do not live by commodity alone, but on hope and dreams. God has promised heaven, even though in actual life we are condemned to labor. Adam's apocalyptic vision ending *Paradise Lost* is his first sustaining hope for himself and his race.

The relationship between labor, dreaming, and the fall is defined by God immediately after Adam's ruin in *Paradise Lost*. In man's nature God sees a powerful yearning for heaven--the consequence of his uncertainty after the fall. God satisfies this yearning by inspiring "propitious" dreams that presage "some great good" (XII,612-13). Glimmers of Edenic unity and reward are, therefore, the kind of dream-sleep Adamic man will experience after apple-picking and eating. While labor is his lot, the dream of essence is still his consolation and hope. Dreams, like God's "motions" in the heart, may be the remnant of prelapsarian power in our nature.

In the lines, "One can see what will trouble/ This sleep of mine, whatever sleep it is," Frost is slyly playing around the edges of Romantic and Miltonic notions of dreaming and prefigurative visioning. Ascertaining "whatever sleep it is" is to appreciate the subtleties of the poem. In Milton Eve asks a similar question about the nature of her dream of the tree of knowledge of good and evil, for it gave her "offense" and "trouble." It was a prefigurative dream of her eating of

157

the fruit and the consequences attendant on it, but she remains uncertain whether the dream is real or fanciful. Her vision of the tree is related to Frost's concern for essence, heaven, and dreams--suggested by his idealized vision of apples. She remarks: "fair it seem'd,/ Much fairer to my Fancy than by day" (V,52-53). Moreover the apple makes gods of humans because of its knowledge-bestowing power, allowing us to "Ascend to Heav'n" (V,80). Eve replies that hers is no ordinary dream of "works of day past, or morrow's next design" (V,33) but a supernaturally inspired, prefigurative vision. Frost questions the type of sleep coming on, whether a "Long sleep, as I described its coming on/ Or just some human sleep"--that is, a common, altogether human, waking dream; or a deeper visionary insight. Important to note is the speaker's awareness of the dream "coming on," to which the magnified apples and the drowsy review of the day's events are apparently preliminary. Will the dream be the essence of apples and Edenic knowledge, or merely the illusory phenomonon of apples? Frost does not say but is testing the thin-iced edges of Romantic visionary experience.

Keats, too, could ponder the nature of his dreaming at the end of his Nightingale Ode: "Was it a vision, or a waking dream?" Keats's equivocation is in the tradition of surmise, to which Frost's poem fits. He is asking the same questions as Keats, but at the inception of the dreaming rather than after its conclusion. Perhaps his woodchuck[61] is the diminished version of Keats's nightingale, also owning special knowledge of beauty, poetry, and the ideal.

Unlike Keats's indolent dreamers who have "visions for the night," Frost earns his dream through labor and experience. Imagination depends on these. Frost therefore denies Keats's dictum, "What the imagination seizes as Beauty must be truth--whether it existed before or not."[62]

While Keats professes autonomic creation, Thoreau in *Walden* says the immediate labors of the day account for the mind's intuitions of "higher laws"; Thoreau's idea of imagination depending on direct, sentient experience is at the intellectual core of Frost's poem. "From exertion comes wisdom and purity," "Higher Laws" states; then follows a description of the tired John Farmer, whose work inspires daydreams. Hearing flute music while thinking of his work, he begins to "re-create his intellectual man." He withdraws into himself, "his mind still running on his labor." These thoughts, coupled with an imagination awakened by music, result in a vison of "higher laws" and of a "glorious existence," and a yearning to reach that spiritual realm.[63] Rooted in the mundane, this spiritual insight, although clearly prepared for and determined in his day's work, arises spontaneously, not in conscious effort. These same ideas are implied in the quality of the dream vision and the character of Frost's incipient dreamer in "After Apple-Picking." If labor and experience help expand the mind of John Farmer and Frost's apple-picker, they also provide an intimation of heaven or some ideal. Frost's dream achieves a reconciliation of the real and ideal worlds, much like the balance attained in "Going and coming back" in "Birches."

One problem remains. Why does the woodchuck know what kind of sleep is imminent, and what role does he play? He owns some special knowledge, for he apparently dreams and "could say" what manner of dreaming he and man have. The woodchuck has harvested, like the apple-picker, and goes into the earth to dream, in a long sleep of earned indolence. He is like the poet of fatted imagination, whose dreams also arise from earth and experience. Both are instinctively thorough in preparing for their long sleep. Frost perhaps borrows Thoreau's description of the poet as marmot, i.e ., woodchuck, in *A Week* . . . :

> The poet is he that hath fat enough, like bears and marmots, to suck his claws all winter. He hibernates in this world, and feeds on his own marrow . . . [a] happy dreamer . . . gone into winter quarters of deep and serene thoughts, insensible to surrounding circumstances; his words are the relation of his oldest and finest memory, a wisdom drawn from the remotest experience.[64]

The poet's reward for labor is a depth and serenity of thought, dream-visions based on earthly experience and recreated in the retirement, as it were, of his winter sanctuary, visions reshaped and recollected in tranquility.

Frost hopes that poetry and vision are therefore the "essence of winter sleep," while at the same time suggesting that the long sleep of death is a consequence of overexertion. If it is "just some human" restorative "sleep," the poet-marmot would know that also. But he cannot predict the issue of overexhaustion. Poems may be such stuff as dreams are made of, and our little sleep may often be rounded with a dream. That dream coming on is as ambiguous and mysterious as any Romantic dream-experience. But the strength and beauty of "After Apple-Picking" lie in its having created a flawless, suggestive description of the origins of dreaming--the dream beginning in the laborer's mind--the mystery attached to its coming on, and the character it will take. Will the laborious harvest be poetically fruitful? Frost does not say, and the marmot-poet speaking cannot, for the dreaming after apple-picking has not yet unfolded or defined itself as either some human sleep or a dream-vision. In any event the core of the poem is in the labor, from which all things imaginative, psychic, and spiritual issue.

7. SURVEYING THE WILD: "BEECH"

> Where my imaginary line
> Bends square in woods, an iron spine
> And pile of real rocks have been founded.
> And off this corner in the wild,
> Where these are driven in and piled,
> One tree, by being deeply wounded,
> Has been impressed as Witness Tree
> And made commit to memory
> My proof of being not unbounded.
> Thus truth's established and borne out,
> Though circumstanced with dark and doubt--
> Though by a world of doubt surrounded.

In "Beech" we turn from physical field labor to intellectual activity, surveying at the border of farm and wilderness. Such measuring is yet another of Frost's metaphors for the ordering process of a philosopher-poet intent on surveying the limits of knowledge. Being more a craft than husbandry but no less demanding in effort, surveying is a rational act establishing, demarcating, and making permanent the known. The imaginary line and pile of rocks defining

VIII - Labor, Art, and Imagination: "Beech"

it are the sign and factum of our labor and intellect imposing a "square" line of truth. The poem celebrates an ability to establish boundaries between known and unknown, measured and immeasurable, finite and infinite, ordered and chaotic. In fact, the poem may even dramatize Emerson's definition of the intellect; it "is Aristotle's: 'that by which we know terms or boundaries.'"[65] Establishing the limits of what we can know is one intention of "Beech"--and Frost's art as a whole.

To know and toe that line without venturing into the unknown and thereby risking disorientation and confusion is the intellect's major challenge. A risk-taking visionary, unbounded by circumferential limits, steps heedlessly into the unfamiliar and immeasurable, tempting a fate like that of the poet in Alastor, [66] who, we recall, perishes in his mental wilderness. This launching out into the illimitable is akin to the Romantic compulsion for dream and illusion. If modern man is "torn between the will to know and the will to dream," it is the Romantic who attempts "to achieve . . . that illusioned view of the universe and of human life which is produced by an imaginative fusion of the familiar and the strange, . . . the real and the ideal, . . . the natural and the supernatural."[67] Frost consistently is concerned with the first of these pairings, standing on the side of the real, the known, and the measured,--yet attracted to their opposites, as we see in the pillared dark of "Come In" and the wooded vastness of "Into My Own." Frost's inclination, however, places him on the surveyed farmside of reality. From a known, established vantage point he heeds that imaginary line, seeing that fact, measurement, and science do not fully define the universe and the mind, yet understanding that Alastorian forays into the unknown, the wild, and the illusory bring risk.

"Beech" stands firmly in the prophetic and Romantic tradition of regarding humanity as at the border of all realms; we are borderers able to draw the line between matter and spirit and are ourselves their meeting place and boundary.[68] Possessing a thoroughly mediating mind, we demark, in a creative act, where matter ("a pile of real rocks") stands for spirit ("my imaginary line"); and in doing so we reconcile the dualities of our nature and define the limits of our knowledge. The spine and Biblical cairn mark God's presence--the infinite located by the finite.

A common, beautiful tree, the beech has associations with

visionary experience and with witnessing the limits of a poet's goal. It is a favorite tree of Frost's most admired writers, Thoreau, Emerson, and Vergil. Thoreau identifies the tree as the known landmark and trysting point in the wilderness: "I frequently tramped eight or ten miles through the deepest snow to deep an appointment with a beech tree."[69] In the Eclogues, it is Vergil's favorite tree, under which shepherds converse, mediate, and pipe tunes. There, the shepherd Tityrus, attended by Melibaeus, thinks of a life beyond the boundaries of his land and state.[70] Emerson's essay "Thoreau" singles out the beech as exemplary in beauty[71] Though significant, the tree itself is not the poem's central figure.

The principal metaphor of surveying harkens back to Thoreau, the exemplary artist and artisan, who was indeed a surveyor, using this detailed craft to analogize the art and intent of writing. Surveying reasserts an order over an ever encroaching chaos: "What I had been doing all my life [was] making bounds, or rather finding them, remaking what had been unmade, where they were away."[72] Surveying, like gardening, reduces the wild to useful, discernable proportions; it is precisely unsurveyed woods--being symbolic of desolation, disorder, mystery, and even death--that the poet refuses to enter. The woods, then, are "the background in hugeness and confusion shading away from where we stand into black and utter chaos."[73] The iron spine, the pile of rocks, and the Witness Tree's wound, which fix the surveyor's imaginary line, stand "against the background . . . small, man-made figure[s] of order and concentration."[74] We stay within familiar boundaries rather than venturing into the unknown.

Unlike Ahab and Emersonian Transcendentalists, Frost trusts in quadrants and compasses. Thoreau desires the unsurveyed, illimitable in nature, disdaining "old bound marks" and "reblazed trees," because wildness forcefully affects his imagination.[74] Frost sees blazed boundaries differently, taking strength that he is "not unbounded" and that nature's wounds bear witness to this fact. "Beech" carefully delineates man's limits. He stands bounded in time, space, and intellect.

The poem may counter Thoreau's daring idealism in *Walden*, which trusts boundless dreaming: "If one advances confidently in the direction of his dreams, and endeavors to live the life which he had imagined, he will meet with a success unexpected in common hours. He will put some things behind, will pass an invisible boundary; new, universal, and more liberal laws will begin to establish themselves around and within him; or the old laws be expanded.[76] We will find in the real world support for our dreams: "If you have built castles in air . . . now put foundations under them."[77] But Frost is no such foundation-builder attempting to support the airy stuff of illusions. He *begins*, instead, with fact and accepts the circumstance of "dark and doubt." Dreams belong to the unbounded and uncertain, and that is all. If they come, dreams arise out of fact and labor, as we have seen. Surveying improves us, then, by refining our sense of boundaries. Laboring, the surveyor physically notches the Witness Tree, thereby committing limits to memory. Frost uses *Walden*'s metaphor of marking the right spot and the critical moment for the philosopher seeking truth--"to improve the nick of time and notch it on [his] stick, too; to stand on the meeting of two eternities, the past and future which is precisely the present moment; to toe that line."[78] Frost's notched stick is the Witness Tree. It reminds the poet of bounds. Thoreau's notch, taken from the Greek *Kairos*, a crucial moment in time (orginally it meant a notch of an arrow)[79] indicates the boundless opportunities of the present moment, including spiritual forays into illimitable nature.

Frost finds little evidence of the one life within him and abroad. The pall of inscrutability, rather than illuminating interchange and visionary power, envelops the wilds and shades our little surveyed corner. An uncharted nature flashes no hint of a supernature, gives no cry of what is hoped to be. "Beech" denies the Romantic dream vision, while using Thoreau's very metaphor of surveying to indicate a Frostian truth. Or so it seems. However, there is more to Thoreau's surveying.

Dark and doubt have their precedent in Thoreau's regard for the wild. In the essay "Walking," he remarks that he too loves "a sort of border life, on the confines of a world into which I make occasional and transient forays only."[80] Even his surveying is uncertain. He states, "These farms which I have myself surveyed, these bounds which I have set up, appear dimly still as through a mist. . . . The world . . . leaves no trace."[81] This mist of uncertainty anticipates the darkness and doubt circumstancing the tenuous lines of Frost's surveyor. Both writers are ever at the edge of chaos, barely able to maintain their minds, their lines of survey, for nature can obliterate all human traces.

The repeated insistence on dark and doubt at the end of the poem suggests, if slightly, the circumstance of evil. The mind's ability to check chaos serves as his protector, but a claim can be made that the unbounded realm beyond the surveyor's line represents the prince of darkness and the speaker's own moody, fallen heart. (This is perhaps one reason Frost uses his mother's maiden name in the pseudonym, "THE MOODIE FORESTER.") Thoreau equates Satan, darkness, and surveying in a passage condemning materialism, and those who, lost in their surveyed property, worship possession rather than nature: "I . . . saw him [man] standing in the middle of a boggy stygian fen, surrounded by devils, and he had found his bounds without a doubt, three little stones, where a stake had been driven, and looking nearer, I saw that the Prince of Darkness was his surveyor."[82]

"Beech" depicts inner landscape, that of the mind and spirit. Both writers include stones and stake to indicate their being bound to the reality of evil, the moral darkness within and around us. Frost has assayed the circumstance of his world well. But in the sequel poem, "Sycamore," he qualifies the tonal darkness of "Beech," our bounded condition, and the demarcations of truth, as he posits the possibility of visionary experience. Zaccheus' sycamore tree is a Witness Tree allowing him, a man of short height and therefore sight, "Our Lord to see."

8. THE VISION OF "THE WOODPILE"

"The Woodpile," one of Frost's most impressive early works, summarizes in the metaphor of labor many of his ideas on creativity already discussed in this chapter, and it also has ties with his Romantically influenced poems of visionary quest. The woodpile, as the evidence of man's "handiwork on which/ He spent himself the labor of his ax," echoes "Two Tramps in Mud Time."   If the poet-axman's labor is an ordering act, the woodpile symbolizes its results. Indeed, the lost swamp-tramper regards the pile as the only evidence of a truth he has been searching for long and with difficulty.

164

Frost emphasizes that it is a concentrated form, set in the wild, like Stevens's jar in Tennessee:

> It was a cord of maple, cut and split
> And piled--and measured, four by four by eight.
> And not another like it could I see.

Human power is the only earthly thing capable of such form-making, even if the structure is only a "momentary stay" for "someone who lived [i.e., "thrived] in turning to fresh tasks."

The wood-pile contains Frost's basic ideas on mind and art, particularly the spiritual comfort we derive from creative labor. Out of confusion and aimless wandering comes the speaker's vision of the wood-pile. The scene enacts Frost's statement on art and imagination: "When in doubt there is always form to go on with. Anyone who has achieved the least form . . . is lost to the larger excruciations. I think it must stroke faith the right way. The artist, the poet, might be expected to be the most aware of such assurance. But it is really everybody's sanity to feel it and live by it.[83] The wood-pile, a form amid chaos, offers the perplexed speaker such assurance; though certainly not a Romantic vision, it nonetheless is a comforting reward (all that he will get in the wild), sparing him of "larger excruciations."

The order inherent in the wood-pile helps order the speaker's mind. He understands the efficacy of labor and our deep need for form, to be sure, but this "vision" is achieved only after a struggle. Up to the point where the speaker sees the wood-pile (about halfway through the poem) he is disoriented; at the same time, he expects to see or learn something: "'I will turn back from here./ No, I will go on farther--and we shall see.'" His uncertainty is additionally suggested by his struggle in the hard snow and by the sameness of the trees near and far. The remark, "The view was all in lines/ Straight up and down of tall slim trees/ Too much alike to mark or name a place by," implies that he has not struck a line of purpose across experience. Though played down and partially masked, his efforts are those of a visionary quester lost in the forest of the mind.[84]

The vision of the wood-pile redeems the speaker from his struggle and confusion and dramatizes Frost's remark that labor and art function as consoling, ordering agents: "The background in hugeness and confusion shading away from where we stand into black and utter chaos; and against the background any small man-made figure of order and concentration. What pleasanter than that this should be so?[85] A man-made, concentrated form, the wood-pile counters the outer chaos of woods and the inner confusion of mind. It warms the swamp "with the slow smokeless burning of decay," a materialistic, natural process making all stays momentary. Frost also may be guarding against Romantic wishful thinking about art and permanence, and beliefs in a World Soul pervading man and nature,[86] for, ironically, decay--rather than spirit or correspondence--rolls through all things.

The episode of the bird further indicates Frost's rejection of nature's instructive purpose and its correspondence with us.[87] Meaning and order are achieved solely by creative labor. Between the materialism of science and the ideals of Romanticism we stand, our steady labor bridging the two realms. "The Wood-Pile" records this middle state and--however toned down from romantic moments of epiphany--illustrates the quality and extent of our moment of understanding.

CHAPTER IX
FOUR POEMS OF ORIGINS AND ENDS: THE ROMANTIC HERITAGE

Man is a stream whose source is hidden. . . . When
I watch that flowing river, which, out of regions I see
not, pours for a season its streams into me, I see that
I am a pensioner; not a cause but a spectator of this
ethereal water; that I desire and look up and put
myself in the attitude of reception, but from some
alien energy the visions come. (Emerson, "The Over-
Soul)

A man's life should be fresh as a river. (Thoreau, Journal)

Those shadowy recollections . . .
Are yet the fountain-light of all our day,
Are yet a master-light of all our seeing . . .
(Wordsworth, "Intimations" ode)

"The Trial by Existence," "The Master Speed," "Too Anxious for
Rivers," and "Directive" testify to the Romantic heritage of Thoreau,
Wordsworth, and Emerson. These four visionary poems spanning an
entire poetic career summarize well the cloud of poets at the center
of Frost's concern with his spiritual and poetic origins and ends. In
these poems, a stream of light or water (the spirit in its earthly course)
leads Frost back to the pulsing source of his spiritual and imaginative
life. That stream has the same symbolic value as "West-running
Brook"; that is, "time, strength, tone, light, life, and love,"--human
essences which spend themselves as they emanate from a
mysterious source. The brook's white wave flinging itself against the
black stream characterizes our resistant nature and impulse to lean
backward toward origin. Finding himself in the stream of life, Frost
glances both ways. Earthbound and waterborn, he can at moments

transcend time and space, looking forward to ends and backward to origins. In these instants he is like a white wave riding a black stream--moving but motionless--balanced between downward pull and backward thrust, much like the climber of birches who ascends on black branches along white trunk, only to be swung downward again to his starting place. If Frost were a true Shelleyan or Platonist, he might have ascended all the way to heaven. But in one poem at least, "The Trial by Existence," he takes us back to the source of our spiritual being.

1. "THE TRIAL BY EXISTENCE"

Except for the Masques, "The Trial by Existence" is Frost's only poem about the abstractions of transcendental philosophy and a theology justifying God's ways. In contrast to dozens of poems that darkly contemplate teleological purpose, "The Trial by Existence" is baldly visionary, dramatizing a radiant spiritual realm. The poem also accepts human responsibility for choosing a world of trial and suffering, and it foreshadows a repeated theme: the delineation of the lost Eden. That Eden is the destination of other seekers of unity in a fragmented world, such as the quester in "A Boundless Moment" and the birch climber.

Not surprisingly, "The Trial by Existence" is an amalgam of allusions to Romantic literature, including Shelley, Wordsworth, Yeats, and Emerson,[1] whom Frost uses to contrast their paradisiacal world with our shattered, earthly existence. We have noted this fragmentation in the trials of the beleaguered speaker of "Birches," who would surmount, briefly, the trees' dome of many colored glass and aspire to Shelley's white radiance of eternity. "Adonais" and the "Intimations" ode[2] provide the Platonic language Frost incorporates in his poem. Whereas Shelley looks forward to the radiance beyond death as an ultimate goal, and Wordsworth looks backward behind birth to the "celestial light," Frost argues for the glory and heroism of our earthly existence (as he did in his labor poems), justifying choice, freedom, bewilderment, and woe as the necessary "essence of life here." Frost draws on Romantic idealism to celebrate not the desirability of the soul's existence in a spiritual world, but its incarnation in a world of pain--thereby turning around the Platonism of Wordsworth and Shelley and gently countering Thoreau's earth-anchored philosophy. We should not be soaring but digging. There is nobility and heroism enough in the endeavor, just as much glory in the soul's earthly "agony of strife," Frost posits, as in its return to heaven via the Shelleyan route of death or the Wordsworthian path of recollection and imaginative re-creation.

Frost's remarkably Shelleyan description of heaven derives from the distinction between eternity's "white radiance" and life's "dome of many colored glass" in "Adonais." Thus, "The light of heaven falls whole and white/ And is not shattered into dyes." Similarly, Frost borrows from the "Intimations" ode to shape the rest of the second stanza; and Wordsworth's treatment of light and dark--distinguishing heavenly from earthly existences--provides Frost a pattern of imagery around which to organize his whole poem. "The light forever is morning light" echoes the ode's eastern "celestial light" which garments the meadows. Frost's "Angel hosts with freshness go" captures the following from the ode: "the glory and the freshness of a dream." The hosts "seek with laughter what to brave," just as "the heavens laugh with" the children in their "jubilee" (39). In contrast to heaven's morning light and "white shimmering concourse" (vss.9, 29), Frost's earthly life of trial is an "obscuration." Even in the ode, darkness accompanies human birth and growth: "shades of the prison house begin to close/ Upon the growing boy: (68-69) as his vision "fades." His recollections are "shadowy" and finally erased. These very "obscurations" are aspects of the Frostian soul's imminent trial, which begins with the dimming of heaven's light as it is "shattered into dyes."

Attending the ritual are "slant spirits trooping by / In streams and cross-and-counter streams." These apparitions remind us of Nature's winds which visit the child in *The Prelude* : "in lights and shades/ That marched and countermarched about the hills/ In glorious apparition." (12:96-98). Wordsworth eventually discusses man's feebleness, suffering, and pride, the subjects of the last three stanzas of "The Trial by Existence." And the voluntary "spirit" awaiting birth and "stand[ing] simply forth,/ Heroic in its nakedness,/ Against the uttermost of earth" is akin to Wordsworth's "soul" that "hath had elsewhere its setting" (61). That "elsewhere" is the Platonic elysium from which the soul goes to its trial. Frost's naked soul, too, "cometh from afar/ Not in entire forgetfulness/ And not in utter nakedness,/ But trailing clouds of glory" (62-65).

The notion of partial forgetfulness prompts Frost to reflect on memory and choice, subjects which end the poem on a knotty, philosophical note. Wordsworth says, "Our birth is but a sleep and a forgetting" (59) of the "visionary gleam . . . the glory and the dream" (57-58) because we not only fall into the experiential world but also develop and fulfill ourselves out of difficulty, uncertainty, and the dubious comfort that choice is necessary. Too, the Wordsworthian child's "heaven-born freedom" (123) is soon tempered with "strife" (126). In "The Trial by Existence" God states that in "agony of strife," we shall not be comforted in the memory of having chosen earthly life. Fate "admits no memory of choice/ Or the woe were not earthly woe." (We would, of course, inevitably turn back for consolation to our time of primal unity and innocence.)

So, Frost endorses the Wordsworthian idea of the value of earthly immersion in strife, pain, and evil. One is "wholly stripped of pride" when he relinquishes memory of choosing earthly existence. The soul must be stripped for the earthly test of the soul to be valid. In our life's progress we bear only the certainty (crushing as it is) of mortality with its puzzlement and pain. This idea of the inevitability that the soul forget its choice conforms to Wordsworth's consolation for childhood's lost vision:

> Though nothing can bring back the hour
> Of splendor in the grass, of glory in the flower
> We will grieve not, rather find strength
> In what remains behind. (178-81)

What remains is primal sympathy, or love, involving a chastening awareness of suffering, faith, and knowledge. These are the noble results of our trial, the sturdy rock replacing the lost memory of Paradisiacal choice. Frost's consolation is remarkably close to Wordsworth's, but it rests on freedom and volition, without which humanity could not really be tested.

2. "THE MASTER SPEED"

"The Master Speed," written twenty years after "The Trial by Existence," shows Frost's continued interest in Platonic regard for the soul. It is a sonnet on the mind's power to perceive, in a mutable world, a permanence or unity of being. Swiftly climbing back up the stream of radiant spirit and of time, the mind affirms its celestial, fountain-like origins. But Frost never forgets mortal time while making these spiritual sallies; for he has learned from Thoreau that earth's the right place for love, as the labor poems affirm. This master speed of psychic power, by linking the self with the informing spirit of the universe, protects the individual from being swept away by the world's chaotic flow. The marriage of two true minds endowed with this "master speed" achieves an ever fixed, eternal mark of love. Through this truly creative power that triumphs over time, we achieve an intimation of immortality.

The poem is consistent with Frost's other works on the preservation and comfort we derive from imagination. This grand theme of the Romantic writers finds its stateliest expression in the "Intimations" ode, from which Frost's poem draws its theme and imagery. The "master speed" is equivalent to Wordsworth's swift recollection of the visionary gleam and childhood's oneness with nature. This recollection saves him from the painful sense of mortality and separation and--coupled with the remembrance of celestial light--provides spiritual strength: "the thought of past years in me doth breed/ Perpetual benediction" (134-35). Wordsworth's "primal sympathy" (182), which is identical with the sense of original unity, remains forever with him, offering consolation and spiritual order in every past and present recollection:

> those first affections
> Those shadowy recollections,
> . . . . .
> Are yet the fountain-light of all our day,
> Are yet a master-light of all our seeing,
> Uphold us . . . .   (148-53)

The mind's "shadowy recollections" are Wordsworth's "master-light" and Frost's equivalent "master speed." According to Frost, the radiance in Wordsworth's child can be recaptured, for memory can "climb/ Back up a stream of radiance to the sky." "The master speed" can take him"back through history up the stream of time" as swiftly as the Wordsworthian souls that "have sight of that immortal sea/ Which brought us hither,/ Can in a moment travel thither" (163-65).

Whereas Wordsworth sees the mind as the visionary power unifying man and nature, Frost regards mind and the love for a woman as twin master forces allowing an intimation of immortality:

> Two such as you with such a master speed
> Cannot be parted nor be swept away
> From one another once you are agreed
> That life is only life forevermore
> Together wing to wing and oar to oar.

"One," "once," and "only" are deftly iterative in reenforcing the theme of unity. "Only" is especially understated in conveying the idea of exclusivity. As in "Two Look at Two," Frost amends Wordsworth's claim of the correspondence and oneness of man and nature, insisting that a purely *human* love between man and woman is the source of spiritual unity and a much more relevant correspondence than between man and nature. Thus Wordsworth's exclamation, "And O, ye Fountains, Meadows, Hills, and Groves,/ Forebode not any severing of our loves!" (188-89), is modified by Frost, who makes the means to immortality an alliance with a woman. She is the source of love and unity. Wordsworth's "primal sympathy" is, for Frost, marital love; the participants speed to immortality, navigating "Together wing to wing and oar to oar." How apt that this verse became the epitaph to Frost's tomb.

3. "TOO ANXIOUS FOR RIVERS"

In contrast to "The Master Speed," "Too Anxious for Rivers" looks downstream and to the end of all things. It is a companion piece to "Directive," which points us upstream to our origins. Death, the condition of life--its darkness, mystery, uncertainty--and teleology are the philosophical considerations of the poem. But Frost is not "anxious" over these matters exclusively; as in "Directive" he is concerned also with myth, imagination, and poetry as the vital source of knowledge, for they are the channels of his highest "effort," investing life with nobility. In comparison, mere science cannot match the power of poetry and imagination.

The "essay of love"--creative effort--is our sustaining activity in life. Ends are not our primary concern. "A Prayer in Spring" celebrates this fulfillment in action, as does "Two Tramps in Mud Time." The making of a life or a poem is a trial, a performance, an attempt, an endeavor, a composition--an "essay" (in its root meanings). An active, physical involvement with the world is the initiator of all essays, whose issue is a poem. As "After Apple-Picking" shows, work gives rise to the dream-poem.

"Too Anxious for Rivers." a complex poem, should not be reduced to the convenient didacticism of the last line or the bare statement on science found in line 17 ("And how much longer a story has science[?])." The subjects of imagination, teleology, and death refer respectively to Romantic, Christian, and Epicurean modes of thinking originating in Thoreau, Bunyan, and Lucretius, from whom Frost's mythmaking freely adapts. The poem comes from this cloud of poets.

It is cast in dactyls after *De Rerum Natura* . The first half is concerned with mountain and stream and valley, and thoughts of death. The second half describes the "howdah" world of the Hindus, the challenge of science, and a Lucretian view of nature and purpose, ending with (or retreating in) the comforting Frostian maxim that earth's the right place for love. Bunyan and Lucretius provide the intellectual foundation for the first and second part, respectively, with Thoreau's presence arching over the whole.

Like West-running Brook, this river represents life, consciousness, and the soul's vigor. Thoreau similarly asserts: "A man's life should be fresh as a river. It should be the same channel, but a new water every instant. Some men have no inclination; they have no rapids nor cascades, but marshes, and alligators, and miasma instead."[3] Frost's line "I never saw so much swift water run cloudless" suggests the purity and vigor of the speaker's life. Just as speed prevents clouds and miasma, a proper tempo and temper avert stagnation of soul, body, and mind.

Let us for the moment limit the meaning of the river to that of life's progress to death or eternity. Frost's initial anxiety lies in not knowing its proper course, reversing the easy confidence of Thoreau, who writes: "I shall not mistake the direction of my life; if I but know the highland and the main,--on this side the Cordilleras, on that the Pacific,--I shall know how to run. If a ridge intervene, I have but to seek, or make, a gap to the sea.[4] Thoreau sees "victory" and glory in the seaward flow of the soul, which "will cut its own channel, like the mountain stream," seeking its own level, though "the gods make it meander."[5] Frost can voice no such Romantic optimism over a glorious end. The force that runs through human life, like gravity pulling down on rivers, no one can change or interfere with. He, therefore, need not be too "anxious" about fate, purpose, and ultimate ends.

Although nonchalance seems a virtue in this poem, Frost's life shows that he worried deeply about these philosophical matters. He feared fateful blows and various emblematic "mountains" which might block life's stream from the immortal sea. The figure for this sense of separation and uncertainty parallels Thoreau's Journal entry on the death of a friend: "My life is like a stream that is suddenly dammed and has no outlet; but it rises the higher up the hills that shut it in, and will become a deep and silent lake. Certainly there is no event comparable for grandeur with the eternal separation--if we may conceive it so--from a being that we have known. I become . . . sensible of the meaning of finite and infinite.[6] Frost admits an earlier anxiety over the soul's passage through the mountain barrier at the long valley's end. Is it the Biblical valley of the shadow of death? The mountain which is "the end of the world" (2) indicates the limit of finitude, a notion deriving from an oriental myth (the first of several in the poem) Thoreau mentions in "Walking." "The eastern Tartars think that there is nothing west beyond Thibet. 'The world ends there,' say they; 'beyond there is nothing but a shoreless sea.'"[7]

The journey motif through a forbidding landscape recalls Christian Everyman's spiritual progress. *The Pilgrim's Progress*, which Frost admired as a supreme work of literature,[8] may underlie the poem. Are the valley, canyon, darkness, and mountain Bunyan territory, where the spirit is tested? Christian's perilous advance over emblematic mountains to the Celestial City, or Mount Zion, is the supreme "effort" and "essay of love," as is Bunyan's poetic account of that progress in his dream-narrative. Frost's poem refers to both spiritual and artistic effort, and Bunyan is his presider.

If Frost's sense of personal unworthiness and overwhelming fear of death and God's punishment sometimes obsessed him,[9] the poem combats these tendencies, calling for the release from worry about matters spiritual, salvational, and theological. He resolves his tensions by cleverly playing Bunyan's own game: Frost invents the allegorical canyon "Of Ceasing to Question What Doesn't Concern Us." His spiritual terrain is different from Bunyan's in thought yet radically dependent on the good Puritan's vision of *The Pilgrim's Progress From This World To That Which Is To Come.* Like its story, "delivered in the similitude of a dream, "Too Anxious for Rivers" possesses a visionary quality and, in fact, defends dreams as a way to truth.

Though answers to ultimate questions, then, need not concern us, our commitment to the "effort" and "essay of love" places value in hope and fortitude. We recall that "Hopeful" is Christian's travelling mate as he progresses over the mountain. Just so, Frost says that hope alone relieves the too anxious soul; it sustains daring and bravery from the very beginning of our "trial by existence."

Though final causes remain an utter mystery, we can construct answers to some questions. Poetry, myth, and imagination are his "essays" at interpretation, understanding, and wholeness of vision that science alone cannot provide. The poem celebrates the power of the imagination and myth-making as our ways of knowing. The myth-making poet explains the world in vivid, easy to apprehend figures, such as:

> The world as we know is an elephant's howdah;
> The elephant stands on the back of a turtle;
> The turtle in turn on a rock in the ocean.

Ecologists and physicists may describe delicate balances in our world, too, but not in this way; indeed, the poem skillfully illustrates the ability of poetry to express truth. Thoreau's influence on Frost is again instrumental; in "Walking," he writes: The Hindoos dream that the earth rested on an elephant, and the elephant on a tortoise, and the tortoise on a serpent; and though it may be an unimportant

175

coincidence, it will not be out of place here to state, that a fossil tortoise has lately been discovered in Asia long enough to support an elephant.[10] He then defends the authenticity of myth and imagination, saying, "I confess I am parital to these wild fancies, which transcend the order of time and development. They are the sublimest recreation of the intellect."[11] The vitality of poetry is therefore dependent on the vitality of a culture's mythology (and vice versa) and not only its rational systems. This is a major point in Frost's poem.

Thoreau thinks science is a "blight" on imagination[12] and wildness in poetry. Frost would agree, though he was himself avid about science and drew upon it for metaphors. The dreams of children, a Romantic symbol for the purest imaginative visionings, fade before the account of science, as Frost's question implies:

> And how much longer a story has science
> Before she must put out the light on the children
> And tell them the rest of the story is dreaming?

The common task of Frost and Thoreau is to rekindle that fading light of imagination. Thoreau anticipates and even resolves Frost's misgivings about all-powerful science, asserting that poetic genius always will be the true light of knowledge:

> Genius is a light which makes the darkness visible, like the lightning's flash, which perchance shatters the temple of knowledge itself,--and not a taper lighted at the hearth-stone of the race, which pales before the light of common day. . . . The science of Humboldt is one thing, poetry is another thing. The poet to-day, notwithstanding all the discoveries of science and the accumulated learning of mankind, enjoys no advantage over Homer.[13]

In short, all revelation is ours through poetry. The supreme myth-maker Homer illuminates truths for an entire civilization, and no story of science can put them out. Through imagination, the cloud of Romantics attempted to find truth, and Frost, following Thoreau's example, fits in their tradition by affirming the primacy of imagination.

176

IX - Origins and Ends: "Too Anxious for Rivers"

To summarize, Frost is anxious over the future "stream" of poetry in a scientific age. He asserts that children's dreams contain prophetic truths, the kind which science labors for years to extract. A child's light will continue to be shed, carrying on the "story" of the "howdah" world. The line, "'You children may dream it and tell it tomorrow'" answers the question whether science will be the dominant knowledge and proclaims a faith in vision--the dreaming of children--and the future telling of it ("tell it tomorrow"). The passage also suggests prophecy; we recall that the children of "Directive" own the visionary goblet like a Grail and therefore possess the same imaginative powers as in "Too Anxious for Rivers."

In contrast to poetry's short, vivid, and precise account of the "howdah" world, science merely tells a long, dreary, incomplete story. Frost follows Thoreau's ideas on the prophetic "telling" which dreaming poets and children have:

> The wildest dreams of wild men, even, are not the less true. . . . It is not every truth that recommends itself to the common sense. . . . Some expressions of truth are prophetic. . . . The geologist has discovered that the figures of serpents, griffins, flying dragons . . . of heraldry have their prototypes in the forms of fossil species which were extinct before man was created, and hence 'indicate a faint shadowy knowledge of a previous state of organic existence.'[14]

Plumbing the mysteries of phylogeny, the poetic mind recreates the vanished truth of the past. The poet's dream apprehends swiftly a "story" which a scientist's methodical and rational labors piece together slowly. The poet's knowledge of the origins of all things is the "something we knew all about to begin with." Lucretius, for one, is the perfectly integrated poet, myth-maker, and philosopher, possessing an imagination that in his great poem *De Rerum Natura* brings together a unified vision of human nature and purpose. This poetic "essay" is an imaginative account of ontological matters, such as Nature's origins and processes, based, in part, on an atomic theory of philosophy. While modern science can trace, describe, and

177

theorize on our geologic and planetary origins, the poet-philosopher Lucretius explains, synthesizes, imagines: "Time was we were molten, time was we were vapor."

The reference to Lucretius helps clarify the meaning of Frost's last five lines and knits the themes of the poem together neatly. Following the ideas of his mentor Epicurus, Lucretius dismisses as false and even harmful all speculative thinking on an afterlife. All we can know are the fixed limits of mortal existence--concrete, objective reality--and we therefore address our efforts to this world and to this life. Matter and space are the only realities, with "the gliding fires of ether" sustaining all life.[15] Epicurus based his philosophy on two entities: Space, or "void," and atoms. While our senses attest to the existence of atomic matter, it is only through inference that we know space to exist. On this theorem stands Epicurean philosophy. Epicurus had to "fare into space" and contemplate it in order to affirm the goodness, desirability, and preferability of earth--or concrete reality. We needn't go through all that, according to Frost; we trust reality to be self-evident and good. The strong say nothing till they see, arriving at the knowledge that life, matter, the world, and work are our primary concerns rather than the void of philosophy, teleology, salvation, and other uncertain matters of the spirit. Of course, neither Frost nor Lucretius rules out these endeavors as a valid part of life's essay. But Lucretius states, "Why not rather make an end of life and labor?"[16] These are properly "the effort, the essay of love."

Indeed the expression and celebration of that labor are the function of poetry and imagination. The poetic act is itself a constant essay of thought, beginning in the mind's confrontation with realty, not in an Epicurean essaying of the void. Earth the right place, not sirius' disc. We need not fare into space to know who we are and what we are; nor should we be concerned about where we are going. Death is the fulfillment of life, as Lucretius asserts, and therefore needn't make us too anxious. Equipped with this philosophical understanding, Frost relieves his anxiety.

"Too Anxious for Rivers" is a directive of sorts, a reminder that the "essay" is our primary undertaking and comfort, especially for the poet. Just as a poem may not be "worried into being," so too one's life and end need not be anxiously contemplated. Lines in "Kitty Hawk" repeat this theme:

> Someone says the Lord
> Says our reaching toward
> Is its own reward.

The reward of striving is implied in the doctrine of works. The "someone" certainly could be Thoreau who champions the poet's essay of heroic striving for an ideal: "The mere vision is little compared with the steady corresponding endeavor thitherward. It would be vain for us to be looking ever into promised lands toward which in the meanwhile we were not steadily and earnestly travelling, whether the way led over a mountain-top or through a dusky valley."[17] Frost's, Thoreau's, and Bunyan's mountains of trial need not concern us, though they may loom on the horizon. Let us find ourselves in our work rather than lose ourselves in thoughts and places too far in the distance.

4. "DIRECTIVE"

> So forth and brighter fares my stream,
> Who drink it shall not thirst again.
> (Emerson, "Two Rivers")

"Directive" guides us, in a mysterious upland road and backwoods farm area, to Frost's Hippocrene, the origin of all language, thought, and form. In every particular he is accounting for the origins of his imagination and poetry; it is a historical and psychic going back in time to the literary roots of Frost's life, centering in the spring and Grail-like goblet. These symbols are the legacy of Wordsworth, Thoreau, and the Bible. The poem is, then, a tribute to the sources sustaining the poet's mind and art through an entire creative life.

Frost's intention is to redeem the past through imagination and memory,[18] whereby he summons aptly from the vast chaos of all he has lived through and works into form. That the creative act can redeem and is itself evidence of final unity are truths Frost imparts to others who would come after him; and so the poem is, in part, a directive to those who would be poets. It also illustrates how we gain knowledge and "get saved" by understanding a poet's parables. And it, finally, is about Frost's beliefs. Like Thoreau, who shows "an

179

unwillingness to exhibit to profane eyes what was still sacred in his own, and knew well how to throw a poetic veil over his experience,"[19] Frost writes cryptically--as we have seen earlier--"to keep the over curious out of the secret places of [his] mind."[20] To be wary of coming too much to the surface is not merely a point of poetic style in "Directive," but it is also part of Frost's belief. From the meditative Thoreau of "Former Inhabitants" and "Winter Visitors," Frost learns to evoke the past and give it form. In this sense the poem is an imaginative "departure" or excursion to primal roots, where the poet draws his life. Thoreau directs "that we should air our lives from time to time by removals, and excursions. . . . Do not sit so long over any cellar-hole. . . . So live that only the most beautiful wild-flowers will spring up where you have dwelt."[21] Seen in this light, the "belilaced cellar hole" of "Directive" suggests at once the pastness of the poet's provenance and the vitality and beauty springing from it.

An excursion backward seems, appropriately, a pilgrimage. The powerful effect of the past on the poetic mind has its precedent in Wordsworth.[22] For Wordsworth, the revisited landscape of Tintern Abbey provides "tranquil restoration" and "life and food/ For future years," by which the mind becomes a "mansion for all lovely forms. Likewise, the moral landscapes and themes of *The Excursion* and "Michael" are an inspiration and source for the pastoral setting of "Directive." In addition to referring to the waters of *Walden*, Frost subtly takes us back to Wordsworth's landscapes in order to account for both of the village cultures lost and faded into one another--they are the British and American "cloud of poets" which shapes Frost's moral vision.

Common to *The Excursion* and "Directive" are a broken goblet near a spring, a ruined house, an interest in the relation between legend and imagination, and the impact of nature, wreckage, and human suffering on the poetic imagination. The subject of *The Excursion* is the human mind, its epic journey through the ruins of nature, time, and human suffering, and its power to give meaning to this broken world. Guided by faith, the enlightened spirit overcomes "what we feel of sorrow and despair/ From ruin and from change, and all the grief/ That passing shows of Being leave behind" (1:949-51). Both Frost and Wordsworth combine legends, history, and folklore into a meaningful order through imaginations fed by faith and hope. Frost

IX - Origins and Ends: "Directive"

maintains that "art-belief,"--the trust in intuition--flows from "God-belief": "The belief in God is a relationship you enter into with Him to bring about the future."[23] As shall be seen, the goblet-grail that is the object of the quest in "Directive" represents all of these beliefs, including "art-belief" and imagination. Using creative memory, the excursive mind sees nature and the past as something other than a meaningless graveyard. In this regard, Frost follows the example of his predecessors: Wordsworth finds his imagination's nourishment in the ruins of the past (namely the story of Margaret's tragic existence), and Thoreau conjures up the past in order to bring Walden's deceased denizens to life.

The poet begins in the voice of a guide directing us out of the confusing present, the "now"; the world is too much with us. We retreat to "a time made simple by the loss/ Of detail, burned, dissolved, and broken off." To surmount and see order in this fragmented world is Frost's burden as guide and teacher. He goes beyond "the lesson for today," that

We are all doomed to broken-off careers.
And so's the nation, so's the total race.
The earth itself is liable to the fate
Of meaninglessly being broken off.

Amid broken tombs, nature, and careers; among glacier ruts, ruin, dilapidation, a broken goblet, erosions, and shattered dishes; at a house upon a farm within a town, there is a waiting vision. He directs us up a road to the source of knowledge.

As guide, Frost follows the example of Wordsworth in "Michael," whose prologue leads the reader up isolated country to the wellspring of his moral imagination, establishing continuity between past and present and between his life as a writer and future "youthful poets, who among these Hills/ Will be my second self when I am gone" (38-39). In "Directive," Frost is Wordsworth's "second self," the pastoral poet and scion of Romantic stock leaving the same poetic legacy to his successors as does the speaker of "Michael." It is no wonder that the introductory lines to "Michael" are a model directive for Frost. Wordsworth's invitation to climb his rough mountain past is remarkably life Frost's appeal for the reader to retreat up "the road

181

there, if you'll let a guide direct you":

> If from the public way you turn your steps
> Up the tumultuous brook of Green-head Ghyll,
> You will suppose that with an upright path
> Your feet must struggle; in such bold ascent
> The pastoral mountains front you face to face.
> But courage; for around that boisterous brook
> The mountains have all opened out themselves,
> And made a hidden valley of their own.
> No habitation can be seen; but they
> Who journey thither find themselves alone
> With a few sheep, with rocks and stones and kites.

. . . ^F^Corth's tale. The quarry-like road (mysteriously linked also to the graveyard marble of line four) begins Frost's excursion and is similar to the stony opening of "Michael." It may also refer metaphorically to the primal source of all things to which humans bend. In "The Snow-Storm" Emerson identifies the "fierce artificer" as the north wind coming "out of an unseen quarry." This artificer is like Frost's mythic god, the enormous Glacier "that braced his feet against the Arctic Pole" and chiseled earth. (However, Emerson's north wind built artwork out of snow.) In "Education" Emerson remarks, "The end of life is that the man should take up the universe into himself, or on the solitude of the Hermit (Thoreau's meditative self). The Hermit is presently judging the distant town folk as being "born too far into life for me" (he is thus similar to the withdrawn speaker in "Directive"), and finds his "water from the spring" sufficient to this needs. At this point the poet advances on him: "Hark! I hear a rustling of the leaves. . . . It comes apace; my sumachs and sweet-briars tremble.--Eh, Mr. Poet, is it you? How do you like the world today?"[31] In *Walden* the hermit-philosopher uniting thought and expressive ability, becomes the poet. The role and presence of the poet-philosopher in "Brute Neighbors" help illuminate the three lines in question. Frost himself comments on the impact "Directive" had on his status as a poet and on his reception by fellow poets, whose belated excitement and enthusiasm for him may be figured in the rustle of leaves in the general "woods" of poetry: "'This is the poem that converted the other group. The one these fellows have taken to build my reputation. The boys [followers of T.S. Eliot] call it great. They have re-estimated me. This is great and the rest, trivia."[32] Elizabeth Shepley Sergeant notes the seriousness locked into the teasing-mournful tones with which Frost hurriedly made these remarks.[33] He knew that the "upstart inexperience" in his audience (and peers) would be an ordeal--a severe trial and judgment--even for him, a true, self-reliant philosopher-poet, and that his works would not, of course, be understood; more likely it would be ignored. Indeed, for a long time, his work was considered simple nature poetry, unfashionably unlike Eliot's--though Frost's use of tradition itself is in the very grain of his poems, as this study has shown. Little wonder that in his later years of fame ("Directive" was published in 1947) he could ironically remark, "Where were they [enthusiastic readers] all not twenty years ago?" Those two decades measure a time of adversity and prosperity, obscurity and fame.

Frost's symbols of the woods and leaves also have ties with Romanticism's lofty trees, a figure for a humanity elevated by poetry. Keats speaks of the metaphorical poet who raises and spiritualizes so that "humanity instead of being a wide heath of Furze and Briars with here and there a remote Oak or Pine, would become a grand democracy of Frost Trees!"[34] Thoreau includes leaves as symbolic evidence of the creative spirit in all things, comparing earth to "living poetry, like the leaves of a tree."[35] Trees are representative of the world of poetry. By implication, then, those who "think too much of having shaded out/ A few old pecker-fretted apple trees" are the dominant poets[36] who have overshadowed the dying "leaves" of Victorian or other previous poetry, already weakened by decay. (The rustle of leaves, therefore, is the vitality and vigor of new poetry, though its writers are still upstarts in their inexperience.)

Out of the confusion of the past--a gauntlet of doubt and uncertainty--the poet finds comfort in form-making. His directive is: "Make yourself up a cheering song of how/ Someone's road home from work this once was." The poet's song should comfort, console, and defend. Both in its spiritual and aesthetic "adventure[s]," the path leads to a "height/ Of country where two village cultures faded/ Into each other." These cultures, as we have seen, refer to Wordsworth and Thoreau, sources which developed the speaker's mind, helping to form and inform this poem. The art and thought of Frost's mentors are the highest "culture," the best Romantic and Transcendental ideals. Along with Emerson and others, they joined in a movement that crossed continental boundaries and became one before the two streams indeed faded into each other in the century that bore Frost. Their writing is the record of a "culture"[37] rooted in a common idealism and belief in nature. These ideas shape Frost, are the spring from which he drinks and thereby becomes whole, are what contribute to his self-culture.

Are these cultures fully and finally lost for the rest of us? No, says Frost, for if we are lost and confused, we can find ourselves by their example. Like Thoreau, Frost says to rely on utter solitude and meditation for spiritual guidance and then to make poetry out of the experience:

> And if you're lost enough to find yourself
> By now, pull in your ladder road behind you
> And put a sign up CLOSED to all but me.
> Then make yourself at home.

The best one can do is emulate *Walden*. Only when we lose our egotism, abandoning ourselves to art and meditation, can we find ourselves in spiritual thought. The imagination thrives when all outer, material occupations are sundered. Then we live in the economy of the self. There is a parallel between the "CLOSED" sign in "Directive" and *Walden*: both suggest that metaphoric language is necessarily obscure and private.[38] (As a consequence of figurative expression, even the Bible's parables are not understood by all.)

The high poet makes himself at home with his past, the remembrance of which he summons up and then reshapes in poetry. His home is the land, ruins, and spring of the spirit, which "Directive" describes in detail. The field is "no bigger than a harness gall," or a harness sore on a horse. A gall, like the "dent dough" describing the cellar hole, is evidence of our slight impress on nature, whose cattle we tame by harness. This metaphor subtly reenforces the subject of poetry that arches the poem, and derives from Thoreau's association of art as a gall:

> Is not Art itself a gall? Nature is stung by God and

> the seed of man planted in her. The artist changes
> the direction of Nature and makes her grow according
> to his idea. If the gall was anticipated when the oak
> was made, so was the canoe when the birch was
> made. Genius stings Nature, and she grows
> according to its idea.[39]

Creativity and previous art have cleared a little space, and Frost
would dwell alone as poet in this field and at this height reached by
past artists.

Still standing intact amid the ruins of the past is the children's
make-believe house, for in Frost's estimation play and playacting
make up the house of poetry. A poet retains this child-like vigor of
make-believe that is the core of imagination; "Some shattered dishes
underneath a pine," then, alludes to language--identified as the
"playthings in the playhouse"--by which the imagination materially
enacts its fancies. Writing of poetic language in "The Constant
Symbol," Frost identifies "playthings given" as "data," that is,
"vocabulary, grammar, prosody, and diary," which the mind as "baby
giant"[40] uses as stepping stones of communication. The mind as a
baby giant "provident in the cradle" reaffirms the child-like vigor of
imagination in "Directive," and helps clarify the relationship darkly
drawn between the children's playhouse, language, and fancy ("make
believe").

That the children's playthings are shattered dishes illuminates
Frost's ideas on poetic language. "Form in language is such a
disjected lot of old broken pieces it seems almost as nonexistent as
the spirit till the two embrace in the sky."[41] The shards (matter, data,
playthings) represent a fragmented language that cannot gather into
a final unity because it lacks metaphor, the form-making essence and
incarnation of poetry. This fallen state of language mirrors the fallen
state of both nature and our creative spirit. Clearly, Frost is
Emersonian in his belief that language depends upon nature and
spirit, for he assumes that purity, wholeness, and simplicity of soul
generate vivid, concrete, symbolic language: pure poetry. In the
chapter "Language" in *Nature*, Emerson remarks:

As we go back in history, language becomes more

IX - Origins and Ends: "Directive"

> picturesque, until its infancy, when it is all poetry; or
> all spiritual facts are represented by natural
> symbols. . . . A man's power to connect his thought
> with its proper symbol, and so to utter it, depends on
> the simplicity of his character, that is, upon his love of
> truth, and his desire to communicate it without loss.
> The corruption of man is followed by the corruption of
> language.[42]

If nature is now fragmented and language shattered, reflecting the infirmity of imagination, then Frost would go back to the primitive sources of poetry and spiritual power which Emerson praises. In the broken goblet lies the waters of linguistic, poetic, imaginative, and spiritual wholeness.

The playhouse is also tied to literary history. It is distinguished by make-believe, not a fully mature poetic "school" because fancy uninformed by a philosophical base remains simplistic. This is Frost's estimation of the impotency of imagism; its practitioners watched other poetry move beyond their inadequate aesthetics. They played imaginatively with fragments, like the shattered dishes in the playhouse which are not pieced into a unity. That is, they had no organizing metaphors. The shards therefore represent verbal formlessness--"a disjected [*i.e.,* 'torn apart' and 'scattered'] lot of old broken pieces." Frost describes Amy Lowell and the imagists as children, "Little ones with no more apparatus than a tea-cup [who] looked on with alarm"[43] when modern poetry was dilating in matter and form.

The poem's focus returns to ruins, this time directing us to weep for "the house that is no more a house." Frost is affected in the same way as is Wordsworth surveying the remains of Michael's sheepcote or Margaret's house, which harbor stories fitting for imaginative exercise and moral edification. He makes himself at home in the basic material of poetry--ruin, the chaos of the past, and humanity's tragic fall. While these chasten the contemplative imagination, Frost acquires fortitude from the example that the condition of life is ruin. The house in "earnest," then, is the real house of life that cannot stand because its time is past, but remains alive in Frost's memory as a valued, rich mansion. It is a rich dwelling of memory because it contains the cloud of Wordsworth's verses of consoling wisdom. Frost's mind is like Dorothy Wordsworth's, "a mansion for all lovely forms,/ Thy memory be as a dwelling-place/ For all sweet sounds and harmonies." That cloud of sustaining memories is what keeps Frost's faith in a spiritless age. Finding comfort and reward in what is left behind is Wordsworthian:

> We will grieve not, rather find
> Strength in what remains behind;
> In primal sympathy
> Which having been must ever be
> In the soothing thoughts that spring
> Out of human suffering;
> In the faith that looks through death,
> In years that bring the philosophic mind.
> ("Intimations" ode, 180-87)

If Frost is concerned with truth and mysteries of the spirit, he finds in reviving the past--making inroads to it-- the very materials by which he can arrive at eternal verities. Likewise, in "Winter Visitors" (*Walden*), while Thoreau laments the common practice of covering up wells, his noticing the act gives rise to meditations about the death of philosophic discussion, of the spirit, and even of life itself:

> What a sorrowful act must that be,--the covering up
> of wells! Coincident with the opening of wells of
> tears. These cellar dents . . . are all that is left where
> once were the stir and bustle of human life, and 'fate,
> free will, foreknowledge absolute,' in some form . . .
> discussed.[44]

In recovering the past, the true poet perforce must think of lofty matters.

The well, or stream, is associated with origins and ends; the mind's intercourse with the past--in history and in literature--is the source and spring of Frost's creative labor. Thus, the lines, "Your destination and your destiny's/ A brook that was the waters of the house" refer to hearkening back to the rudiments of things historic,

IX - Origins and Ends: "Directive"

philosophic, poetic, and spiritual. And the most nourishing spring of all is philosophic literature which treats the self's relation to the cosmos: a Miltonic "'fate, free will, foreknowledge absolute.'" The brook, "cold as a spring as yet so near its source/ Too lofty and original to rage," is a characteristic Romantic metaphor. It is reminiscent of Walden's waters of purity and inspiration and Emerson's Over-Soul, whose "stream" and "flowing river" are the sources of all knowledge and being. "The soul gives itself alone, original and pure, to the Lonely, Original, and Pure, who on that condition, gladly inhabits, leads, and speaks through it."[45] Influenced by Emerson, Frost believes that perception, knowledge, creativity, understanding, and faith are born in the "original" stream of spirit, the "Over-Soul," which is "your destination and your destiny."

The stream also alludes to "Michael's" "boisterous" and "tumultuous" brook of Green-head Ghyll, raging down from the pastoral uplands that are the source of Wordsworth's moral understanding. And Thoreau, in a summary of *Walden*, best describes the animation of spirit as a flowing stream: "The life in us is like the water in the river. It may rise this year higher than man has ever known it, and flood the parched uplands."[46]

In the last eight verses of "Directive" the speaker confidently assumes the role of sage and prophet, showing us the way to salvation. His gospel derives from *The Excursion* and the Bible, the one providing an inroad to draw meaning out of the past, and the other offering exemplary parables by which such meaning is carried. He directs us to a "goblet like the Grail," located, appropriately and literally, at the root of life, the "instep arch/ Of an old cedar." The Grail-goblet is the container of faith and knowledge. Its mystery (quests for it have traditionally been perilous) embraces the unfathomability of image containing idea, of figure shaping meaning, of verbal matter expressing spirit.

The interdependence of faith, imagination, correspondence, salvation, and poetry dominates the last six lines of "Directive." As Wordsworth's second self," the poet speaks in a "homely" voice that resonates like its visionary forebear "for the delight of a few natural hearts" and for "youthful Poets" ("Michael," 36-39). In *The Excursion* Wordsworth is a solitary sage who can

> see around me here
> Things which you cannot see: we die my Friend
> Nor we alone, but that which each man loved
> And prized in his peculiar nook of earth
> Dies with him, or is changed. (1:469-73)

Mentioning love and "broken brotherhood" he identifies his thoughts with the flowing waters of the house's spring. He drinks from it and sees the dilapidations of time within the grounds, the house, and "the useless fragment of a wooden bowl" (1:493), which represents grail-like evidence of the world's fallen condition that the poet alone can overcome. Fortified by faith, it is only the poet, "obedient to the strong creative power/ Of human passion" (1:480-81), who can tie together ruins of time. Out of the fragments of the past, Wordsworth--and after him Frost and Eliot[47]-- builds meaning, value, and order through poetry. This heritage is our creative blessing and salvation.

In the "house in earnest," as in the ruins of Margaret's cottage and Michael's sheepcote and the cellar holes of former inhabitants in *Walden*, the poet traces the past and is able to rescue it, seeing it whole again through art and faith. It is Wordsworth who exemplifies for Frost the poet's role as propitiator, guide, and mediator (or redeemer). Showing Frost the way, Wordsworth rests on the "breast of Faith" (1:955) as the rock and stay against despair, ruin, and change; but Frost's faith is qualified, resting on correspoondence and the incarnate power of words.

Suggesting that he will be the truth-bringer through a poetry of parable, Frost is like Christ, who was the embodied Word. The poet's goal is foremost "to say one thing in terms of another . . . spirit in terms of matter; to make the final unity. That is the greatest attempt that ever failed. We stop just short there. But it is the height of all poetry, the height of all thinking."[48] "Directive" takes us back to that creative height, dramatizing the mandate of form-making that is akin to faith and the testament and triumph over disorder; for "In us nature reaches its height of form and through us exceeds itself."[49] Those who "get saved" understand metaphor, whose half-hidden meaning is the dark glass testing their perception, as "Revelation" suggest. They are the believers and servers in the cause of truth, St. Mark clearly says in 16:16. And just as Christ redeemed the world by rising from the sepulchre and inspiring disciples to preach and "confirm the word" (16:20), Frost would redeem the past--symbolized at the outset by burned and broken "graveyard marble"--and thereby inspire his followers to do likewise from the ruins of their pasts.

The poet's role as minister to would-be communicants is particularly strong in the last two directives: "Here are your waters and your watering place./ Drink and be whole again beyond confusion." Truth, as Transcendentalists regard it, flows from an ever-replenishing source and has its word in the poet. As minister and mediator to that primal truth, he confidently can promise wholeness beyond confusion to those who do not know the way upward, or have lost the path since childhood. These are the same original, sustaining waters to which Thoreau directs us in "Civil Disobedience":

> They who know of no purer sources of truth, who
> have traced up its stream no higher, stand, and
> wisely stand, by the Bible and the Constitution, and
> drink at it there with reverence and humility; but they
> who behold where it comes trickling into this lake or
> that pool, gird up their loins once more, and continue
> their pilgrimage toward its fountain-head.[50]

This has been the direction and directive of the poem; here we are at its literary and inspirational waters. Frost, however, uses the Bible as a spring-like tributary to the thought and craft of "Directive," reinforcing its evangelical tone. To be saved and to apprehend truth, one must understand the words of the poet, just as in its tribal days Israel was exhorted to heed its prophets.

In the Gospel according to St. Mark, there are a number of parables on the clear waters[51] that sustain spiritual life, on the innocence of children, on divided houses that cannot stand, on sickness, unbelief, and healing--parables which Frost weaves into the fabric of his poem because of his faith in the oneness of God, self, and art-beliefs. The prophetic voice and parabolic mode of the following passage represent Frost's traditional attitudes toward the poet and poetry: "For whoso shall give you a cup of water to drink in my name, because ye belong to Christ, verily I say unto you, he shall not lose his reward (9:41). The verse repeats Matthew 10:42, which tells of a "cup of cold water" given to "these little ones." Similarly, Frost promises wholeness to his audience, just as Jesus did in drinking and eating with sinners, saying: "They that are whole have no need of the physician but they that are sick: I come not to call the righteous, but sinners to repentance" (Mark 2:17). Frost also is physician to those parched in spirit. Indeed, the ruins of the house to which Frost takes us may refer to St. Mark's figure for the grievous split we know before finding healing water. Mark warns, "If a house be divided against itself that house cannot stand" (3:25). In a related way, "Directive" regards aesthetic wholeness as integral to spiritual unity.

Not only are the metaphors and tone of St. Mark relevant to the meaning of "Directive," but also his account of Jesus' attitude about his own people and land strongly suggests a parallel to Frost's relation to his American audience. Speaking of himself, Jesus acknowledges that "A prophet is not without honor, but in his own country, and among his own kin, and in his own house" (Mark 6:4). If Frost identified with Hannibal's lost cause, he also saw a kinship with Christ who, finding himself unappreciated in his own country, complained of his people's failure to understand his parables and "marvelled at their unbelief" (6:6). One can see why Frost might identify with Christ; time and again he deeply felt the need to explain what his poetry of parables meant, stating rather off-handedly what must be reckoned as deadly serious underneath: "It takes a lot of in and outdoor schooling/ To get adapted to my kind of fooling." The fooling and play hide any teaching and preaching in his poetry. Of this playing with meaning both in and out of school (which only the "right person" attuned to metaphor could understand), he remarks: "St. Mark said, 'These things are said in parables' (that is, poetry, figures of speech), 'so the wrong people cannot understand them, and so get saved.'"[52]

Frost would minister to a faithful, attuned, but limited audience--the elect--guiding them to the waters of faith and poetic truth just as Jesus, healing and teaching, ministered his "mighty work" upon "a few" (Mark 6:5). Jesus instructed his disciples to go forth into the world and teach; Frost guides those few who would be saved in the Romantic sense of psychic and spiritual wholeness. He leads us to the sources of creative, intellectual strength. Its waters fill the grail, or form, of poetry--a poetry that is "the renewal of words forever and ever" through the language of metaphor, a poetry "by which we live forever and ever."[53]   The grail containing these waters is our destination and destiny, the sum of everything that we can know and believe.

The waters are the origins of Frost's cloud of other poets--Romantic and Biblical--out of which he creates his major poetry. This cloud has been our focus and subject which reaches its most subtle and complex form in "Directive," at once Frost's grand, concluding statement of his Romantic heritage in his art and thought.

𝒩𝒪𝒯𝐸𝒮

CODE FOR CITATIONS

C *The Complete Works of Ralph Waldo Emerson,* 12 vols., Centenary Edition, Edward Waldo Emerson, ed. (Boston: Houghton Mifflin, 1903).

J *The Writings of Henry David Thoreau,* 20 vols., Walden Edition (Cambridge, Mass.: Houghton Mifflin, 1906) The Journal, vols. 7-20 of this edition (ed. Bradford Torrey) are also numbered separately 1-14. I have used the latter numbering, preceded by *J*.

L *Selected Letters of Robert Frost,* ed. Lawrance Thompson (New York: Holt, Rinehart and Winston, 1964).

RF Lawrance Thompson, *Robert Frost: The Early Years, 1874-1915* (New York: Holt, Rinehart and Winston, 1966).

RF 2 ...., *Robert Frost: The Years of Triumph, 1915-1938* (New York: Holt, Rinehart and Winston, 1970).

RF 3 Lawrance Thompson and R. H. Winnick, *Robert Frost: The Later Years, 1938-1963* (New York: Holt, Rinehart and Winston, 1976).

SP Selected Prose of Robert Frost, eds. Hyde Cox and Edward C. Lathem (New York: Holt, Rinehart and Winston, 1966).

W *The Writings of Henry David Thoreau,* 20 vols., Walden Edition, (Boston: Houghton Mifflin, 1906).   The writings of Thoreau, exclusive of the Journals, are in vols.1-6, which I have designated *W*.

𝒩𝒪𝒯ℰ𝒮

𝒞ℋ𝒜𝒫𝒯ℰℛ 𝐼

1. *Robert Frost: Poetry and Prose,* ed. Edward C. Lathem and Lawrance Thompson (New York: Holt, Rinehart and Winston, 1972), pp. 420-21.

2. "Introduction to *The Arts Anthology: Dartmouth Verse, 1925* (Portland, Me.: Mosher Press, 1925), p. vii. Rpt. in *Robert Frost 100,* ed. Edward Connery Lathem (Boston: Godine, 1974), p. 65.

3. By Romanticism I simply mean a body of literature written by those American and English writers mentioned in this chapter. Though not always successful, that literature shows the mind attempting to impose value on the external world. It strives to connect the self to nature through immediate experience; the poet's purpose is to reconcile man with his surroundings through imagination, which is the bridge between the categories of the objective and subjective, the world and self. The assumptions behind many representative romantic poems are the poet's awareness of his separation from the world he is contemplating; it is a world unrelated, indifferent or even inimical to him. His desire is to join the two in an act of creation. The most informative commentary on Frost's romantic qualities as a poet is in Charles Carmichael, "Robert Frost as a Romantic," *Frost: Centennial Essays,* ed. Jac. L. Tharpe (Jackson: Univ. Press of Mississippi, 1974), pp. 147-65.

4. J, 13:87; 11:331-32.

5. *Robert Frost: Poetry and Prose,* p. 420.

6. He also remarked in earnest joking, "my latest book is just made out of my old books." Reginald Cook, *Robert Frost: A Living Voice* (Amherst: Univ. of Massachusetts Press, 1974), p. 42.

7. *RF* 2, p. 65.

8. *W*, 1,108-9

9. John Aldridge, *The Devil in the Fire: Retrospective Essays on American Literature and Culture 1951-1971* (New York: Harper and Row, 1972), p. 138.

10. Jay Parini, "Emerson and Frost: The Present Act of Vision," *Sewanee Review* 89 (Spring, 1981), 206-7.

11. *The Portable Matthew Arnold,* ed. Lionel Trilling (New York: Viking Press, 1949), p. 299.

CHAPTER II

1. Parini, 207, describes Frost's romanticism as having a poetic field of vision . . . best defined in terms of its special relation to Emerson's." Frost's "poetry represents a continuing dialogue with his great predecessor" (226). Frost acknowleges his debt to Emerson in "On Emerson." *Daedalus* 88 (Fall, 1959), 712-18, rpt. in *SP*, pp. 111-19.

2. *SP*, p. 78. The "Word" is from John 1:1.

3. *SP*, p. 24.

4. *C*, 1:34.

5. "A Defense of Poetry," *The Complete Works of Percy Bysshe Shelley*, eds. Roger Ingpen and Walter E. Peck (New York: Gordian Press, 1965), 7: 137.

6. *C*, 1:24.

7. *C*, 1:23. An "abstract" is the material distillation of the alembic.

8. *SP*, p. 106.

9. *C*, 2:273.

10. See Meyer Abrams, *The Mirror and the Lamp: Romantic Theory and the Critical Tradition* (New York: Norton, 1958), pp. 272-285.

11. *C*, 2:276.

12. *C*, 2:279.

13. *C*, 2:280.

14. *C*, 2:288-89.

15. *SP*, p. 45.

16. *C*, 2:281-82.

17. *C*, 2:286-87.

18. *The Letters of John Keats* 2 vols., ed. Hyder Rollins (Cambridge, Mass.: Harvard Univ. Press, 1958), 1:184-85.

19. Quoted in Hyatt H. Waggoner, *American Poets: From the Puritans to the Present* (Boston: Delta, 1968), p. 324.

20. James M. Cox, "Introduction" to *Robert Frost: A Collection of Critical Essays,* ed. James M. Cox (Englewood Cliffs: Prentice-Hall, 1962), p. 3.

21. *W*, 1:112.

22. Reginald Cook, *Robert Frost: A Living Voice* (Amherst: Univ. of Massachusetts Press, 1974), p. 51; *L*, pp. 278, 182.

23. *RF*, p. 549 n4.

24. *RF*, 347-48.Frost also took part in a public discussion of *Walden,* the record of the dialogue appearing in "Thoreau's *Walden,*" *The Listener,* 52 (August 26, 1954), 319-20.

25. *RF*, p. 218.

26. *C*, 10:476.

27. *W*, 2:179.

28. *J*, 11:304.

29. Much criticism on Frost has been to discern similarities and differences with Wordsworth, Emerson, and Thoreau, showing in what ways Frost develops as a nature poet and the extent of his

intellectual kinship with these previous writers. For a summary of this criticism see Donald J. Greiner, *Robert Frost: The Poet and His Critics* (Chicago: American Library Assn., 1974), pp. 141-81. Still the best study of Frost for clarity and for first establishing the Romantic context for many of Frost's poems, Reuben Brower, *The Poetry of Robert Frost: Constellations of Intention* (New York, Oxford Univ. Press, 1963), has examined some of the poems in the light of other writers, notably Emerson, Wordsworth, and William James. The results are illuminating. However I think the parallels made are often to general and sweeping to allow a full appreciation of the craft, subtlety, and depth of Frost's adaptations and the shaping of them into his poems. Frost's poems ride the older poetry in order to test the Romantic view of nature and also to reconsider many aspects of Romantic orientation. Frost's responses are varied in their playing against the heritage of the past poetry. This study intends to focus on the art of Frost's poems as they are informed by the previous literature.

30. "A Tribute to Wordsworth," *The Cornell Library Journal* 11 (Spring, 1970), 77-99.

31. *P.* 79.

32. *L*, p.244.

33. *RF*, p. 427.

34. Samuel Taylor Coleridge, *Biographia Literaria*, 2 vols., ed. John Shawcross (London: Oxford Univ. Press, 1907), 2:12.

35. *SP*, p. 41.

36. *L*, p. 467.

37. *The Complete Works of Percy Bysshe Shelley*, 7:137-38.

38. *The Letters of Robert Frost to Louis Untermeyer*, ed. Louis

Untermeyer (New York: Holt, Rinehart and Winston, 1963), p. 255.

39. *SP*, p. 107.

40 *SP*, p. 106.

CHAPTER III

1. *C*, 2:282; I:48.

2. *C*, 1:24. Italics added.

3. *C*, 1:40.

4. *C*, 1:4, 3.

5. *C*, 1:62.

6. *C*, 1:62.

7. See Peter L. Hays, "Frost and the Critics: More Revelation on 'All Revelation,'" *English Language Notes* 18 (June, 1981), 287, and Richard Poirier, *Robert Frost: The Work of Knowing* (New York: Oxford Univ. Press, 1977), pp. 20-22. Brower, p. 141 n., presumes some exact, scientific experiment. Following Brower's lead in interpreting the poem to be about the searching mind are: Frank Lentricchia, *Robert Frost: Modern Poetics and the Landscapes of Self* (Durham: Duke Univ. Press, 1975), pp. 4-7; and Carmichael, "Robert Frost as a Romantic," p. 159.

8. *C*, 1:40-41, 42.

9. *C*. 1:42-43.

10. Brower, p. 141, perceptively notes: "the ray is very mind-like."

11. *C*, I:27. This passage is precisely the "correspondence" that Frost considers the heart of all relationships and meaning. "Correspondence is all" (*SP*, p. 61). Dorothy Judd Hall, *Robert Frost: Contours of Belief* (Athens: Ohio Univ. Press, 1984), pp. 80-81, describes the poem as "a rhetorical enactment of the difficulty of correspondence between man and the universe--and, also, between poet and reader."

12. *C*, 1:29.

13. *C*, 1:29.

14. Sherman Paul, "The Angle of Vision," *Emerson: A Collection of Critical Essays*, eds., Milton Konvitz and Stephen Whicher (Englewood Cliffs: Prentice-Hall, 1962), p. 162.

15. Ibid. p. 168.

16. *C*, 1:36.

17. *J*, 2:403.

18. *J*, 12:23-24.

19. Emerson, "Montaigne: Or the Skeptic," *C*, 4:150. See also "Fate," *C*, 6:33, for another use of the rider metaphor.

20. *SP*, pp. 18, 20. Frost follows Emerson in his view that idea precedes feeling in the genesis of a poem, for a poem must have something to be wild about, and that is theme. Frost's use of the equestrian metaphor apears in his remark that the poet's knowledge is got "cavalierly and as it happens in and our of books" (p. 20).

21. *C*, 3:21.

22. *C*, 3:27.

23. *C*, 3:30.

24. "The Runaway" and "The Cow in Apple Time" see the need for domesticity and tractability and human control, without which untamed animal nature would harm itself.

25. *C*, 3:34.

26. *C*, 3:33.

27. *C*, 3:12-13.

28. *C*, 3:42.

29. Epigraph to "The Poet," *C*, 3:1.

30. *C*, 3:21.

31. *C*, 3:37.

32. Coincidentally, the cliffs in the woods are the site to which Thoreau repeatedly withdraws for meditation and silent observation, as his Journals show. His poem "Cliffs" records the wreathing and mingling of nature's inspiring breath with the poet's. See *J*, 1:51-52.

33. *C*, 1:37.

34. See Chapter VIII, pp.151-58.

35. "Uses of Great Men," *C*, 4:5-7.

36. Harold H. Watts, "Robert Frost and the Interrupted Dialogue," *American Literature*, 27 (March, 1955), 78-81, regards the factory as symbolic of all institutions which Frost would reject.

37. *RF*, p. 155, notes that *The Tempest* is one of the plays Frost read and studied with special care, extracting "essential meanings."

38. *C*, 2:181.

39. *RF* 2, p. 637.

40. *W*, 2:336.

41. *W*, 2:337-38.

42. *W*, 2:339.

43. *W*, 2:341.

44. The relation between nature's frostwork and the poetic Frost-work reaffirms the Romantic notion of correspondences, expressed in a punning that appears in his poems. Another example of imagination's secret ministry of Frost is to be found in "The Quest of the Purple-Fringed," as we shall note. Robert Graves has observed in the lines "Something there is that doesn't love a wall" that "the frozen-ground-swell is 'frost.'" *Selected Poems of Robert Frost* (New York, Holt, Rinehart and Winston: 1963), p. xiii. Ronald Sharp, "Robert Frost at Midnight," *Papers on Language and Literature*, 15 (1979), 311-16, finds "frost" the punning link between "An Old Man's Winter Night" and Coleridge's "Frost at Midnight."

45. *W*, 2:340-41.

46. *W*, 2:340.

47. *J*, 6:89.

48. *W*, 1:75.

49. *J*, 3:232.

50. *C*, 1:52.

51. *L*, p. 353.

52. Fragment, IV, vi, *The Poetical Works of William Wordsworth*, 5 vols., ed. Ernest de Selincourt (Oxford: Clarendon Press, 1949), 5:343.

53. *J*, 2:252-53.

54. *J*, 13:17-18.

55. Quoted in Elizabeth Shepley Sergeant, *Robert Frost: The Trial by Existence* (New York: Holt, Rinehart and Winston, 1960), p. 410. Poirier, pp. xiv-xv, regards the tent, the beloved, and the poem as having common characteristics.

56. *L*, p. 467.

57. *C*, 2:188.

58. Emerson describes love as that "which create[s] all things anew; which [is] the dawn in him of music, poetry, and art" (*C*, 2:175). Thoreau also regards the emotion of love as the kindling impulse and "generating force" behind all great writing, exhorting poets to "yield" to it (*J*, 3:253). When beginning a poem Frost compares the delight to true love; this comparison and the "figure" a poem makes perhaps derive from these writers.

59. Robert Frost, "Introduction" to *Threescore: The Autobiography of Sarah N. Cleghorn*, (New York: H. Smith and R. Haas, 1936), p. xii.

60. *Poetical Works of Wordsworth*, 2:409.

CHAPTER IV

1. "To the Daisy," *Poetical Works of Wordsworth*, IV, 68, 414 n.

2. *RF*, p. 558.

3. "Spoils of the Dead" (uncollected poem), *RF*, p. 559.

4. See *J*, 5:255, for an instance of this claim.

5. *C*, 1:8.

6. *J*, 5:184.

7. *J*, 2:309.

8. *J*, 5:283.

9. *J*, 4:289.

10. See *Hyperion*, 3:73-74, and "Epipsychidion," 384, for examples.

11. Frost himself uses the word "play" to describe figurative capability. See *SP*, p. 67.

12. "Ode: Intimations of Immortality . . ." 202-3.

13. "Walking," *W*, 5:240.

14. *W*, 1:184. The title of the poem, "Rumors from an Aeolian Harp," indicates a concern for the soul's unity with nature, the harp being a favorite Romantic symbol of the mind and its harmony and interchange with spirit.

15. As for example in Thoreau's spiritual vale, Blake's vales of Har, and Wordsworth's vales of Esthwaite and the Wye, whose Tintern Abbey redeems and recreates the "blessed mood" by which "we see into the life of things."

16. *W*, 1:404.

17. *W*, 1:407.

18. *W*, 1:403.

19. *W*, 1:408.

20. The first edition of *A Boy's Will* identifies the flower as "butterfly weed," but in the *Collected Poems* (1949) Frost deletes the couplet, perhaps because it is too specific, limiting, and obvious. The description "A leaping tongue of bloom" may serve (among other possibilities) as a fairly accurate figurative description of the orchises Snakemouth, Dragonmouth, or Rose Pogonia, described elsewhere as a "spear . . . tipped with wings of color." In his Journal Thoreau in fact describes the orchis as a tongue of color and leaping flames. The fact that the tuft of flowers grows in the wet margin "beside a reedy brook" conforms to the place where the orchis thrives, that is, in moist areas. Thoreau notes that it grows "along the shaded brooks and meadow's edge" (J, 5:345). In "The Tuft of Flowers" the speaker contemplates solitude and fraternity, with the flowers playing a mediant role to his understanding; they are the externalization of his best thoughts. The flowers resolve Thoreau's idea in *Walden's* "Solitude" that "a man thinking or working is always alone, let him be where he will. Solitude is not measured by miles of space that intervene between man and his fellows. . . . I am no more lonely than a singel mullein or dandelion in a pasture." (W, 2:150, 152). Frost's flowers, of whatever genus, are the reconciling evidence of man's solitude and fraternity.

21. Frost may not have been knowledgeable about flowers in his early years, according to George Monteiro, "Frost's Quest for the 'Purple Fringed,'" *English Language Notes* 13 (March, 1976), 204-20, but the description of the purple fringed orchis is quite precise, conforming to Frost's botanical hornbook, Mr. William Starr Dana's *How to Know the Wild Flowers* (1893), which relies on Thoreau's Journals for accounts of the flowers. Frost did not

mistake the purple fringed orchis for the gentian.

22. *Encyclopaedia Britannica* (1929),16:850.

23. *J*, 4:104.

24. *J*, 6:338.

25. *J*. 6:338.

26. *J*, 6:401.

27. *J*, 4:103. Michael West, "Versifying Thoreau: Frost's 'The Quest of the Purple Fringed' and 'Fire and Ice'" *English Language Notes* 16 (June, 1979), 41-42, identifies this passage, quoted in Mrs. William Starr Dana, *How to Know the Wild Flowers*, as the source for Frost's poem. West sets the time at midsummer, but the last stanza clearly indicates "summer was done."

28. *J*, 4:200.

29. *J*, 4:76.

30. *J*, 4:81.

31. The advent of frost may be taken doubly, referring to ice crystals and the poet. We noted already "something" that "doesn't love a wall"--Frost; the poet takes delight in verbal disguise. He also puns on his name in the phrase "lurking frost" in "Two Tramps in Mud Time," for subtle purposes, as I shall note later.

32. "Frost is defined as the condition of atmospheric calm and clarity that precedes hoar-frost, a formation involving a cooling of the air near the earth's surface. The poem's description of the climate and day favorable for frost is meteorologically precise. It is a day "with no breath of air"--atmosphere permitting the flowers' "perfect poise the livelong day." The moisture-laden earth, where alder trees (and orchises) thrive, sets an appropriate spot for the

earliest frost.

33. L, p. 20. The import of the equinox in Shelley's thought helps illuminate the poem's Romantic orientation. See Earl R. Wasserman, *Shelley's 'Prometheus Unbound: A Critical Reading* (Baltimore, Johns Hopkins Press, 1965), pp. 39-48.

34. See Keats's "I stood Tiptoe upon a little hill," 163-80.

35. Frost puns on the word "right" in "Design" also, where the assorted characters "begin the morning [rite].

CHAPTER V

1. *C,* 1:73-74.

2. Lentricchia, p. 102-3.

3. Commentary on this cryptic poem is almost non-existent. Reginald Cook, *The Dimensions of Robert Frost* (New York: Rinehart, 1958), p. 103 regards the poem to have a private "special significance" for the poet.

4. Wordsworth expresses a dissociation of imagination and sensibility in this exact manner in many of his poems, notably the "Intimations" ode.

5. *C,* 1:26.

6. Frost expressed an early admiration for Yeats. See *RF,* pp. 361-62, 412-14.

7. *SP,* p. 41.

8. *J,* 11:210-11.

9. *J,* 3:51; 10:157.

10. *C,* 1:11.

11. *C,* 1:8.

12. *C,* 1:9.

13. *C,* 1:9.

14. *C,* 1:11.

15. *C,* 1:9.

16. *W*, 1:65.

17. *J*, 1:66.

18. "Essay, Supplementary to the Preface," *Poetical Works of Wordsworth*, 2:426.

19. Lawrance Thompson, *Fire and Ice: The Art and Thought of Robert Frost* (New York: Holt,1942), p. 131, deftly observes that "the creator of poems is quite as much interested in the problem of communication as God himself."

20. *C*, 2:278.

21. Abrams, *The Mirror and the Lamp*, p. 272.

22. *SP*, p. 65.

23. Frost greatly admired Arnold (*RF*, pp. 500, 304) perhaps because Arnold's backward regard for Romanticism has so much in common with his own poetry. Arnold is the English poet of diminished vision and Frost his American counterpart.

24. *C*, 1:29.

25. *C*, 2:291.

26. *C*, 2:34.

27. *C*, 2: 280, 273.

28. *C*, 2:269.

29. *C*, 2:286-87.

30. *C*, 2:290.

31. *J*, 5:144.

32. *J*, 5:247.

33. Shelley's skylark has "skill to poet" and is a teacher of gladness. See the last six verses.

34. See Waggoner, p. 297; and Brower, p. 30.

35. *J*, 10:344.

36. *J*, 10:411-12; 6:251.

37. *J*, 2:9.

38. *J*, 5:229.

39. *J*, 4:285.

40. See Brower, p. 30; and C.R.B. Combellack, "Frost's 'The Oven Bird,'" *The Explicator* 22 (Nov., 1963), art. 17.

41. *J*, 4:282.

42. William H. Pritchard, "Diminished Nature," *Massachusetts Review* 1 (1960), 483; and Brower, p. 82.

43. *J*, 4:38.

44. *J*, 9:313-14.

45. Waggoner, pp. 313, 316, 324, 327.

46. *J*, 3:486.

CHAPTER VI

1. Many critics differ in their regard for Frost as a nature poet, treating him as a philosopher instead of regarding him on his own terms as a "philosophical poet." For a summary of the variety of critical responses to Frost as a nature poet and his concepts of nature see Greiner, pp. 207-46, and Kerry McSweeney, "Frost's Commentators: The Weak and the Strong," *Critical Quarterly* 24 (1982), 19-25.

2. *W*, 1:182.

3. Poirier, Brower, John F. Lynen, *The Pastoral Art of Robert Frost* (New Haven: Yale Univ. Press, 1960), Sidney Lea, "From Sublime to Rigamarole: Relations of Frost To Wordsworth, *Robert Frost*, ed. Harold Bloom (New York: Chelsea House, 1986), pp. 85-110, and Barry D. Bort, "Frost and the Deeper Vision, *Midwest Quarterly* 5 (Autumn, 1963), 59-63, discuss the Romantic reference in Frost's nature poetry, noting that the poet understands the Wordsworthian voice and his debt to it, but that the claims for a unity or correspondence between man and nature are no longer tenable for the modern poet. Lea argues Frost's reduction of possible sublimity to bald earthiness, of "poem as redemption into poem as 'rigamarole'" (p. 86). Brower shows that the poet is not beguiled by the Romantic mythology of the landscape, citing Wordsworth, Thoreau, and Emerson as guides to Frost's achievement. Lynen argues that Frost is anti-Romantic in that the poetry shows the contrast and separation between man and nature. George W. Nitchie *Human Values in the Poetry of Robert Frost: A Study of a Poet's Convictions* (Durham: Duke Univ. Press, 1960) and Alvan S. Ryan, "Frost and Emerson: Voice and Vision," *Massachusetts Review* 1 (Oct., 1959), 5-23; argue that in rejecting the Romantic concept of nature, Frost's final position is fully humanistic in outlook. They fault him unfairly for not having a clear system of convictions, forgetting that poems reflect varying moods of the moment; the poet is not a coherent philosopher but engaging in outdoor fooling indoors.
    While I am indebted to these critics, they, except for Lea, tend

to be too reductive and sweeping about Frost's nature poetry. My focus is the artistry of the poems and their organic ties to certain works of Romantic quest literature. Each in some way tests the mind's subtle relation to nature and can best be read and understood from a Romantic frame of reference. Each poem is unique and deserves to be discussed individually.

4. The "principle of generosity" is essential to any Romantic interchange between mind and nature. See Geoffrey Hartman, *The Unmediated Vision: An Interpretation of Wordsworth, Hopkins, Rilke, and Valery* (New Haven: Yale Univ. Press, 1954), pp. 9, 26.

5. *J*, 5:135.

6. *Interviews with Robert Frost*, ed. Edward Connery Lathem (New York: Holt, Rinehart and Winston, 1966), p. 21. The advice is originally Thoreau's in *J*, 3:253; he urges that the poet suffer himself to be affected by the moon.

7. *Interviews with Robert Frost*, p. 18.

8. *P*. 21.

9. *C*, 1:8.

10. "We animate what we can, and we see only what we animate. Nature . . . belong[s] to the eyes that see [it]." (Emerson, "Experience," *C*, 3:50). Wordsworth made the same assertion in "Tintern Abbey" wherein nature and the language of the sense conspire to create value--"the mighty world/ Of eye and ear--both what they half create,/ And what perceive" (105-7).

11. *SP*, p. 61.

12. *C*, 1:73-74.

13. *C*, 1:74-75.

14. *C*, 1:75.

15. *C*, 1:76.

16. The Journal for Jan. 1 and 2, 1853, indeed describes the bent, ice-bound birches after a winter storm (*J*, 4:438,440). The source for "Birches" and its "Thoreauvian eyes" have been discussed by George Monteiro, "Birches in Winter: Notes on Thoreau and Frost," *CLA Jounal* 12 (Dec., 1968), 129-33.

17. This parenthesized verse appears in the first edition of *Mountain Interval* but is omitted in *Complete Poems* (1949).

18. *J*, 4:48.

19. *SP*, p. 18. See also Thompson, *Fire and Ice* , p. 32, rpt. in part in "Robert Frost's Theory of Poetry," *Robert Frost: A Collection of Critical* Essays, p. 28.

20. *W*, 2:229.

21. *W*, 2:203, 206-7, 209.

22. *W*, 2:209.

23. *W*,1:17.

24. Brower identifies the image as "a poet-Zeus crowned with leaves" (p. 137), but perhaps a poet Apollo would be more appropriate, being god of poetry, and associated with inspiration, the muses, and Helicon.

25. *RF*, p. 130.

26. *RF*, p. 132.

27. *J*, 11:292-93.

28. *C*, 1:51.

29. *C*, 1:48.

30 *C*,1:50.

31. *C*, 1:51.

32. *RF* 2, p. 361.

33. Poirier, pp. 161-65.

34. Brower, pp. 131-34; Lynen, p. 148.

35. Roy Harvey Pearce, "Frost's Momentary Stay," *Kenyon Review* 23 (Spring, 1961), 269.

36. See *W*, 2:143.

37. *W*, 2:136-37. Italics added.

38. *J*, 4:492-93.

39. *J*, 4:492-93

40. *C*, 1:74.

41. *RF* 2, p. 361.

42. *C*, 1:76.

43. "Robert Frost Reads From His Own Works," Yale Series of Recorded Poets, Decca, DL-9127.

44. *J*, 2:25.

45. *C*, 1:76.

46. *RF* 2, p. 361.

47. *W*, 3:132.

48. *W*, 3:122.

49. *W*, 3:115.

50. Poirier, p. 164.

51. *C*, 4:39.

52. *C*, 1:73-74.

53. *J*, 9:216.

54. *W*, 2:294. Even in winter, verdure and warmth may be found in it. Robert Penn Warren, "The Themes of Robert Frost," *Selected Essays* (New York: Random House,1958), p. 125; Malcolm Cowley, "The Case Against Mr. Frost," *Robert Frost: A Collection of Critical Essays*, p. 43; James M. Cox, "Robert Frost and the Edge of the Clearing," *Virginia Quarterly Review* 35 (Winter, 1959), 80; and Lentricchia, pp. 87-100, see the woods as Frost's symbol of the dark landscape of the soul.

55. *W*, 5:228.

56. The entry for Jan. 4, 1853 (*J*, 4:449), reads: "My temple is a swamp." On Oct. 31, 1857 (*J*, 10:150), he writes: "If you are afflicted with melancholy . . . go to the swamp," and see its "concentrated greenness." Thoreau's and Frost's swamp is identifiable with the Wordsworthian concept of the "omphalos: the navel point at which powers meet," a Delphic-like site of vision. See Geoffrey Hartman, *Wordsworth's Poetry: 1787-1814* (New Haven: Yale Univ. Press, 1964), pp. 122-198.

57. See, *e.g.*, *J*, 3:319, 342, 349; 5:43, 65.

58. See Coleridge's "The Eolian Harp." This harp, or lyre, is a favorite Romantic analogue for the mind, in its creative relationship with nature. See also Abrams, pp. 51-52.

59. *J*, 10:116.

60. *J*, 12:58.

61, *W*, 2:196; 206-7.

62. *W*, 2:358.

63. *W*, 2:313.

64. See Waggoner, p. 316. Parini, p. 220, claims Frost is deriding "false visionaries."

65. *W*, 1:47-48.

66. Frost can therefore "contain" both visionary questing and merely limited vision in his poem. According to Reginald Cook, *Robert Frost: A Living Voice*, pp. 279-80, Frost accepts the position of "containment" of opposites, holding contrary beliefs in "a dialectical tension."

67. The gloss reads: "To know definitely what he thinks . . . about science." Frost did not reprint the gloss to this or other poems in subsequent editions because, as he suggested, they restrict the poems' implicit meanings. See Thompson, *Fire and Ice*, pp. 100, 102; and Nitchie, pp. 85-86.

68. *RF*, p. 326.

69. See *NED* under "Demiurge," 1.

70. *L*, p. 584.

71. Emerson's "Forerunners" may also provide a frame of reference

for an understanding of the poem.

72. *RF*, p. 36.

73. *L*, p. 221.

CHAPTER VII

1. Cook, *The Dimensions of Robert Frost*, p. 177 and *Robert Frost: A Living Voice* pp. 280, 282. "'Truth,' Frost stated, emphatically 'is a dialogue.'" and a dialectical tension which contained contrary beliefs and opinions.

2. See *L*, p. xvi, which discusses Frost's inveterate maskings and ironic style. See also Waggoner, pp. 305, 315-16.

3. Reginald Cook, "Frost on Frost: The Making of Poems," *American Literature* 28 (Mar., 1956), 62, describes Frost's elastic, ready mind:

   "Addicted to stichomythia, or the art of the sharp verbal exchange, colloquially called the 'come-back,' he had the eloquence of rejoinder. 'I like a quick answer,' he says. 'They're often in self-defense.'"

4. Quoted in Cook, *The Dimensions of Robert Frost*, p. 205.

5. Sidney Cox, *A Swinger of Birches: A Portrait of Robert Frost* (New York: New York Univ. Press, 1957), p. 25.

6. Cook, *The Dimensions of Robert Frost*, p. 213.

7. Watts, p. 69.

8. *C*, 3:32-33.

9. *C*, 3:32.

10. *W*, 5:235, 234.

11. *J*, 2:37-38.

12. Lentricchia, p. 75.

13. *C*, 1:76.

14. 13 May, 1932. *L*., p. 386.

15. Quoted by Emerson in "Thoreau," *C*. 10:484.

16. *C*, 2:294.

17. "A Dream of Julius Caesar," in *RF*, p. 102.

18. Of "Kubla Khan" and other verses, Frost said "Those are the top places in poetry" (Cook, *The Dimensions of Robert Frost*, p. 50.)

19. *RF* 2, p. 207.

20. *C*, 2:281.

21. *C*, 2:282.

22. *C*, 3:26.

23. *C*, 2:283-84.

24. *C*, 2:282.

25. *C*, 2:286.

26. *C*, 2:267.

27. *C*, 6:9.

28. *C*, 2:294.

29. Matthew 7:7. In "The Over-Soul" Emerson takes Matthew's figure of effective prayer and applies it to transcendental communication.

30. Matthew 6:6.

31. See *RF*, pp. 337-38, 347. Though it has "Yeatsian echoes," the poem is dominantly Coleridgean. The biographical occasion for the poem is outlined on pp. 377-79.

32. Robert Orenstein, "Frost's 'Come In,'" *The Explicator* 15 (June, 1957), item 61, claims bird and song embody "the sensuous appeal of nature," with the song as stimuli evoking "a literary response." "Frost's thrush and Keats's nightingale are birds of a feather." Brower, p. 32, hears the song as a "Romantic invitation . . . into a night retreat of Tennyson or Keats," with overtones of remoteness, death, and transport in the phrase "'a call to lament.'"

33. Warren, p. 127.

34. *J*, 4:190-91.

35. See *SP*, pp. 18-20.

36. *J*, 2:19.

37. *J*, 5:292-93.

38. *J*, 2:416.

39. *J*, 2:440.

40. *J*, 2:446 (Sept. 2, 1851).

41. *Prelude* (1850), 13:16-17.

42. *J*, 6:38.

43. *J*, 2:413-14.

44. *W*, 1:413.

CHAPTER VIII

1. This theme is discussed in Leo Stoller, "Thoreau's Doctrine of Simplicity," *New England Quarterly* 29 (Dec., 1956), 443-61.

2. For a discussion of this chapter in *Walden*, see John B. Pickard, "The Religion of 'Higher Laws,'" *Emerson Society Quarterly* 39 (1965), 68-72.

3. *W*, 2:246.

4. The metaphor of work is not simply the arduous process of knowing, of getting down to the reality of nature and the feel for facts, as Richard Poirier, pp. 277-85, has remarked. He does not go far enough. Work is a metaphor for the whole process of creativity, and the ordering of art; and it is best understood in the context of Frost's relation to Thoreau, as I intend to show in this chapter.

5. Charles Kaplan, "Frost's 'Two Tramps in Mud Time,'" *The Explicator* 12 (June, 1954), item 51.

6. See my discussions herein of "A Hillside Thaw," The Quest of the Purple-Fringed," and "Mending Wall" for other instances of Frost's implicit punning on "frost."

7. *J*. 3:244-45.

8. *L*, p. 467.

9. *J*, 3:165.

10. *J*, 3:165.

11. *W*, 1:108-9.

12. See Samuel Taylor Coleridge, *Biographia Literaria,* 2 vols., ed.

John Shawcross (London, 1907), 2:12.

13. *J*, 8:314.

14. *SP*, p. 19.

15. *W*, 1:74.

16. *SP*, p. 46. See Emerson, "The Over-Soul," about the inter-relationship of man's various beliefs.

17. *SP*, p. 46.

18. Priscilla M. Paton, "Robert Frost: The fact is the sweetest dream that labor knows," *American Literature* 53 (March, 1981), 43-55, investigates the relation between work, metaphor, and knowledge, and what constitutes "truth." Frost himself said of this "one line" that it summarizes "my own philosophy of art" and poetry (Cook, *Robert Frost: A Living Voice*, p. 133.

19. Sidney Cox, "The Courage To Be New--A Reappraisal of Robert Frost," *Vermont History* 22 (Apr., 1954), 119-26, discusses the relevance of fact and labor to Frost's view of poetry: "The laborer brings a fact into being. *Factum* means made. The height of satisfaction is achieved in a causing-to-be something useful or delightful which was not before" (p. 122). Frost reveals the profound importance of creative effort and self-culture in his "Letter to The Amherst Student."

20. *W*, 2:101.

21. *J*, 1:18.

22. *C*, 1:17-18.

23. While "The Pasture" is representative of the kind of poetry Frost writes, its pastoral mode, which contrast country and city, is not the essential element of the poem, as Lynen, pp. 19-22,

maintains. Nor is the poem devoid of metaphorical meaning. We needn't see the pasture simply as a better world because "it is more natural, more neatly organized" (p. 23); it is the farmer who organizes, maintains it through a special cooperation with nature. Lentricchia, p. 24, observes that the act of enclosure reflects the act of the imaginative man.

24. Quoted in Cook, *The Dimensions of Robert Frost*, p. 102.

25. E. A. Richards, "Two Memoirs of Frost," *Touchstone* 4 (Mar., 1945), p. 20.

26. *SP*, p. 106-7.

27. *W*, 2: 179.

28. *J*, 1:313.

29. *Prelude* (1850), 1:35. See also 40-45 and (1805 ed.) 11:9-12.

30. *Prelude* (1850), 1:37.

31. *Prelude*, 1:43, 45.

32. *Biographia Literaria*, 1:74.

33. *Prelude* (1850), 12:127-31.

34. *Prelude* (1850), 12:93, 95-101.

35. *J*, 4:274-75.

36. *SP*, pp. 106-7.

37. On this theme see "To the Right Person."

38. *SP*, p. 20.

39. *C*, 1:64-65.

40. See Lynen, pp. 9-16, 127, 131.

41. *C*, 3:204, 215-16.

42. Laurence Perrine, "The Meaning of Frost's 'Build Soil,'" *Frost: Centennial Essays*, p. 234., summarizes a number of themes in the poem, among which are self-reliance and "a rich mind for writing good poetry."

43. *The Letters of Robert Frost to Louis Untermeyer*, p. 255.

44. P. 255.

45. *J*, 11:304.

46. Frost often referred to his occupation of farmer and is supposed to have written "farmer" on his income-tax forms.

47. *J*, 11:304.

48. *W*, 2:181.

49. *C*, 2:75.

50. *C*, 2:75.

51. *C*, 2:49-50.

52. Calling the poem a "masterpiece," Warren, pp. 127, 130, notes the poem's similarity to "Mowing," and that "the dream will relive the world of effort." John J. Conder, "'After Apple-Picking': Frost's Troubled Sleep." *Frost: Centennial Essays*, pp. 171-81, discusses the poems complicated feats of word association, but does not discern the overall coherence of the poem, which is dependent, in part, on the cloud of previous poets.

53. *J*, 3: 126.

54. *J*, 3: 123.

55. *C*, 2:333-34.

56. *C*, 1:34-35, 42.

57. *C*, 1:42.

58. *C*, 1:61-62.

59. *C*, 1:73-74.

60. Joe M. Ferguson,"Frost's 'After Apple-Picking,'" *The Explicator* , 22 (Mar., 1964), item 53; Nitchie, p. 92; Poirier, p. 298. References to the myth abound in Frost's poetry: "The Grindstone" ties the apple tree to knowledge, and "Away," "The Oven Bird," "Nothing Gold Can Stay," "Kitty Hawk" and many other poems allude to the primal fall.

61. Ferguson, item 53, argues that man's sleep is inferior to the woodchuck's. I am inclined to agree, but with qualification. The woodchuck's sleep has special symbolic value and will be discussed forthwith.

62. *The Letters of John Keats*, 1:184.

63. *W*, 2:245-46.

64. *W*, 1:101-2.

65. "Education," C, 10:147.

66. Frost read Shelley in 1892 (*RF*, p. 136). "Kitty Hawk" refers to *Alastor* and presumably to one kind of flight implicit in the poem.

67. Hoxie N. Fairchild, "Definition of Romanticism," *Romanticism:*

Points of View, eds. Robert Gleckner and Gerald Enscoe (Englewood Cliffs: Prentice-Hall: 1962), pp. 99, 101.

68. See Hartman, *Wordsworth's Poetry, 1787-1814,* p. 198, for a discussion of this theme.

69. *W*, 2:292.

70. The lines from Eclogue I are: "Tityrus, you, recumbent beneath the shades of a spreading beech, meditate your rustic muse on a slender pipe: We abandon the boundaries of our country, and our pleasant fields. We fly our country." The beech is associated with poetry and thoughts of distant lands, and may provide a source for Frost's poem.

71. *C*, 10:483.

72. *J*, 10:232.

73. *SP*, p. 107.

74. *SP*, p. 107.

75. *J*, 10:233-34.

76. *W*, 2:356.

77. *W*, 2:356.

78. *W*, 2:18.

79. Northrop Frye, *The Great Code: The Bible and Literature* (New York: Harcourt Brace Jovanovich, 1982), p. 7.

80. *W*, 5:242.

81. *W*, 5:242.

82. *W*, 5:260.

83. *SP*. p. 106.

84. The precedents for this metaphor in literature are many, including Dante, the poet in *Alastor*, Endymion, or the disoriented Wordsworth at Simplon Pass in *The Prelude*.

85. *SP*, p. 107.

86. See Lynen, pp. 144-45, for the Wordsworthian implications of the poem.

87. Waggoner, pp. 308-9.

CHAPTER IX

1. Brower, p. 124, sees Emerson's "Fate" (essay and poem) involved in Frost's poem. Richard Ellmann, *Eminent Domain* (New York: Oxford Univ. Press, 1967), pp. 6-7, notes Yeats's influence in stanza 8.

2. *RF*, p. 556 n.8, notes that stanza 2 echoes "Adonais" but does not examine the thematic relationship between the two poems or Frost's subtle, meaningful weaving of Shelley's language into his poem. The same may be said for Marion Montgomery, "Robert Frost and His Use of Barriers: Man Vs. Nature Toward God," *Robert Frost: A Collection of Critical Essays*, p. 144, which notes that Frost seems to have had Wordsworth's "Intimations" ode in mind when writing "The Trial by Existence."

3. *J*, 1:347.

4. *J*, 1:258.

5. *J*, 1:244-45. Cf. *W*, 1:312-13.

6. *J*, 9, 249.

7. *W*, 5:218.

8. *RF*, pp. 307, 347, 524.

9. *RF*, pp. 258, 295, 559.

10. *W*, 5:233-34.

11. *W*, 5:234.

12. *W*, 5:232.

13. *W*, 5:231-32.

14. *W*, 5:233.

15. "Lucretius: On the Nature of the Universe," *The Intellectual Tradition of the West*, eds. Morton Donner, Kenneth Eble and Robert Hebling (Glenview, 1967), 1:134.

16. *P*. 148.

17. *J*, 10:202.

18. Brower, pp. 227, 234-40, considers this the theme of the poem. It is "a journey into inner as well as outer history, into one's own" (p. 233); but the inner history involves, mainly the cloud of other poets--major literary experiences in Frost's complex intellectual life, which is, as I shall point out, the inspiration of the poem. Pearlanna Briggs, "Frost's 'Directive,' *The Explicator* 21. (May, 1963), item 71, interprets the poem as a biographically larded account of the ordeal by which Frost became a poet. James M. Cox, "Robert Frost and the Edge of the Clearing," p. 87, sees the poem as the path Frost has followed as a poet and a poetic ground he has possessed. S.P.C. Duvall, "Robert Frost's 'Directive' Out of *Walden*," *American Literature* 31 (Jan., 1960), 488, is the first to show the relationship between the two works, noting that *Walden* is "one of the great watering places of American Literature" from which Frost drew metaphor, imagery, and wit. But with regard to the themes of imagination and the career of the poet, *Walden* offers many more clues to the subtlety and meaning of "Directive." Greiner, *The Poet and His Critics*, pp. 173-74 summarizes criticism to "Directive" to 1974. See also George W. Nitchie, "Robert Frost: The Imperfect Guru," and John F. Lynen, "Du Cote de Chez Frost," *Frost: Centennial Essays*, pp. 46-49, 573-91; Lentricchia, pp. 112-242.

19. *C*, 10, 476.

20. *L*, p. 385. (19 April, 1932)

21. *J*, 12: 343

22. Brower, p. 238, refers to the Wordsworthian flavor of "Directive"; but more than a parallel exists. There is an organic tie vital to the poem's meaning. Frost adopted Wordworth's belief that the past is redeemable through memory, imagination and retrospection, and through these powers of mind an order and continuity are given to one's life. It is the past that provides the material for that order and the faith to endure. See also Lea, pp. 95-107.

23. *SP*, p. 45.

24. *C*, 10:131.

25. *J*, 10:465.

26. *SP*, p. 27.

27. *W*, 2:268.

28. *J*, 11:, 326.

29. *SP*, p. 78. Italics added.

30. See, for example, Jud. 9:8-14; Isa. 61:3; Matt. 3:10.

31. *W*, 2:247-48.

32. Sergeant, p. 394.

33. P. 394

34. *The Letters of John Keats*, 1:232.

35. *W*, 2:341.

36. Briggs, item 71, interprets the lines as referring to Pound and the Imagists, who have in literary history "shaded out" Georgian poetry.

37. Thoreau gives implicit reasons why the former inhabitants of Walden did not thrive. They created no artifacts, the bases of culture and self-culture, which would sustain them economically and in spirit, causing the backwoods wilderness to thrive in creative industry. All things flourish in art. He remarks: "Might not the basket, stable-broom, mat-making, corn-parching, linnen-spinning, and pottery business have thrived here, making the wilderness to blossom" (*W*, 2:291). Frost clung to this concept of self-culture.

38. This parallel is noted by Duvall, pp. 486-87.

39. *J*, 7:10.

40. *SP*, p. 28. See also pp. 65, 67, 78, 107 for Frost's recurrent use of "play" as poetry and figure-making.

41. *SP*, p. 28.

42. *C*, 1:29.

43. *SP*, p. 72

44. *W*, 2:290.

45. *C*, 2:268, 296.

46. *W*, 2:366.

47. For the relation between "Directive" and Eliot's poetry, see George Knox, "A Backward Motion Toward the Source," *Personalist* 47 (Summer, 1966), 365-81.

48. *SP*, p. 41.

49. *SP*, p. 106

50. *W*, 4:385-86.

51. Thoreau and Emerson no doubt borrowed from the Bible the metaphors of water and drinking. The Bible is in many ways the great nimbus for the thought and symbols of American and English Romantics.

52. Lathem, *Interviews*, p. 162.

53. *L*, p. 462.

Volumes of Frost's Poetry

Index of Names, Etc.

Index of Names, Etc.